CW00968706

God's Ecology
and the Dawkins Challenge

A Scientific Guide to the Spiritual Habitat
by
Jon Freeman and Juliana Freeman

In the attics of my life
Full of cloudy dreams unreal
Full of tastes no tongue can know
And lights no eye can see
When there was no ear to hear   You sang to me

I have spent my life
Seeking all that's still unsung
Bent my ear to hear the tune
And closed my eyes to see
When there were no strings to play   You played to me

In the book of love's own dreams
Where all the print is blood
Where all the pages are my days
And all my nights grow old
When I had no wings to fly   You flew to me

In the secret space of dreams
Where I dreaming lay amazed
When the secrets all are told
And the petals all unfold
When there was no dream of mine   You dreamed of me

Robert Hunter   *Grateful Dead : American Beauty*

Published by :SpiralWorld

PO Box 7088

Ashley Heath

Ringwood BH24 9DT

www.spiralworld.net

© Jon Freeman and Juliana Freeman 2008

All rights reserved.   Excerpts up to 200 words in length may be quoted without explicit permission where acknowledgement is made of authors and publisher. This excepted, no part of this book may be reproduced or stored and retrieved in any form without explicit permission in writing from the publisher.

Printed in the United Kingdom by Biddles Ltd., King's Lynn, Norfolk

ISBN 978-0-956-0107-0-4

CONTENTS

God's Ecology

1. Introduction

Politics and Religion are dead. The time has come for Science and Spirituality.

J. Nehru

The purpose of this book is clear and simple. It is to meet an intellectual and scientific challenge to the validity of spiritual thought and religious experience. This will require us to establish the true nature of the spiritual universe and re-position both science and the human relationship with the world of the Divine.

There is a growing convention for science to be given an authoritative voice in the world. There would be nothing wrong with that if scientific understanding truly justified the authoritative opinions that are expressed, but it doesn't. Scientific dogma around religion contains fundamental flaws and leaves large gaps. These errors inhabit scientific thinking and the way science represents the spiritual world. Their strong and increasingly pervasive expression causes humanity widespread damage.

This question has sharpened recently with the popularity of Professor Richard Dawkins' book "The God Delusion", and his associated TV assaults on both religion and alternative medicine. He has issued a highly-charged and very open challenge which should not go unanswered. Richard Dawkins is a brilliant man who fully deserves the praise that he receives for his clarity of thought and for the lucidity of his writing. Indeed we must thank him for making the nature of the debate so clear. To a large extent religious and spiritual thinkers have been reluctant or unable to engage with changing knowledge of the physical universe and have not faced the need to separate deep spiritual truth from tradition, habit and dogma. In consequence there are many justifications for his challenge, but it is now urgent for the spiritual viewpoint to be presented coherently. Some of the authoritative statements science makes are not supportable. In his attacks, Prof. Dawkins does us the service of being a primary spokesman for the flaws that have run through science for a long time. Our view is that a whole dimension is missing from the scientific viewpoint, like a black and white picture awaiting the discovery of colour. Essential information is ignored, or goes unseen. We intend to paint in those colours and supply the missing dimension. We come not to bury science, but to raise it.

This is emphatically not an anti-science book. We are passionate about the value of science. There is great value in requiring some common sense, intellectual rigour, and up-to date recognition of the way the physical universe operates. But there is a belief system of "scientism" which attaches to science just as religion attaches to spirituality. Fundamentalism is a deep problem in all religions and science has its own fundamentalists. There is so much in science that we can and will endorse and plenty of bathwater worth removing from religion, but some fundamentalist scientism is throwing out the baby. The baby is still breathing. Just. It is time for that baby to begin its journey towards adulthood.

The baby is the universe of spiritual consciousness. It's a big baby; indeed they don't come much bigger. That baby lives in the scientific universe, or you could equally say that science inhabits the baby's universe. They are together, intertwined and inseparable and we intend to show how, to reveal a whole network of missed information and rich connectivity.

We don't seek to prove all of science wrong; much of it is brilliant. We do wish to re-frame it though and to call for change in the areas where flaws exist. Humanity has struggled for too long with a polarity of thinking which would have us believe exclusively either in science or in a religious spirituality. It has been made difficult to live fully with both. Yet there is only one universe in which scientific humans and spiritual humans share one world, not two.

In that world, both viewpoints are valid. Both scientists and those who recognise the existence of a spiritual consciousness have portions of the truth. It is time for these two viewpoints to blend and for both the world and for the human beings who inhabit it to be made whole. One does not have to look very far to see the downside of a world in which science operates without the balance of spirituality and which is dominated by materialism and disrespect for nature. Equally the damage sometimes done in the name of religion is blindingly obvious, as Richard Dawkins makes very clear. Both polarities distort human existence. There has to be and indeed there is a way for humanity to live which is free from both these follies. The text of this book is devoted to filling the gulf, to placing the collagen fibres over the wound that divides our world.

This would be an impossible task were it not for the many brilliant people who have already described these fibres. If we can see far it is because, like Newton we stand on the shoulders of giants. Our story will be told largely through their many voices. Our aim is not to claim any authority for ourselves but to weave their strands into a coherent and healing whole.

The basic flaws

We should not go further without setting out the nature of the flaws that scientism articulates. Describing them is simple and for some instances we will use Professor Dawkins' book as an example. It will take the rest of the book to justify our claim that they are errors.

1. A meaningful definition for the Divine. There are several definitions given in the first chapter of "The God Delusion" for different classifications of "God" – personal God, pantheistic God, God as metaphor etc. All of these are demolished. Fundamentally the mistake is to accept a set of "straw men" which others have used to define the spiritual world and then, with great relish, to knock them down. In that demolition it appears that no space remains for any form of spiritual reality. Something inhabits this space which is not covered well by religion and not addressed fully in the choices people are offered. We intend to fill this gap with a substantial, meaningful and coherent definition.

On page 13, Richard Dawkins quotes Steven Weinberg's comment that if you want to say that "God is energy," then you can find God in a lump of coal. He goes on to say that if the word God is not to become completely useless, then the word should be used in its traditional sense to denote a supernatural creator appropriate for worship. Unfortunately, this narrowing of the definition precludes recognition of the real nature of the "divine" and confines the relationship to "worship" rather than "knowing", "experiencing" or "engaging with". If God is omnipresent, perhaps we need a definition which does find the Divine in a lump of coal. Dr. Dawkins suggests (P.50) that the existence of God is a testable scientific hypothesis like any other. We agree. The hypothesis we present for a meaningful "transcendent spirit", for the presence throughout the universe of a creative consciousness is backed by evidence. It is however more subtle than the definitions that he offers us.

2. The spiritual world has physical reality. There is a polarisation in our

language between "spiritual" and "physical". This is an important distinction but also a misleading one when taken to indicate that there is no connection between them. It implies that spiritual events are without physical mechanisms. We will define later what we mean by "spiritual" but for now please understand that we are not referring to a psychological phenomenon nor to a metaphorical one. Our version of "spiritual" is a part of the physical, scientifically describable universe. The concepts of Red and Violet are useful, but not to the exclusion of the orange, yellow and blue which lie between them. The error lies in the polarisation itself, in its self-limiting definition of the physical world.

On page 72 there is a reference to Arthur C. Clarke's statement that "any sufficiently advanced technology is indistinguishable from magic." This is true in the same sense as Patience Strong's homily that a stranger is a friend you haven't met yet". The false separation between spiritual and physical causes us to regard as "supernatural" the phenomena that we have not yet found an explanation for. In a sense there is nothing in reality that is super-natural or it could not exist at all. We will attempt to use more helpful distinctions which see the spiritual world as beyond our ordinary thinking and perceptions. The Divine is "ultra-natural" or even "intra-natural", present around or within ordinary reality. We need to expand our frame of reference to recognise the technology that exists in this realm.

3. Spurious objectivity and inconsistent attitudes to proof. The scientific world claims to work to a principle of "objectivity" and that this objectivity is maintained through the standards it sets regarding what may or may not be regarded as "evidence" or as "proof". The standards have been debated deeply in the past and form an academic subject in their own right, the Philosophy of Science. Some of the roots lie even deeper in philosophy itself, in its examination of what may or may not be "known". In practice we will show that these supposed standards are flawed in their reasoning, and are inconsistently and arbitrarily applied. Indeed it will be apparent that spiritual knowing cannot find a place in science because it is methodologically excluded.

On page 89 we are offered information about the brain and about its susceptibility to optical illusions. We will use similar images. Where the conclusion that Richard Dawkins draws is that human perception of a spiritual reality is akin to an illusion, we will suggest that we need to recognise and work constructively with our sensory limitations. Using our "additional senses" will help. His view, and the conventional scientific view, is that such limitations make any argument from personal experience invalid. But this is a self-fulfilling argument. It is used to deny experience that is common to millions of humans. Under such conditions what could possibly count as validation for our perceptions? Presented that way, it's an impossible task. But we will present sufficient objective evidence to show that there are very strong grounds to trust that people are not as dim as science thinks that they are and that there is a layer of non-ordinary reality that is eminently accessible.

4. The subjectivity of the choice to be objective. When claiming the objectivity above, it should be understood that in itself the choice of this supposed objectivity by philosophers and scientists is a subjective one. There has been huge value in attempting to ensure that we have some means of determining and validating what classes as "knowledge" or "truth", and science has benefited greatly from this. Belief in an ultimate objectivity is however quite mythological and it leads to the spurious claims of objectivity in methodology just noted. Human beings cannot understand the world they inhabit by excluding themselves and their experience from it. This inconvenient truth also leads to the next error.

5. The paradoxical nature of reality. Quantum physics, mathematics and philosophy have all shown the world to be full of paradoxes. This affects the most fundamental aspects of what may be considered "real" or "true" and is among the reasons why complete objectivity is a myth. We will see that paradoxes come and go according to perspective, and that it is impossible for any single view or system of rules to ever provide us with absolute truth. We will also see how wonderful and empowering this is; it opens up a truly creative science, describing a truly creative universe.

6. The significance of information. The scientific model is geared towards that which is material and directly observable. There are good reasons for this approach and it too has deep historical roots. Nevertheless it excludes aspects of the world which are crucial to the relationships between living organisms, aspects which lie in the realm of information and by which those organisms regulate their biology and their behaviour. In humans that information is critical in understanding the nature of the real world.

Some of these flaws can be traced back through millennia of Western philosophy, at least to the time of the Greeks. We don't for a moment suggest that Richard Dawkins is responsible for these errors, and he is not their only spokesperson. However he is a very prominent and passionate advocate. We suggest that these errors have come to inhabit the thinking in our culture. This is true to such an extent that it is not surprising they are now as unquestioned a part of our world as water is for the fish. Nor is it surprising that they are embedded in our language, the common currency of science or of its representatives. We do not define ourselves as philosophers, but the change we are promoting is also a philosophical change and we will inevitably refer to this from time to time.

Nor do we wish to be unkind to scientists as individual human beings. We live in the same world as they do and are also subject to its blind-spots. We also have sympathy where the goal of pursuing science as a career is subject to intense competition with strong pressure on funding, tenure, academic publication processes and teaching curriculum that sometimes make true independence a heroic choice. There are political issues here too. This is neither in essence a political book nor one about market economics but we would be naïve if we did not recognise that there is a political and economic reality that affects the scientific world. In the end, the shift that is required is a cultural shift which will affect all of these areas.

The fundamental challenge is for us to provide evidence to support our claims for a spiritual reality and to allow the spiritual agenda to be subjected to the same scrutiny as any statement or claim that might be made in other contexts. We are delighted that the question is being asked and eager to rise to this challenge. In return we will make suggestions for proper scientific investigation of various phenomena and hope that they will be taken equally seriously.

The fundamental demand of science is that it should be based on evidence. We will provide evidence. Some of that evidence will be based on human experience. Science requires that such evidence should be consistent and that it can be validated by repetition. We will provide an abundance of such evidence and refer to more. We will also illustrate the evidence with personal stories but the evidence should not be dismissed as anecdotal. There is too much of it for that.

At the same time a potential trap is set for us by the inconsistency which is applied to the definition of what may be offered as scientific evidence. The "hardest" of hard science happens in laboratories under conditions which are not particularly compatible with many of the aspects of life that we depict. Many "hard" scientists dismiss "softer" sciences such as those concerned with psychology or social phenomena. A friend, one-time CERN engineer Dr. Vinicio Sergo uses the apt phrase "the religion of Numerical Truth" and describes our slavery to it as a refined Orwellian situation. We would entrap ourselves if we attempt to meet laboratory standards of proof. Readers who will think we have failed if we cannot do this are warned that this would be an impossible task. We cannot overcome diehard skepticism and regard the stance described as anti-scientific; it leads to loss of knowledge. The same friend refers to this as "like the loss of biodiversity – a loss for life".

At the same time many scientific endeavours live outside the laboratory. Professor Dawkins' own discipline of ethology, and the piecing together of evolution through fossil evidence are examples of studies which rely strongly on careful observation of limited information, and on systematic analysis to determine meaning and relationships. We ask only for the same standards to be applied to our evidence.

We see a parallel in meteorology. "Weather" is a term that you could see as vague and hard to define. You can quantify rain, measure temperature and air pressure and come to conclusions about patterns that enable a degree of understanding of climate and prediction of weather events. But you still might struggle to say what weather is.

But we all know it's there. It is meaningful. Today might be ideal for me and too cold for you but subjectively we would agree together that weather exists. Sometimes spirituality exists in a similar frame. We are examining phenomena that live in the realm of human experience. Some of them will be measurable and some less so. If God exists, this is the realm she exists in. You might say that we are engaged in a new science of "deology".

We have used the title "God's Ecology". Ernst Haeckel, who coined the term, defined ecology as "the comprehensive science of the relationship of the organism to the environment". This draws another parallel, the metaphor of treating "God" as an organism and examining the environment in which it lives. Much of today's environmental agenda is concerned with the destruction of habitat and diversity, with an upset to the balance of nature that threatens our present and future lives. Those who inhabit a universe which is in any sense spiritual also find their habitat to be threatened. "The God Delusion" is only one part of a consistent attack on the world of spirituality, holistic health and the validity of belief. In this sense we are eco-warriors for the spiritual environment.

The journey

The territory that we are entering into is vast. Each chapter here represents a whole area of study. As a result we can only pull out core concepts, illustrate a few crucial facts and in doing so hope to construct a road map through several of the larger countries. We can post some signposts, describe a little landscape. It's a "Rough Guide" to the science of spirituality. But we do know where we are going and we will arrive home safely with broadened minds.

The itinerary starts in chapter 2 with our review of the territory in which spiritual experience operates and with some exploration of phenomena which have labels such as intuition and psychic awareness. We will put some definition around these, some examination of what evidence is to be found and what this means for our use of words like knowledge, belief, faith, certainty and truth. We start here because the core to all threads in our tapestry lies in understanding what "consciousness" is. Consciousness and our own inner experience exist at the boundary between subjective and objective experience. There is an information flow which pervades biological and physical worlds. Consciousness lives in the space between what has previously been termed "physical" and "spiritual". This is both why it has been missed and why it is central to our text. This book sets out to illustrate, rather than attempt a precise definition of what we mean by this.

This will lead us in chapter 3 into discussions of the relationship humans have as biological organisms with their physical environment. We will redefine the understanding of the spiritual experience so that it can be understood to be an integral part of that relationship. Scientism tends to treat the body as a biological machine. In doing so it oversimplifies the data and narrows the scientific possibilities. There is a physical component to the way in which consciousness is experienced and the relationship between subjective experience and biological mechanisms is highly complex.

One area of major conflict between science and the world of spiritual alternatives is that of complimentary medicine. We will explore the mind-body-spirit relationship in this context and show how the attack on spirituality and the attack on holistic medicine arise from the same misconceptions and use the same flawed methods. In chapters 4 and 5 we will look at the shamanistic view of the world and what it tells us about the nature of "reality" as well as seeing what it means for the nature of healing.

The boundary between spiritual healing and alternative medical methodology is frequently blurred. There are good reasons for this but it does lead to confusion. The involvement of human consciousness and spirit in the healing process is powerful, complex and sometimes subtle but it is also erroneously dismissed with the phrase "placebo effect". There is so much more involved. In general, science has taken no trouble whatsoever to investigate the evidence or to understand the theoretical under-pinning of holistic medical theory. Frequently its misrepresentations amount to ridicule. At best it ignores huge quantities of systematic evidence-gathering. In Chapter 6 we will use the science of homeopathy as a specific illustration of this general trend, and as a template for understanding "energy" medicine.

This will lead us naturally into the biological sciences, which are the subject matter of section 2. We will look first at the complexity of processes which build and maintain bodies like ours. We then follow the thread of inheritance between generations and change over millennial timescales with a discussion of genetics, inheritance and evolution. We are not about to argue for the biblical creation story but neither do we accept the purely mechanistic view of this process which books like "The Selfish Gene" and "The Blind Watchmaker" would persuade you to be the whole truth. In chapters 8 and 9 we will challenge some serious over-simplification in the way that science presents the role of the gene and in chapters 10 and 11 provide an alternative to the view of randomness as being at the core of evolutionary change. Consciousness enters into this world too and these chapters also explore the relationship between organisms and their environment and the story of how our experience of consciousness arises and how its relationship with our environment is maintained. There are more powerful reasons than those offered by scientism why evolution has supported human "spiritual" experience and provided it with adaptive advantage.

In section 3 our perspective switches from the human to the cosmic as we enter the world of the tiniest particles and the largest scales of time and space. This is the realm of other best-sellers, particularly Stephen Hawking's "Brief History of Time". In the face of the failure to unite these extremes through a physical "Theory of Everything" we will once again be placing consciousness in the middle. Albert Einstein famously (if metaphorically) said that "God does not play dice with the Universe". In these chapters we will show how an active and creative consciousness sits with quantum randomness in the realm of the small and how chaos theory unites the impact of the small with the unfolding of the large. We will also indicate how human consciousness takes part in this creative flow and answer the question of why humans engage in prayer.

In section 4 our final chapters return to our starting-point in order to draw together all these scientific strands with regard to the wide varieties of human experience. We will go deeper into our way of defining "reality" and take a brief look at the social and cultural aspects of our relationships with the world. It will be a major achievement here if we can demonstrate how foolish has been the scientific dismissal of many varieties of human spiritual experience, but this is our secondary goal. The primary goal is to weave all the strands of our thinking into a framework for future scientific understanding and investigation and even more into a tolerant, inclusive, broad and flexible basis for choices about how to live life.

Human religion has had its own evolutionary path. Historically, religions have evolved to meet a variety of needs. They created tribal bonds and community cohesion, and provided moral guidance to curb individual extremes. At their best these developed into governance and moral cohesion to unite countries and continents. At their worst they became the vehicles for many types of extreme in the exploitation of power and dominance or the fight for territory. Religion has retained too much of the primitiveness of its roots and quite often still exhibits an intolerant form of tribalism. It has not so far evolved at a large scale in a way which accommodates scientific knowledge or modern forms of thought, though valuable attempts at such an evolved viewpoint have been made, for example by William Bloom in his book "Soulution – The holistic manifesto".

Dr. Dawkins' attacks are part of the process by which religion and spiritual thinking need to evolve. Thinking which is primitive and not equipped to survive deserves to die and he is not hesitant in administering the killing blow to maladaptive thoughts and values. At the same time the implied superiority of intellectual rigour and the Westernised view of Truth are themselves subjective values. Scientific truth is not Absolute truth. The values are not global and the worst of their effects are seen in environmental exploitation, cultural extermination and economic imperialism. Scientism will be felt by many who are at the effect of these forces as another part of the attack on who they are and resistance will become a matter of survival for their very identity. While undoubtedly not the scientists' intention, it is no less dangerous for that.

The recent history of our subject matter is embedded in an "either-or" that lives in the gulf between science and spiritual experience, founded on a definition of spirituality that puts it in a non-physical realm, beyond the reach of science. As a result it can feel warlike and is reflected in our earlier use of the term "eco-warrior". We may feel personally that the battle is only between ideas. But beneath this whole cultures are at stake. If any of us expect others to give up their forms of what we regard as primitive thought we must first abandon our own dogma, deal with the mote in our own eyes and the impairment of our own vision.

The God Delusion continues the missionary tradition with scientism as its new religion. Having barely survived the Christian missionaries, the world may not be keen for a new form of cultural brain-laundering. Perhaps the West does have something to offer with its science and democracy but if others are expected to surrender their existing cultures and identities then we must allow them to develop their own replacement. It is unrealistic, arrogant and dangerous to require that they simply follow us into our limited version of the Promised Land. We would not wish anything we say in this book to be felt as prescriptive. We hope that the closing chapters of this book will be seen as a template within which all cultures may develop in ways which honour their traditions and evolve toward whatever species of culture they need to become.

There is one further thread in these last chapters and it is possibly the most challenging of all to the world of scientism. One of the fundamental activities among religious and spiritual humans is prayer. We referred above to a human engagement with the realm of consciousness as "creative". We will look at what this creative engagement really involves and at what it could mean for a genuinely inclusive, empowered and peaceable human race to live integrally through spiritual science and scientific spirituality.

The territory we are attempting to cover is vast. Inevitably we will skim. We will have to over-simplify if we are not to be bogged down. This is a book about scientific thinking. For narrative simplicity we will not adopt a text-book approach to references. Even so, everything we say has back-up and the details can be found in the major texts that we refer to.

Where we delve into scientific detail, we are aware that we risk "losing" lay readers. We believe that we have avoided this most of the time, but there are perhaps five chapters that may provide an intellectual challenge to non-scientists. We have attempted to provide some graphical support, but if it still feels too difficult we encourage readers to skim rather than give up. Sometimes the penny will drop later. But you can gain great value even if you don't grasp everything and we believe that our overall theme can be understood even if some of the detail is fuzzy. We also believe that it is of psychological value to know that the underpinning is there and could be revisited if necessary.

A New Way of Seeing

A story is told of scientist and poet Johann Wolfgang von Goethe as a young man. On returning from an educational journey To Italy, he was asked by his father if he had seen anything new. He replied "No father, but I have learned a new way of seeing." We have been brought up in a world which sees itself in a particular way. The errors that science makes are built in to that mode of seeing. While we are frustrated with science when it dismisses evidence unjustly or deliberately ignores it, the polemical views that we are challenging are merely an expression of the same flawed way of seeing that much of the world grows up with. So our task is to present a new way of seeing. We can offer a few images of this, and it is one theme that will run throughout our journey.

A simple dialogue with Dr Dawkins will not accomplish this task. Meeting his challenge to provide a science of spirituality will be impossible in a "he says black, we say white" way. His facts are not wrong, but some facts are missing, leading to mistakes of interpretation. We must make a shift of perspective, to see his black and our white at the same time. And then we must paint in the colours to see the whole in its richness. His view provides a valuable framework into which we will weave our threads and we thank him for providing such a clear base to work from.

As a teenager Jon was fascinated by the drawing here, which he repeatedly reproduced during dull lessons at school. Those who are familiar with the drawings of Maurits Escher will recognise its central dilemma of our human perspective. In the drawing it is possible to see a squared-off, two-legged figure and a rounded three-legged one, depending on where you focus your attention. Escher's endless staircases and confusing buildings are a brilliant elaboration on the theme.

We do not see the world as it is. The back of our eye is a curved surface, a few millimetres in depth on which rays of light draw a picture that represents hundreds of metres of height and depth. Our inner conceptions of the world are subject to similar limitations. We cannot change our eyes, but we can change

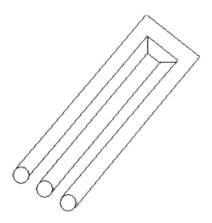

our concepts. This is an exercise not in vision, but in visioning. We have to use imagination to reframe our images.

The facts are not new. Many of them will be familiar. It is like the type of movie where the whole story is in front of you, but you do not understand it until the "MacGuffin" moment when the partially hidden motivator is made obvious. It's the territory of Hitchcock's "Charade" and Shyalaman's "Sixth Sense", and as with the latter all the clues were there, but you just didn't see them the right way. Most of our clues have been there all along. It's obvious when you watch the film twice, or when you review the facts. It's the film "Usual Suspects" once you know who Keyser Söze is. Our MacGuffin is not news either. Goethe knew it. Proust knew it too when he said "The true voyage of discovery consists not of seeking new landscapes, but having new eyes." You have been watching this movie all your life. If you don't already know the MacGuffin, here are your new eyes.

The MacGuffin

The usual story is that human beings are creatures who inhabit reality. The things of the world – whether the inanimate chairs and tables or the scuttling beetles – are objects that are separate from you. They are as they are and exist independently. You see them, touch them. You the subject make decisions about them, the object. It is a subject-object world. You make decisions about your experience. There is an external reality and you "know" things about it based on your interpretation of the information that your senses give you about it.

Science seeks to give complete definition to this external "reality" by getting beyond those sensory experiences and the decisions we make about them into a realm where all aspects of reality can be measured and understood independently of our personal experience. It seeks laws that define the way reality works – laws which hold true regardless of any of our experiences.

This works very well within certain boundaries and has taken humankind a long way in mastering its physical universe. This knowledge put men on the moon and mapped the chemical sequences of our chromosomes.

This story does not work for an intuitive world, for a prayerful world, for a world of energy healing. There is no science of human experience because human experience is outside the boundaries of science. There would be no problem with this if science were to accept that it has placed an examination of "God" outside of its methodology. It would be quite acceptable for science to say "we have no knowledge of this, it's not our remit, none of our business." The scientific attack on spirituality and holistic medicine steps across this boundary. In the "God Delusion" Richard Dawkins makes it his business and ours. The challenge to provide a science in which prayer and energy healing are intelligent and meaningful can only be met by extending the scientific realm as Goethe sought to do and as we do here.

Our view is that the "subject-object" divide is a human invention and has nothing to do with what is "real". It implies a separateness between us and the rest of the universe which is quite illusory. In consequence the view of what constitutes scientific objectivity and the presentation of our subjective experience as unreliable are both equally misguided. If you choose to stand in a valley you have only one possible perspective on the terrain. A helicopter view is quite different. The terrain has not changed. When you look at life from within a definition that assumes everything to be separate, you cannot see connectedness. Once you know that the connectedness is there, everything looks different. Reality lives not in subjects or objects, but through and in-between all of creation. Connectedness is our MacGuffin.

The hypothesis that this generates is that all "spiritual" experience takes place in the realm of this connectedness. The connection is not amorphous. It operates through information which is retained and exchanged throughout material creation. This information actually informs and defines the shape and nature of all material things. Information and our consciousness of it are inseparable. We would see it as what physicist Sir Arthur Eddington meant 80 years ago when he said "The universe is of the nature of a thought or sensation in a universal Mind... To put the conclusion crudely — the stuff of the world is mind-stuff". Throughout this book we will present evidence that demonstrates the presence of this information, its universality, and the way in which humans in particular interact with it. This is the realm in which spiritual experience takes place.

Spirals and levels

Throughout this book we will use a pair of images as a skeleton for our presentation. The two images, which you can see on pages 43a and 43b belong together and depict several elements of the world we are about to describe. The texture will emerge as our narrative develops, but we present the outline here. You will find it helpful to refer to the diagrams as we explain.

The images are a spiral with multiple layers and a disc of concentric rings. We would like you, if you can, to imagine them as if the disc is horizontal and the spiral is vertical, placed at its centre, like a cup and saucer or an ice-cream sundae glass. It is important to have a sense of the three-dimensionality of this image. While it is represented on a flat printed page, it has movement side-to-side, front-to-back and bottom-to-top.

Our ways of thinking are often in polarities. We see and speak in opposites, black or white, visible or not visible, good or bad. Things are present or absent. We may know that there are shades of grey and gradations of goodness but this either-or quality is typical of our thought and communication.

Science also presents us with polarities. It sees subjects (us) and objects (the other things and people in our worlds). It presents us with matter and energy, with particles and waves. Our entire world-view is constricted by this mental, philosophical and linguistic habit.

Accepted scientific truth has already gone beyond this limitation. Since Einstein we have been aware of the way in which matter and energy are interchangeable and a whole generation of writers about physics like Fritjof Capra and Gary Zukav has drawn out the parallels with mysticism in titles like "Tao of Physics" and "Dancing Wu-li masters". The underlying unity is acknowledged. In some ways though, it remains static. It does not give a picture that includes living, evolution, complexity and time.

To get that picture we have to increase the dimensions. In the spiral, the right-to-left view is broadly representative of the interplay of matter and energy. This is shown at the sub-atomic level where particles and wave functions are interchangeable. It is sustained, on one side through the various manifestations of physical, chemical and biological form – the ways that matter is configured – and on the other via different configurations of energy interchange in electromagnetic fields, chemical reactions and cellular life.

From the bottom to top we have a picture of complexity – and in effect of time also - since the complexity arose over the vast time-scale of cosmic creation from the "big bang" forward. Its range encompasses the entirety of both non-living material development and evolution into living forms that began with amino-acids and to date has reached the trillion-celled combinations that write and read books. Thus the spiral layers present an imprecise and arbitrary map of this development, from fundamental particles through atoms and complex molecules to living cells, organs and multi-celled organisms. Many of these layers are likely to have their own spirals of internal development; for instance the whole periodic table of elements might be represented in this way. We will see later that there are further spirals above this one which govern the dynamics of social evolution.

None of the two-fold picture so far would challenge orthodox science. Side to side and top to bottom, our picture holds a conventional materialistic view. There is no spiritual element, nothing beyond the standard picture of random particles interacting in magically and mysteriously wonderful ways. But when we seek to explain a world in which people have intuitive or spiritual experiences, and in which humans find something that they are inclined to call "God" then the picture as described so far is inadequate.

Our intention in this book is to bring the front-to-back dimension of this cone to life. This is the hardest to visualise from a flat page. The dynamic of existence does not simply swing from one side to the other but rather it loops around, developing, expanding and growing. While it grows more complex, it also self-balances. The loop connects each layer of the spiral to the next in a continuous thread. The elements in that balancing process are represented in the rings of our disc.

Outside the disc we have shown the overall dynamics of structure and flow, which correspond to the matter-energy polarity in physics. The third element is the balancing process itself. Maintaining balance is at the core of an ecological view of the world. The image of an ecosystem is of interactions between multiple species of plants and animals, inhabiting specific conditions of climate and terrain. The question of how this governance of equality and balance comes about in life as a whole is central to this book.

The right and left "sectors" of the discs contain labels which broadly correspond with those to the right and left of the spiral. The same sense of developing complexity should be apparent as those rings progress from the philosophical "subject-object" polarity through waves and particles, matter and energy, into the more conceptual aspects of our biology – our body and feelings, the forces of our spiritual "will" energies. In the social realm this reaches a corresponding dynamic balance that deals with the interplay of individual freedom with social collective mutuality.

This balance is not an accident of random interactions. It is held in a context of information that the universe contains about itself and which manifests as consciousness, as mind and in social governance that are depicted in the upper sector. Throughout our story we will present the picture of what this information is, where it is and how it affects all of the processes that science recognises, but cannot fully explain. We will also encompass all the manifestations that are not recognised by science but are the core of spiritual experience, religious belief and holistic medical alternatives.

While our habits tend towards polarity, the three-fold view that this diagram presents is not new. It can be found in a Freudian view of the psyche with its ego, super-ego and id. Rudolf Steiner's three-fold social order with its "rights" realm has the social aspect of governance quite explicit. His three-fold view of man presents our interactions with the world through facts, feelings and ideas. It is present in the context that is used by much of alternative medicine as represented by the name of the UK "Mind-Body-Spirit" exhibition. It is also fundamental to Robert Pirsig's presentation of the philosophical significance of "quality" in "Zen and the Art of Motorcycle Maintenance" and to the discussion of "qualia" in other developments within philosophy. Some philosophers see qualia as another word to describe what we will call "consciousness". But despite such pre-figuring, the implications for a fully integrated view of science that encompasses the spiritual nature of the universe have not previously been offered in the way that we present them here. This could be the biggest MacGuffin you will ever encounter.

Every chapter in this book will explore aspects of this integrated universe. We may cover one or more layers of the spiral or explore one or more rings of the disk. As we do so we intend that a picture will emerge showing how all the aspects come together as a unified whole.

We could not possibly represent all of the connections in the diagrams. As said at the start of this section, the spiral and disk merely provide a skeleton. We can only paint some of the muscles, nervous systems, organs and circulatory processes which make this living universe. But in the diagram we have drawn attention to three strands of connectivity which are most important in our story. These form the vertical bands through the spiral layers and we draw your attention to them here.

In our chapters exploring the phenomenon of "intuition" we will illustrate the way in which the information that the universe holds about itself is accessible to humans. The ability in our individual minds for "inner sensing" that accesses the information realm has no boundaries. We will give evidence for the ways in which this knowing provides access to every level of existence. We will also provide the evidence for mind-over-matter interaction in this realm, the experiments that demonstrate conclusively that there is a complete and active connection down to the smallest levels. We could have used other labels than "intuition" and our descriptions of information and consciousness address the same realm.

Some of the connectivity that runs through layers of the spiral is provided in the realm of body chemistry – in the chemical messengers that provide one level of cellular communication and in the rhythmic chemistry of cellular life-process that supports coherence and co-ordination. This strand will run through our chapter on the neuro-endocrine system and through the biological picture of life's rhythms.

Another part of the connectedness is provided by a layer of function that we have called "photon and liquid crystal coherence". This strand is present also in the understanding of quantum physics and the orchestrated organisation of our brain function that emerges there. Throughout the text we will be building background understanding for the nature of this connectivity and giving scientific proof for it.

In all of this we will show, illustrate and provide evidence for a world-view that makes sense of spiritual experience, psychic knowledge, energy healing and for a vision of the world as a connected whole. To offer a comprehensive depiction of the world, we have to deal with many different scales of existence and to encompass a hugely complex picture. The small diagrams accompanying most chapters attempt to position each piece within the overall map. Our goal is that some simplicity will emerge on the far side of the complexity. At the same time, the fact that we are including a spiritual world that is invisible by its very nature, requires us all to engage our inner senses and our poetic side, to operate alongside our intellectual and analytical forms of understanding.

One aspect of our presentation will be to require an expansion in science itself. As indicated earlier, the scientific flaws that we have described derive from an attempt to achieve an impossible level of "objective" proof and a choice to exclude data which might derive from human experience and therefore by definition be "subjective". Our early chapters will provide the evidence that this complementary viewpoint is essential and requires us to place the "subjective" alongside the "objective" in order to achieve a complete view of what "reality" might be. This is the perspective from Goethe and others who tell us that to see something new sometimes demands a new way of seeing. As a Sufi parable about coffee would have it "He who tastes, knows; he who tastes not, knows not." You cannot know all there is about coffee (and by extension about the world) from its objective or physical properties.

The result of this exploration is an overarching map of creation which we believe is more complete than most views on offer from philosophical, spiritual and scientific perspectives and which combines all three in a coherent whole. We don't hype our message with a claim that "this book will change your life" but thinking of the world this way has certainly changed ours – and for the better. We invite you to join us in this exploration and hope that you enjoy it.

2. The Sight Within

A man born and bred to the so-called exact sciences, and at the height of his ability to reason empirically, finds it hard to believe that an exact sensory imagination might also exist.

Johann Wolfgang von Goethe

Science and metaphysics therefore come together in intuition. A truly intuitive philosophy would realize the much-desired union of science and metaphysics.

Henri Bergson

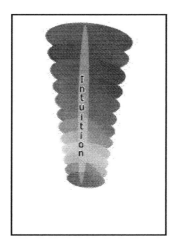

Theme

Our introductory task is to illustrate aspects of the conscious connectedness we are describing. In this chapter we give some personal experience and strong evidence from others which reveal core features of the "top-to-bottom" nature of this connection as revealed by human experience. These features are:-

There is a thread of connectedness through all levels of material reality

This connectedness allows human access to information about the world

The information is specific and externally verifiable

Access is both open and "targeted" as well as being received spontaneously or by deliberate enquiry

Information arrives via pathways which resemble our external sensing.

The thread of connectedness does not acknowledge time boundaries

The connectedness is not simply a matter of passive or active receiving. There is also very strong experimental evidence that humans can "transmit" and that transmission has physical consequences

A personal background

A book about spirituality has a personal core, however strong our central intention to address scientific questions may be. The path we are taking mirrors personal journeys. It will support your understanding to know who is writing and why and this knowledge is particularly relevant to our starting point.

Jon's personal journey began with a background of atheistic upbringing, an intellectually challenging father and an interest in sciences which led via A-levels in maths and physics to the study of Human Sciences at Oxford. This subject included elements of genetics and evolution, ethology (a young Richard Dawkins being one of his lecturers), Human Biology plus various other disciplines with mankind as their central subject. Mysticism, religion and spirituality were not part of this package and the extra-curricular focus was a combination of student politics and classical music.

Clearly something happened to change this atheist, but there was no voice from the heavens, no blinding experience on the road to Damascus, no conversion by charismatic evangelists. The experience which brought this shift was low-key and undramatic while at the same time being ultimately as powerful and life-changing as any of those options. Jon describes it as follows.

"After leaving University, having skirted one path that led to research work in chimpanzee behaviour and another in the Philosophy of Science, I pursued a fascination with the world of computers, then in its infancy. An initial impulse towards the use of computers as an educational tool had been displaced by learning what they could do in the commercial world and I was enjoying the experience of taking drudgery from people's daily working lives. I was also on the conventional life-path with a wife and two children.

Another part of this conventional path was stress, both in over-work and from the marriage which was not going well and this led me to take a course in relaxation techniques and creative visualisation. At least, that is what I though it was. Over the four days it became apparent that there were much deeper intentions in the training which had to do with extending sensing abilities towards intuition in order to assist people to address their own and other people's health issues. By the end of the course, I was told, we would experience ourselves as having the ability to gain knowledge psychically.

I did not believe this possible, at least not through training. I might have allowed the possibility of extraordinary gifts but saw myself as the least likely person to be capable of such a thing. Even so, I went along with the training process in an open-minded and curious way. On the last afternoon we each went through exercises, using the techniques we had been taught. In these exercises we would be given the name, age and approximate location of an individual, known to one other of the participants who had written down some basic facts about that individual. This information was in the hands of a third person.

My experience during the exercise was of "tuning in" to the subject individual (David, a 27-yearold male living in Devon) using the techniques we had practiced. For a long time I was getting nothing until I tried a particular approach in which rather than trying to "see" the person or "hear" information about them in my mind, I visualised what it would be like to be that individual. The effect was instant. I had the strong feeling of there being pain in the rear left side of my head and spontaneously grimaced. I asked the observer if the person had pain from some condition like a brain tumour and was told that this was exactly what was written down. I used other techniques to attempt to send healing (this being the real purpose of the training) before bringing my attention back and participating in the experiences of other students.

Of the twenty or so people in the room, all but two had some kind of success in this kind of detection – enough that they knew with confidence that they had detected something that they could not have known by any "normal" means. I therefore had to recognise not just my own experience but that of several others, none of whom had given any indication of previous training or gifts in such areas.

For a while this experience was simply a curiosity and I did not know what to do with it. later it began to bother me. All my scientific training told me that there was no known mechanism by which such things can happen. There was no physical medium by which such information is known to pass. There was no way known to science in which the information itself is "published". There was no way to understand in any scientific terms how I could have located the correct individual based on just a name, age and location. Yet in true scientific spirit my questions were "evidence-based".

Basically, this meant that the science I had been taught had to be flawed in some way. Although I subsequently observed other courses in which larger numbers of people went through a similar experience, and even though I later trained as a teacher for the method and saw those whom I taught having the same success, it was the personal experience that was transformational. I have spent over two decades since then pulling the loose thread in the scientific knitting. The explorations which that led to are central to all that follows."

Juliana will introduce herself in Chapter 6.

Flat-earthers and the global reality.

Our first step on the journey requires that we deal with a major challenge that humans face as soon as a subject like intuition is raised. We are biological creatures whose existence runs from birth through life toward death and our concepts of time and space fully reflect this view of reality. Scientifically speaking, reality is not so simple. Mathematicians and physicists work with a model of the real world which has more than our three dimensions of space (up-down, side-to-side, front-to-back) and which does not view time as running in one direction.

Throughout biological creation it is obvious that organisms rely for their survival on understanding space and time very well. You know this each time you cross a busy street. It is a fact which appears to have driven the evolution of sensory apparatus in predator and prey species and we are used to relying on these senses. For humans the physicist's perspective is also psychologically threatening. Potentially it challenges our identity, our sense of self, to imagine a world of ten dimensions in which time's arrow does not apply.

Perhaps it will help to imagine a reduced number of dimensions and to see ourselves like "Mr. Square", the being imagined by Edwin Abbott, a Victorian-era mathematician who created a world whose inhabitants could only see in two dimensions. They could see forward and back. They could see left and right. Up and down did not exist for them. If you put such a being on a globe and started him walking straight forward, he would eventually arrive back at his starting point with no notion of how this was possible. They resemble the humans who expected sailors to fall off the edge of an Earth that was presumed to be flat. Mr Square could see the third dimension but had trouble conveying this to others.

When the medieval flat-earthers were told that the Earth was a globe they at least had a concept of spherical objects to relate to. They had pebbles, apples and oranges. The information that we present here requires a bigger shift. As Mark Twain said "It ain't what you don't know that gets you into trouble. It's what you know for sure that just ain't so". We have to let go of what we think we know. The metaphor of thinking "outside of the box" is very strongly applicable here and as Twain also said "you can't depend on your eyes when your imagination is out of focus".

While the background is that scientifically the box didn't exist anyway, we need to tell some other stories which will illustrate how the linear "cause and effect" chain is broken. We want to make it easier to grasp. But we also need to follow this up with some experimental evidence. Stories don't help if they are then treated as myths, mistakes and coincidences. The research evidence is limited because very little research gets funded – the catch-22 consequence of not being seen as scientifically possible. But there is some quality that makes up for the lack of quantity. It is good enough to deserve being taken seriously.

Skilled medical intuitives

The next two examples are also about medical intuitives – in both cases people who can be regarded as having marked natural abilities, honed by years of practice. Where Jon is a two-fingered pianist plonking out "chopsticks", these are virtuosi playing Rachmaninov. The first example comes in her own words from Dr Caroline Myss who has progressed from being perhaps the best-known modern medical intuitive to being one of the world's most inspired and clear-thinking spiritual teachers.

By way of introduction, this is what Dr Norman Shealey, M.D, Ph.D says of her:-

"There have been, throughout the ages, talented intuitives and mystics who have sensed the power centres of the human body. Alice Bailey, Charles Leadbetter and Rudolf Steiner have all written in this field, but no-one has captured the breadth and depth of our electromagnetic spiritual framework as well as Caroline. Never before has the anatomy of the spirit been so powerfully revealed. Herein lies the foundation for medicine of the twenty-first century. ...

Quantum Physicists have confirmed the reality of the basic vibratory essence of life, which is what intuitives sense. Human DNA vibrates at a rate of 52 to 78 Gigahertz (billions of cycles per second). Although scientific instruments cannot yet evaluate any one person's specific frequency or the blocks to the flow of such energy, two basic facts cannot be denied. First life energy is not static, it is kinetic; it moves around. And second, talented intuitives such as Caroline can evaluate it, even though neither the human mind nor the energy system can yet be accurately physically measured.   Indeed in my twenty-five years of work with intuitives throughout the world, none has been as clear or accurate as Caroline."

What follows is our précis of Caroline's own description of her experience, which starts in 1982 when she has recently started a publishing company and is still a smoker, coffee-drinker and "not at all primed for a mystical experience".

"I gradually recognised that my perceptual abilities had expanded considerably. For instance a friend would mention that someone he knew was not feeling well, and an insight into the cause of the problem would pop into my head. I was uncannily accurate and word of it soon spread through the local community.

Soon people were phoning the company to make appointments. To say I was in a fog would be a gross understatement. I was confused and a little scared. I could not figure out how I was getting these impressions. They were and still are, like impersonal daydreams that start to flow as soon as I receive the person's permission, name and age.   Their impersonality, the nonfeeling sensation of the impressions, is extremely significant because it is my indicator that I am not manufacturing or projecting these impressions. They are clear but completely unemotional.

She describes the sensation of wondering with each consultation whether "it" would work together with the fear of failing people by being inaccurate and the tension this led to.

> "Deep in my soul, I knew that I was connecting with something that was essentially sacred, and that knowledge was splitting me in two. On the one hand I feared that I would become incapacitated, like mystics of old; on the other, I felt destined for a life in which I would be evaluated and judged by believers and sceptics. No matter how I envisioned my future, however, I felt I was headed for misery.

> But I was fascinated by my newfound perceptual ability nonetheless, and was compelled to keep on evaluating people's health. In these early days the impressions I received were mainly of a person's immediate physical health and the related emotional or psychological stress. But I could also SEE the energy surrounding that person's body. I saw it filled with information about the person's history. I began to realise something I had never been taught in school: that our spirit is very much a part of our daily lives; it embodies our thoughts and emotions, and it records every one of them from the most mundane to the visionary. Although I had been taught, more or less, that our spirit goes either "up" or "down" after death, depending on how virtuously we have lived, I now saw that our spirit is more than that. It participates in every second of our lives".

Caroline continues with her story describing a deep experience in which she was "guided" from within, entirely without warning, through the explanation to a woman facing terminal cancer of all the events in her life – in "every detail" - which had led to her current illness. It is a dramatic and revealing story which we regret having no space to reproduce. We deeply recommend "Anatomy of the Spirit" and all of Caroline's considerable body of work.

> "Since that autumn day in 1983 I have worked wholeheartedly as a medical intuitive. This means that I use my intuitive ability to help people understand the emotional, psychological and spiritual energy that lies at the root of their illness, disease, or life crisis. I can sense the type of illness that has developed, often before the individual is even aware of having an illness at all. The more I have used my intuition, the more accurate it has become. Now it feels almost ordinary to me, although its workings will always remain a little mysterious."

As Dr Shealey pointed out, Caroline is not the only medical intuitive but there are several special features about her material. Her partnership with Dr Shealey is one significant element in this. Over many years he would telephone her about his patients As a result the accuracy of her work was confirmed by true medical diagnosis with a practitioner who could follow cases in detail. Also significant is the nature of Caroline's perceptions and the way in which it captures not just immediate information in the "here and now" but past information.

At the risk of taking too much time with "medical intuitive" stories we also wish to bring in the perspective of Dr Mona Lisa Shulz who is an M.D. with a Ph.D. in neuroanatomy and behavioural neuroscience as well as a practicing intuitive. Where Caroline Myss presents the Spirit-to-mind connection with such clarity, Mona Lisa is able to apply her deep knowledge of the mind-body chemistry in order to map the mind-body relationship in distinct operational terms.

It is not possible to convey the complexity of this map in a single quotation. It forms a tapestry that weaves through her book "Awakening Intuition". At the centre is her intricate understanding of the way in which the development of disease reflects the nature of the life conditions the subject is dealing with, and how this process is mediated physically and biochemically through the way that particular functions become blocked and subsequently break down. Here is a typical example. At the beginning of every reading Mona Lisa has only the subject's name and age obtained over the phone to work with.

"The reading. As soon as I began reading Violet, age 38, I saw a life full of joy and exuberance. She seemed to me like a little sparrow sitting on a fence, warbling away. She didn't like to complain and masked everything with her cheerfulness. But underneath her heart, I saw a difficulty, a person who was getting in the way of something Violet wanted. I saw disappointment in her relationship with this person, which was making Violet's healing a challenge. I saw something Violet wanted to do, some life's path she needed to follow, but I saw she was being held back by this person who had authority over her. This person appeared to be extremely goal-oriented and focused on his own needs to the detriment of the feelings of those around him. In fact he reminded me of a cat who's just killed a bird. He's sitting on the porch, surrounded by feathers. And the feathers are the petals of Violet's heart.

I saw that Violet was feeling less and less joy and was slowly becoming angry and resentful. Her partnership was not one of equality; her partner was the authority and she was submissive.

In her body I saw a little scarring in her lungs from past smoking, and occasional bladder infections in the distant past. But in her head I saw a kind of fury, what I call a tornado in the scalp. This whirlwind of anger and hostility was buffeting her heart and causing it to race and skip a beat.

The facts. Violet was a musician who had an intense desire to become an orchestral conductor. She had the opportunity to work and train toward this end with a leading male conductor. Her husband, however, was opposed to this idea. A nonmusician himself, he was threatened by the prospect of his wife's working closely with another man at something in which he could have no part, and he refused to allow her to pursue her plan. Violet was inwardly furious at this, but out of deference to her husband's feelings and jealousy she had put off her training. However she hadn't given up on her determination to become a conductor. She continued privately to plan to do it at a later date, thinking that she could present the idea to her husband in another way so that he would eventually approve it. For the time being, violet had put a lid on her own feelings to keep her husband happy, but her resentment simmered. Meanwhile she confirmed that she had developed an arrhythmia in her heart.

Explanation. Violet had given over authority in the partnership to her husband, but the results of this were causing her great resentment, and this resentment was sitting on her chest. And this in turn was setting the stage for serious heart problems. Sudden death from a heart attack is believed to be due to arrhythmia, a change in the rhythm of your heart. Stress often causes an increase in the production of brain chemicals called catecholamines, which can speed up the heart rate, overstress the heart muscle, wear down its reserves, and enhance the person's chance of developing heart disease."

Dr Shulz's book combines the intricate analysis of different types of illness and their roots in body chemistry with exhaustive investigation into the nature of the intuitive world, drawing on her own experience and that of others. She quotes a study by Patricia Brenner into the intuitive experience of nurses, who are noted for their sensitivity to the condition of patients undergoing close monitoring, detecting features not obviously present in the data they are reading.

"In an extensive study of nurses and intuition, nurse and researcher Patricia Brenner ascribed the intuitive process of nurses in clinical situations to "skilled pattern recognition"....this theory concludes that preciously acquired knowledge, an expertise based on memory and prior experience, is the basis and source of intuition. An nurse detects something in a patient that rings a tiny bell in her mind and reminds her of a previous similar case that leads to her hunch about the current patient's condition.

One of Brenner's own nurse cases however, contradicts this neat theory. It involves a case of pulmonary embolism. As it happens, pulmonary embolism, a blood clot in the lungs that's nearly always fatal if undetected, is one of the hardest things in Western medicine to diagnose, There are virtually no common symptoms and very often no discernible signs that a patient is in danger of a PE. ...Fundamentally it's one of the most fatal medical conditions and tragically, one of the easiest to miss.

The nurse whom Brenner observed saw a patient with cerebral edema, or fluid on the brain. His fluid intake had been restricted, and he was resting quietly. But the nurse was concerned. "Somehow I knew he was going to have a rough time," she reported. There it was, the intuitive hunch. "Somehow I knew he was on the highway to a pulmonary embolism." But what a hunch! How did she make the unbelievable leap to that extraordinary conclusion? It was a case of pole-vaulter cognition. This patient didn't have a problem with a clot in his lungs, he had cerebral edema. It wasn't even a case of right church, wrong pew; this nurse didn't even seem to be in the right state! The only possible symptom she could relate to pulmonary embolism was having overheard the patient's wife say earlier in the day that he was anxious. That night the nurse couldn't stay away from the patient's room, even though he was assigned to someone else's care... She found him "sort of pale and anxious,) and even though he was still conscious she called the doctors, and sure enough, just as the doctor's arrived, the patient began to die. The doctors coded, or resuscitated, him. The pulmonary embolism was caught and the patient was saved."

From these examples we would like to draw out several features of the intuitive experience and begin to highlight some threads which run through the cloth of the connected world we are describing. These threads will recur and be developed as this book unfolds and we will see them from a variety of perspectives.

- There is a connection between one human being and another that enables the transfer of information

- That information is capable of being highly specific

- That information is capable of being accessed without an explicit "address" protocol. That is, Caroline and Mona Lisa can tune in to a person simply by hearing a name even when that name is spoken by a third person.

- There is a connection between the information content and the physical events which take place in the body

- Individuals (e.g. the nurse in the example above) can be aware of this information content even when not explicitly seeking it through a deliberate intuitive intention

- The intuitive sensory mechanisms in the receiver vary. They may deliver through pictures, words, or feelings and sensations, or the receiver may "just know". But all of these mechanisms use existing sensory pathways.

There are passages in Mona Lisa Shulz's book which explore the need for a person who is learning to be intuitive, to recognise the pathway which is most active for them, and to understand the symbolic ways in which information presents. This matches Jon's experience and forms an important part of the process he uses for teaching intuition.

The book also explores the significance of dreams as a communication path for inner knowing about the body-mind. The symbology of dreams is hardly a new discovery, but it has a link with our next example, written of by J.W. Dunne in his 1927 book:-

"An Experiment with Time".

J.W. Dunne (1875-1949) was a British aviation pioneer. As an engineer trained in the classical pragmatism of the late 19th century, he held a number of early British aeronautical patents. He was successful and respected with a comfortable income, to all appearances a normal member of society.

Dunne's book begins by chronicling an experiential journey. Over a period of time he had repetitive incidences of dreams which would in the days following be mirrored back in newspaper stories and headlines of dramatic events. His initial scientific scepticism is documented in great detail, as is the process of analysis by which he sought to test his experiences and to eliminate the possibilities of chance and coincidence or faulty memory and suggestibility. He describes the process with the true engineer's love for precision.

Over an extended period he compiled lists in which he systematically noted correspondences between dreams and events, both when those events were in the past (i.e. before the dream) and when they came after, as if the dream had been predictive. In some cases the dream would be close to the event. In others they were significantly ahead of the time they corresponded to. His eventual conclusion was that dreams were occurring in approximately equal numbers relating to the past and to the future.

Here is one example of a predictive dream with a six-month time-span.

> The dream occurred in the autumn of 1913. The scene I saw was a high railway embankment. I knew in that dream – knew without questioning, as anyone acquainted with the locality would have known – that the place was just north of the Firth of Forth Bridge, in Scotland. The terrain below the embankment was open grassland, with people walking in small groups thereon. The scene came and went several times, but the last time I saw that a train going north had just fallen over the embankment. I saw several carriages lying towards the bottom of the slope, and I saw large blocks of stone rolling and sliding down. Realizing that this was probably one of those odd dreams of mine, I tried to ascertain if I could "get" the date of the real occurrence. All that I could gather was that this date was somewhere in the following spring. My own recollection is that I pitched finally upon the middle of April but my sister thinks I mentioned March when I told her the dream next morning. We agreed, jokingly, that we must warn our friends against travelling north in Scotland at any time in the succeeding spring.

> On April 14th of that spring, the "Flying Scotsman", one of the most famous mail trains of the period, jumped the parapet near Burnisland station, about fifteen miles north of the Forth Bridge, and fell onto the golf links twenty feet below.

The experiments described in the book extended over a period of years and were widened to include numbers of other subjects. Examples and analyses fill the first half of the book. Unless one treats the text as either fraud or fantasy the accumulation of evidence is totally convincing when viewed in the context of the care with which it is acquired and the dry delivery of a Victorian / Edwardian gentleman. He progresses to the following conclusion regarding what he had originally thought might simply be his own "abnormality" in the experience of pre-cognitive dreaming.

> "...in the light of the experiment, I did not appear to possess even a specially well-developed faculty for observing the effect. Those other people had got their decisive results more quickly than I, and in most cases, those results had been clearer.
>
> The outcome of the experiments suggests that the number of persons who would be able to perceive the effect for themselves would be, at least, so large as to render any idea of abnormality absurd"

The second half is devoted to an enquiry into the meaning of these events. What do they tell us about the nature of consciousness and its relationship with linear time? Much of this is presented in mathematical terms, some of it related to the theory of Relativity, which was quite new at the time. Hopefully we can present the core conclusions in a simple and understandable way. While we could short-circuit the discussion by simply saying that, from physics' point of view there simply is no linear time of the kind that we experience, we feel that it is useful to understand more about the nature of our conscious relationship with time and our perceptions of it.

An experience familiar to many is that of sitting on a train at a station. There is another train on the neighbouring track. You notice that your train is beginning to pull out slowly and quietly and you see the neighbouring coaches passing. It is only when the last coach passes that you realise that the station is still there. Your train hasn't moved at all. (Perhaps if you are not familiar with trains, you may have had a similar experience as a car or bus passenger during a stop-start traffic jam.)

Our experience with travelling is that we are usually the ones in motion and that is what we expect. Our minds process the signals from our eyes with this as the in-built assumption. We don't think about it. This tells us something about our position as "observers". We tend to see what we expect to see.

Our view of time also contains expectations. Our everyday waking observer adopts the same view of time that the passenger takes towards scenery. The scenery moves past us and we see one scene after another. Likewise, we experience one moment, then another and then another as time flows. With time we do not think there is any possibility of reversing our journey. We cannot makc time go backwards. Still less can we teleport back and forward across the landscape, frog-hopping from past to future.

A corresponding shift of perspective occurs in the dream-experiences described by J.W. Dunne. Just as when we find it was the other train that was moving, his story requires us to turn our view of time around. Instead of time flowing irreversibly with only the present moment being in our view, the whole vista is made available to us and we can indeed do the equivalent of teleporting ourselves into past or future. We can imagine teleporting because that's like an aeroplane but quicker. We can likewise imagine an H.G. Wells-type time machine where the jump is from now to the past or future.

But dreams are also different because we don't physically move. There's no machine, no Time Tunnel, no Tardis. What there is, is an observer that moves. The conscious awareness can roam in time or space, but our bodies stay where they are. This resembles our experience of memory where we are familiar with an internal journey to images that we have stored, and where our consciousness no longer resides in the present but instead has its focus in that past experience. We know what it is like, replaying the car accident or the embarrassing moment, recalling the moment of joy at a birth, or when we fell in love. There is a resemblance to imagination or fantasy, where we visualise ourselves in the future, shaking hands as we receive the hoped-for promotion, or that moment as children where we scored the winning goal in the cup final.

In pre-cognitive dreaming however, it is neither memory nor imagination. The observer moves not in his / her own personal world but in the landscape of all worlds. The observer, the dreamer, is not part of the experience but is at a distance, seeing the train fall off the track, watching the stones tumble down the embankment.

In J.W. Dunne's presentation there are two crucial features which distinguish the experience. His investigations do not deal much with the similar realms of intuition or telepathy described earlier, but we suggest that the conclusions would be the same.

Firstly, we need to reframe our view of reality. In the dream experience we have stepped off time's arrow and have options not available to our physical selves. Our consciousness can move. In a similar way, the intuitive experience takes the consciousness of the observer into realms where there is access to information that is not presented to the senses we call "physical".

Secondly we need to accept that there are two distinct types of observer. Most of us spend all of our waking time in one mode, being "observer A". There is a "right now" in which Jon is sitting at a keyboard, thinking thoughts, typing words, seeing images appear on a monitor. In a future "right now" insert your name here is reading a book and sharing those thoughts. You can be aware of the book, the place you are in, the chair you're sitting on etc. But there is another observer – an "observer B". This other observer takes a back seat in our consciousness. We may never be aware of their observations at all, or we may experience them in dreams, or we may receive them as intuitive experiences. This other observer can roam in space and time; it can see, hear and feel that which is not here and not now. It can know things which are not accessible to observer one.

We do not choose to say what this other observer is. If you have a belief system there may be a language you use for it. Words like inner knowing, gut-feel, soul, spirit, higher self, "I am" presence and even "God self" come to mind. But if none of this instantly fits your belief system then we ask you for now to recognise the evidence that is being put forward and leave a space for a world-view to emerge that will encompass the reality that this evidence is demonstrating.

Who's looking?

Once we accept that Observer B exists, and always has, our questions over "God" and spirituality begin to take on a new aspect. The difficulty with "God" is not one of existence or non-existence, it is one of interpretation and understanding. Most historical views of the Divine are too simple to fit the complex reality of a connected world. Many stem from simpler times and thought structures. There is a need for a 21st Century re-evaluation.

What we have begun to see is that for most people in our society Observer 2 is either unheard, heard and distrusted, heard and ignored (because our science tells us it cannot be real) or simply over-ridden because it does not tell us things that our Observer A personality wants to hear.

Often, while we may hear the inner voice we do not understand the way in which it communicates. For most people the voice is subtle and understanding requires some effort. We have no way of knowing what this experience was like for people 5000 years ago or at the time of Christ or Mohammed. We have little understanding of what it might be for those living now in different ways than we do – the aboriginals, the indigenous peoples who still live close to nature. Perhaps these cultures have been more open and receptive or their members have experienced less competition for their attention. Even where a culture treats intuitive relationship to the world as normal it is too much to expect that such a culture might use our modes of analysis or express those views in concepts that are familiar to us. There are a few exceptions however which may help us over this barrier and we will come to them in Chapters 4 and 5.

For now we simply want to open up the idea that much of what now occurs under the banner of religions and those aspects of spiritual belief in other cultures which are easily criticised and presented as primitive, may arise from attempts to make sense of a complex world seen "as through a glass, darkly". What we hope will emerge through this text is a more coherent way to understand the complexity, the difficulties of interpretation and the nature of "what lies beneath" – or perhaps what reigns above.

As preparation for this we will now present some of the more systematic and explicitly scientific investigations of connectedness. What has been done to prove the ability of minds – of observer 2 – to roam in time or space and to extend the projection of our sensing mechanisms?

If you were to listen to what scientists say, you could be forgiven for thinking that no-one has done any experiments to determine whether psychic activity is possible. Where there are references to such experimentation, they are almost always dismissive. For example, the famous Prof. Carl Sagan, renowned cosmologist and science-fiction author wrote his final book "The Demon-haunted Universe" to defend scientific knowledge in the face of irrational beliefs. But his chapter on telepathy fails to mention any experimental work. His only concession is to acknowledge elsewhere the existence of three claims in the ESP field which deserve serious study, one of which is the claim that by thought alone, humans can affect random number generators in computers.

Unfortunately he does not say what these deserving claims are, despite the fact that just one such proof of even a minimal effect would demand fundamental revision to conventional scientific theory. In the following pages, we describe some of the more convincing work. Our first choice may well be the one he is referring to.

Psychokinesis

One particularly interesting series of experiments was conducted under the supervision of the Professor of Aerospace Sciences, and Dean Emeritus of the School of Engineering and Applied Science at Princeton University. Robert Jahn is the author of "The Physics of Electric Propulsion", a consultant for NASA and the US Defence Department, and had no special interest or belief in the paranormal. However, he was approached by a student of clinical psychology to oversee her project on that topic. The results were of such interest, that in 1979 he founded a laboratory under the direction of Brenda Dunne "to study the potential vulnerability of engineering devices and information processing systems to the anomalous influence of the consciousness of their human operators."

Twenty-six years on, the Princeton Engineering Anomalies Research facility (PEAR) has recently (Feb '07) announced its intention to close. On its website it states

> "Jahn and his colleague, Brenda Dunne, a developmental psychologist from the University of Chicago who has served throughout as PEAR's laboratory manager, together with other members of their interdisciplinary research staff, have focused on two major areas of study: anomalous human/machine interactions, which addresses the effects of consciousness on random physical systems and processes; and remote perception, wherein people attempt to acquire information about distant locations and events. The enormous databases produced by PEAR provide clear evidence that human thought and emotion can produce measurable influences on physical reality. The researchers have also developed several theoretical models that attempt to accommodate the empirical results, which cannot be explained by any currently recognized scientific model."

In one series of experiments, Jahn and Dunne employed a device called a Random event generator (REG). The REG relies on an unpredictable natural process such as radioactive decay, and produces a string of random binary numbers. REG is in principle like a fast coin-flipper which can produce a high number of tosses in a very short time. The statistical expectation is that a large number of throws will tend towards a 50/50 split between heads and tails.

Jahn and Dunne had volunteers sit in front of the REG, and concentrate on having it produce more heads, or more tails. Over the course of hundreds of thousands of trials, they discovered that the volunteers did have a small, but statistically significant effect on the output of the REG. They discovered that the ability was not limited to a few "gifted" individuals. Rather they discovered that the majority of the individuals they tested could produce some effect. In addition to that, they observed that different volunteers produced results that were consistently distinctive. In certain cases these results were so marked, that the experimenters started to regard them as "signatures".

In a further series of experiments, Jahn and Dunne went from the sub-molecular level, to the visibly physical. They used a sort of pinball-like apparatus that allows 9,000 three-quarter inch (2cm) marbles to circulate around 330 nylon pegs, and distribute themselves into 19 different collecting bins at the bottom. The device is contained in a vertical frame 3M by 2M (10' by 6') with a clear glass front. Left un-influenced, the marbles would normally fall more in the centre than the outside bins, and the overall distribution would be a bell-shaped curve.

The experimenters had the volunteer subjects sit in front of the machine, and try to cause more balls to land in the outside bins than in the centre ones, thus flattening the shape of the bell. Once again, over a very large number of trials, the volunteers were able to create a small shift, but a measurable one, in the landing-pattern of the balls. In this they showed that a psychokinetic effect could be achieved, not just at the level of microscopic processes, but on events in the everyday, material world. Furthermore, where characteristic individual "signatures" had been observed in certain subjects during the REG tests, those characteristics were again observable in the pinball-type experiments. This suggested that the Psychokinetic abilities of any individual remain consistent from experiment to experiment. There was still clear variation between individual capabilities. The conclusion drawn by Jahn and Dunne was this.

"While small segments of these results might reasonably be discounted as falling too close to chance behaviour to justify revision of prevailing scientific tenets, taken in concert the entire ensemble establishes an incontrovertible aberration of substantial proportions."

These experiments have several particularly appealing features. Firstly, they did not use "gifted" or "special" individuals. They showed that the results could be achieved even on a wide range of people who had taken no steps to develop such a capability. While it is scientifically significant even if only one being can achieve such results (because the theories of science would still have to allow its possibility and explain its mechanics) it is much more exciting to think of this as part of a generalised reality.

Secondly, these experiments are very hard to "rubbish". In both cases, there is little potential for the experimenters, wittingly or unwittingly, to influence the outcome. It would be particularly hard for the experimenters to produce the consistent "signature" pattern. The procedures were designed in such a way as to be watertight, by a scientist of considerable repute, and no apparent bias. Unless one is willing to accuse the experimenters of deliberate fraud, there is not much room for question.

The only question that might be asked is over what is statistically significant. Perhaps, these minute fluctuations do not seem very exciting. But it is normal in many areas of scientific research to treat small variations in large numbers of samples, as being significant. The likelihood of the effects occurring by chance vary. Of their overall body of work, including that on Precognitive Remote Perception, Jahn and Dunne say "The composite formal human / machine results are of the order of 10^{-12}; the formal PRP results to the order of 10^{-8}". In normal speech these are chances of 1 in a trillion to 1 in 100 million, hugely less likely than a millionaire lottery ticket. Any reasonable assessment would be that the results are enough to show that the behaviour being observed is not random. In the absence of any other plausible explanation, the one proposed by the experimenters should be accepted.

Please don't be misled about the significance of small-scale effects of this kind. Their mere existence is in antithesis to scientific orthodoxy and blows a hole in scientism. In addition we will show later how small-scale effects can be of great practical significance.

We should also note, as we will in other areas of our scientific material, that Jahn and Dunne have experienced huge difficulty in achieving publication of their results in science journals. Science is not a level playing-field. Those interested in more detail can download the "PEAR proposition" paper from the website (www.princeton.edu/pear).

Psychic information-transfer

The second experiment we want to describe, was the subject of an article in New Scientist (15/5/93), by John McCrone. This is how he describes it.

> "Isolated inside a steel-lined cubicle with walls a foot thick, the subject lay back in a chair. Two halves of a ping-pong ball were taped over his eyes, and headphones filled his ears with white noise. Three metres away, in a second padded and shielded cubicle, a "sender" was concentrating on a TV film of an eagle, and trying to transmit the image telepathically. Something seemed to be coming through in the receiver's chamber: "I see a dark shape of a black bird with a very pointed beak with his wings down ... almost a needle-like beak ... Something that would fly or is flying ... like a parrot with long feathers on a perch. Lots of feathers, tail feathers, long, long, long ... Flying, a big huge, huge eagle. The wings of an eagle spread out."

Chuck Honorton, who died in 1992, had set himself the mission of putting the previously disreputable field of parapsychology on a scientific footing, by designing telepathy experiments that would be regarded as rigorous. Maybe he had succeeded. Susan Blackmore, a psychologist at the University of Western England in Bristol, who is a noted debunker of psychic claims, is quoted as saying "He has pushed the sceptics like myself into the position of having to say that it is either some kind of extraordinary flaw that no-one has thought of, or that it is some kind of fraud - or that it is genuine ESP."

Honorton's methodology came from a long history of other experiments which were either shown to be frauds, or were criticised for flaws in their methodology. Initially the "Ganzfeld" technique, as it was known, was subject to as much criticism as any others. From a dialogue between Honorton, and one of his principal critics, came the modifications to methodology that resulted in the most recent, and most convincing experiments.

The principle of the Ganzfeld (from German, meaning "whole field") was the knowledge that if people are subjected to perceptual deprivation, the elimination of outside stimuli to the senses, their internal visual imagery would increase. Since mental imagery is a common way to convey psychic impressions to people it was thought that such impressions would be more easily detected under such conditions and so make research easier.

Also involved in the sensory deprivation, is the shielding of the receiving subject from all normal forms of communication. The room has double-doors and walls. The ping-pong balls mentioned in John McCrone's description have red light shining on them, creating a plain visual field. The subject is encouraged to keep his/her eyes open. White noise creates a uniform background, and an additional acoustic barrier. Honorton's experiment also included copper shielding against radio-wave communication.

The methods used involved use of a computer to randomly select from a selection of four videotapes to be shown to the "transmitter" subject. The experimenter is kept blind to the selection made. The receiver spends 15 - 30 minutes in relaxation / deprivation, describing sensations to the experimenter, before the transmission session starts. After the receiving session, the receiver is shown four video clips - the one seen by the transmitter, plus three others, and has to attempt to identify which one was transmitted. In the latest versions of the trials, over 240 subjects were used. These were not known to be "gifted" and most only made one trial. Overall, where random chance would have produced only 25% of correct responses, the trials yielded an average value of 34% correct identifications of the randomly selected transmission.

That might not sound high, and you have to understand statistics well to argue about how meaningful it is. Suffice it to say, that the more tests that are done, the less likely it is for any result other than the random 25%. So, if there are enough tests, and the result differs markedly from random, then the result is significant. It indicates that some effect is taking place in an area where no effect is believed possible. In short, it is enough to prove that psychic communication is possible, even if it is that communication is unreliable and low-key.

In general, telepathy experiments have been criticised for leaving too many possibilities for inadvertent communication. If the experimenter knows what the receiver is meant to pick up, he may unwittingly influence his choice. In recent experiments, great care was taken to avoid this possibility. Even the VCR is acoustically shielded from the experimenter, so that the amount of time spent fast-forwarding should not be known. A different copy of the tape is used for the playback and selection to the receiver, so that no differences of tape wear should be involved. The sender cannot communicate with any other person, by any method, during the experiment.

In Honorton's experiment, all sessions were recorded, providing a means of corroborating any results. Although this method made fraud difficult, rather than impossible, one has to be very determined to reject the experiment to make such an accusation. So far even hardened sceptics have assumed some "hidden flaw", rather than deceit to be the cause of the successful result. However, no flaw has subsequently been found.

There was another interesting feature of the experiment. The overall hit rate was above chance. But the hit rate among receivers who did not believe in the possibility of telepathy was as low as 8%. This indicates that certain "believer" subjects had achieved even **higher** success rates than 34% and also opens the possibility that the "non-believers" may have had some intuitive knowledge that enabled them (semi-intentionally) to select correctly **less than** 25% of the time

There have been many attempts at Ganzfeld experiments. Not all have been as tight in their methodology, and many have been criticised. Some have been unsuccessful. Evaluation of this evidence is very tricky. There is no scientific acceptance that telepathy is a proven fact. Nevertheless, there is a weight of evidence building that is making it harder than ever to dismiss the possibility.

We want to draw attention to two aspects of these results. One is that whereas these effects are usually called "paranormal", we should be seeing them as normal. The reason we do not think them normal, is only because science has told us they are not and our culture has built that belief in to our development and education. Mechanisms of energy exchange that are not recognised within the terms of accepted scientific theory are required for them to even be possible. We can hardly say this too strongly. Science acknowledges no way - no mechanism at all, by which such events can happen. Psychic communication takes place without any recognised wave or particle to facilitate it. These results and any other evidence of psychic activity, expose physics as incomplete. When the science does not match the reality, it is science that must be revised - it is

Oneness to Complexity Spiral

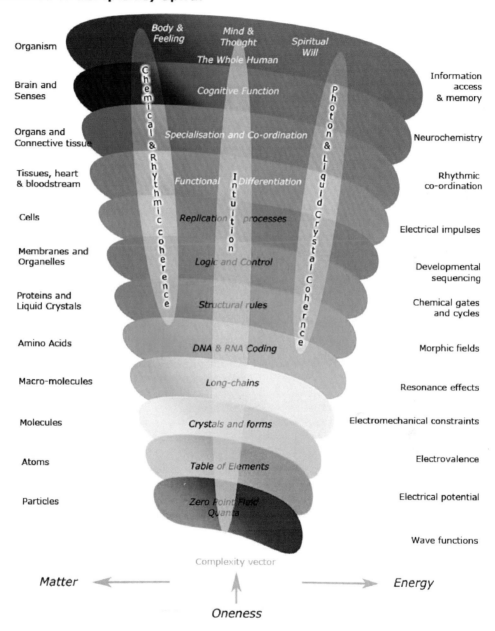

This spiral is not intended to delineate exact boundaries. It illustrates the balance between the energy and matter aspects of creation (r-l) and depicts layering of increased complexity (bottom-top).   The central pillar of labels indictates the successive addition of information content layers to the story of creation and represents the front-to-back dimension. Correspondences between these layers and the material or energy aspects to either side are indicative approximations which inevitably overlap and are superceded and included within later layers.

Aspects of the Creative Impulse

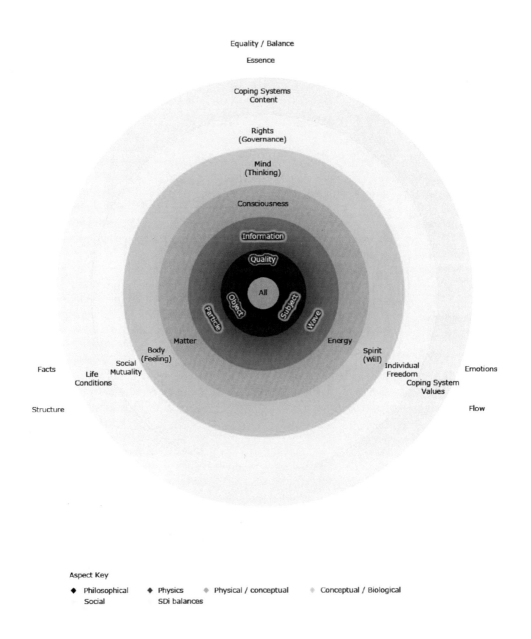

Equality / Balance

Essence

Coping Systems
Content

Rights
(Governance)

Mind
(Thinking)

Consciousness

Information

Quality

All

Object

Subject

Particle

Wave

Matter

Energy

Body
(Feeling)

Spirit
(Will)

Social
Mutuality

Individual
Freedom

Facts

Life
Conditions

Coping System
Values

Emotions

Structure

Flow

Aspect Key

◆ Philosophical   ◆ Physics   ◈ Physical / conceptual   ◇ Conceptual / Biological
  Social   SDi balances

Note that growth is from the centre to the periphery and that each layer includes tho
before it.

Plate 3: Belousov-Zhabotinsky reaction – "quantum clock" – see page 171

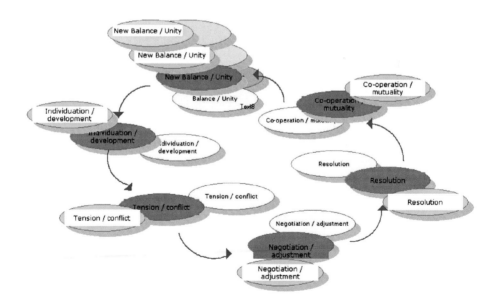

Plate 4: Sahtouris spiral – see page 187

With special thanks to Don Beck

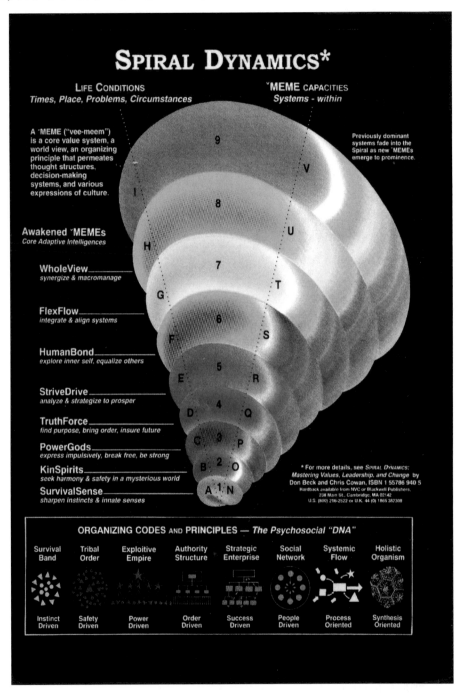

Plate 5. Spiral Dynamics Conditions and Values. P.262

fruitless and unscientific to challenge reality. Later when we look at the world of physics we will discover that it already reveals these gaps, even in its own terms.

It is also important to be aware that small effects could be extremely important. The reason for this will emerge later, after we have looked at physical laws, and what is commonly known as "chaos theory" - the study of how dynamic systems change over time. Sci-fi movies and TV series tend to show "psychic" powers in a dramatic way so it might seem that they are not important when their effects are so small and subtle. This is far from true, but it will take a while to show why. We will come to see these small influences as the "butterfly's wing that causes the hurricane". At the personal level we also need to guard that the "Hollywood effect" does not prevent us from recognising our own intuition. Intuitive knowledge comes less with technicolour special effects and more as a still quiet voice.

We have not reproduced the classic remote viewing experiments of Targ and Puthoff or the detailed Jahn and Dunne PRP material here. This is purely for reasons of space. The experiential aspects are covered by other material in this book. The experimental results can be found in the source texts and are briefly referred to in the PRP probabilities given from the PEAR proposition earlier.

What is Knowledge? What is Science?

The term "Science" has its linguistic root in the latin verb "Scire", which itself means to know or understand. In consequence it is quite tricky to distinguish the two questions posed in the heading above. It is even more difficult when we bring other expressions into play – words such as belief or faith. We may even have multiple shades to a word like "know". I know that the sun will rise tomorrow. I know that I am hungry. I know that Paris is the capital city of Texas (just kidding).

There are people – maybe you are one such - who would claim to "know" God. They would not say "I believe in God". They would not say they have faith (or not merely that). Knowledge has all of these flavours and more. Page 50 of the God Delusion lists seven and these do not include our own view. Science attempts to be something distinct from all of these and to establish a body of facts which are verifiable and true for all people under all conditions or at least for a clearly defined range of conditions.

In order to do this, science establishes principles of measurement. These principles are most comfortably satisfied when the measurement is performed by apparatus. Science likes it best when the only thing for the human being to do is to read the temperature on the thermometer, to weigh the object on a scale. Provided the apparatus is constructed to the correct standards, the measurements can be repeated in other times and other places by other people and the results will be the same.

Relatively little of science conforms to this standard. Readers of Dr. Dawkins' earlier works will be very familiar with the way in which genetics and evolution offer a great deal of data, and that data is not entirely measurable. Great intellectual effort is required in order to analyse that data and there are deep divisions about what it means. Darwin's theory of evolution through natural selection is a scientific theory but it is not an experiment which can be replicated elsewhere by other observers under controlled conditions. (Readers of Douglas Adams will be familiar with the alternative to this statement, which is that the Earth is an experiment constructed by white mice for such a purpose, but we are not convinced that this hypothesis is helpful.)

In other areas of science the processes required to measure or detect that which is not visible require increasing complexity. Things too small to see require microscopes. The composition of the Sun cannot be determined by grabbing a handful – it is established by indirect means. Brain cells, neurons and dendrites are examined through scanners or by means of thin tissue slivers under electron microscopy. The picture of scientific truth is built piece by piece using many different methodologies, layers of technical intermediaries and multiple human observers, and often via deep dispute over what a set of results might mean.

Determining whether knowledge is scientific is not a black and white, yes-no matter. This wide range of data-gathering and disputation involves a systematic attempt to eliminate anything personal, subjective or psychological but it has few absolutes. The truths it uncovers are often relative, often temporary and waiting to be superceded or subsumed, as Newtonian mechanics was by Relativity.

In practice, science is an approach, an attitude to evidence. It's like a police investigation. If you are seen in the neighbourhood of one murder that might mean nothing. If you are placed at the scene of another that might just be coincidence. To be at a third will make you suspect number one.

Science can only measure "things". It might expand the category of "things" on a continual basis to include discoveries like supernovae and quantum particles. It might allow the category of measurement to include the collection of data regarding species and habitats and to enable inference regarding ecological pressure, food-sources, predators, competition etc. Inevitably though, science is troubled by "information". With murder fresh in our minds you might like to think of Iago, whose manipulation of information supply is such as to induce Shakespeare's Othello to jealous murder of the wife he adores. Information has consequences but it doesn't fall into the realm of "things".

When you "know" that you are hungry, that information has the consequence that you are likely to get more closely acquainted with the contents of the fridge / vending machine. Your body is an information processing device. This information is internal and possibly not conscious – certainly based on things that you are not conscious of such as blood-sugar or fat levels. Other information is external – my skin is cold; add clothing or seek shelter. Science can measure some things. It could validate your blood sugar levels or the external temperature. It cannot measure your choice whether to seek shelter or put on clothes. It might have considerable difficulty with your choice when you get to the fridge? Ham? Perhaps you are a vegetarian. Cheese? Maybe a vegan. OK, Hummus. Unless there's chocolate biscuits available, making all other choices irrelevant. The choice lies in the realm of information and is not measurable, but the information affects the world and is more significant when the information persuades you to go to war in Iraq.

We could also have asked "what is intuition?" It is a form of knowing – sometimes remarkably accurate, and still it does not quite fit what we would be comfortable to call "knowledge". And yet it is verifiable. In the research cited above, a scientific attitude to evidence has been present to the greatest degree possible, taking into account the limits to that evidence placed by phenomena which are very hard to detect. In the examples of intuition there is external confirmation of the truth of subjective experience. Even so, that experience lay fundamentally in the realm of information, and science has a limited toolkit for this realm.

We are about to delve further into the subjective worlds and we will have to reach our own view, find our own answer to the question of "what do I know?" How many coincidences does it take before a pattern is acknowledged? How many reports of similar experience, from how many cultures, are required in order to establish a truth as universal? How much data is required before the scientific model of the physical universe has to change, and incorporate the passage of information from one place, one person, one living being to another into its theoretical frame?

Review

We set out to offer evidence to illustrate the way in which information about the universe is accessible to and accessed by human beings. We have shown that aside from our personal experience of such events, there is evidence with external validation which shows that humans can seek and locate specific information and that equally it can be presented to them unasked.

We have shown that this information is presented to human consciousness through sensory pathways that make use of the same mechanisms familiar to us in memory and imagination, but providing data which are not necessarily part of our personal world and which can also be accessed in a way which contradicts our habitual experience of the arrow of time.

In addition we have presented strong evidence from rigorous experimentation of both passive information detection and active information transmission. In the case of transmission we have shown the top-to-bottom feature that is in our diagram, connecting humans right through to the atomic particle level. We have also shown that such active transmission has outcomes in the physical world. This is a feature that we will revisit in the context of energy healing and later in relation to the nature of prayer.

3. I sing the body neuro-endocrine

And all the world is football shaped

It's just for me to kick in space

And I can see, hear, smell, touch taste

And I've got one two three four five senses working overtime

Trying to take this all in

I've got one two three four five senses working overtime

Trying to taste the difference 'tween a lemon and a lime

Pain and pleasure and the church bells softly chime

    Andrew Partridge   *XTC 1982*

I SING the Body electric;

The armies of those I love engirth me, and I engirth them;

They will not let me off till I go with them, respond to them,

And discorrupt them, and charge them full with the charge of the Soul.

    Walt Whitman   *Leaves of Grass*

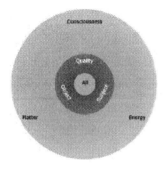

Theme

In this chapter we explore the connectedness that exists at the cellular level in the form of chemical messengers and rhythmic co-ordination. We present one key aspect of the role of "consciousness" in the relationship between matter and energy within complex organisms. We will see that the conventional view that "mind" is located in our brain as the seat of our thinking process is incorrect. Our organs and the cells that compose them have a part to play, as do the cells in our blood. The chemical messengers which circulate our bodies influence our physiological states and the ways in which we experience those states as emotions.

We will also encounter the truth of the age-old perception that the heart is not just a pump, but a co-ordinator of feelings and decisions. The heart has a particular role in the processes that we describe as "mind" and in our overall intelligence. All of this brings an extra dimension to the connectedness, one that integrates our emotional states with our values and decision-making. It resembles our intuition as an internal, subjective experience carrying personal meaning, but also forms part of our relationship with the external reality. This relationship includes the part played by biochemistry in our spiritual experience.

Sense, emotion and human experience

The chapter title does not sound as good as the Walt Whitman line quoted, but one suspects he would have absolutely adored the story that this chapter tells, like us finding it rich, subtle, delicate and full of wonder.

The field of science we are about to explore is relatively new. Genetics only began in earnest with the discovery of the double-helix structure by Franklin, Watson and Crick and has taken fifty years to the point of mapping the human genome. But where it might be said to be in early adulthood, the discipline which studies the chemical nervous system is barely a teenager. The field which has acquired the name "psychoneuroimmunology" (PNI) started with a paper published by Candace Pert and Sol Snyder in 1979. It was a slow starter. The name was coined in 1984 but even two decades later the full significance is just emerging.

We are about to delve into some intricacies of biology. In case this focus seems odd in a discussion of spirituality, we should explain the importance of what is to come. Everything that we are describing in the realm of spirituality is expressed through human experience. Everything that is sensed is sensed by bodies and all that is described comes through a language that derives from a physical process and is reported in terms of our senses. This is how we experience our relationship with the material world and it is also how we experience the world of unseen energies that can be called "spiritual".

Albert Einstein, when asked to describe how radio works, reportedly (and perhaps mischievously) said

> "You see, wireless telegraph is a kind of a very, very long cat. You pull his tail in New York and his head is meowing in Los Angeles. Do you understand this? And radio operates exactly the same way: you send signals here, they receive them there. The only difference is that there is no cat."

It is tempting to try and describe spiritual experience as if it is a radio or TV program. It would seem easier and perhaps more "scientific" to leave the person out. The TV is seen as inert, as a window through which the program is viewed. We trust the technology, that if we watch a program we are seeing that which the director filmed and the TV itself has not altered the original content. In this analogy, with intuition, spirituality and all the related phenomena we describe, the receiver (TV) is an active part of the process. There is a human where the cat..... isn't.

Even more than that, when we describe Candace Pert's work, we are in an arena of both biology and communications. The content of the communication, the ways in which it is mediated are at the heart of human experience – subtle, intricate and powerful. The internal relationships and the external ones are intertwined. We will not understand them adequately unless we understand them in their connectedness. This also relates to homeopathy and to other complementary healing approaches including "spiritual" healing.

It's not just a computer

Most of us, even younger readers, will have been educated in an old model which viewed the brain and nervous system as being like an electrical circuit or a computer. There is a system of that kind present within you. It is critical to instantaneous actions such as motor functions. If you touch a hot object you need an instant response through specific muscles if you are to avoid a burn. The kind of co-ordination that is required for sports needs rapid decision-making based on visual clues and a direct pathway between decision-making and muscular action. We know that damage to nerve fibres can be catastrophic. For this reason the computer-like model is powerful and persuasive.

That model doesn't give the whole picture though. There is much more happening in the body and a great deal of it is not instantaneous and is not happening in a single location. Living alongside the electrical network is a nervous system composed of molecules and sensors. The sensors are not just in the brain. Every cell is a little part of this network of intelligence.

While second to be discovered, the chemical system was there first. It exists in creatures without brains and is therefore more basic – more fundamental to life. There is a primitive single-celled creature, the tetrahymena, which is widely used in laboratories for experimental study. This creature makes many of the same substances, including insulin and the endorphins as we are about to describe in humans. On its single-cell surface can be found opiate receptors just like the ones in human brains.

At the operational heart of this chemical system are peptides, complex molecules which travel throughout the body and act as messengers. Francis Schmitt of MIT coined the broad term "informational substances" because they distribute information throughout the organism. The responses elicited by these molecules can be multiple and complex and they are classified under a wide variety of categories, including hormones, neurotransmitters, neuro-modulators, growth (and growth-inhibiting) factors, gut peptides, interleukins, cytokines and chemokines. Fortunately we don't need to know precisely what each of these does but it is valuable for us to recognise the complexity. Some of these messenger names may be familiar such as insulin for its part in blood-sugar regulation or oestrogen and testosterone for their part in sexual differentiation and fertility regulation.

For a long time it was expected that the brain would be central to communications and control, even if there was a new agent in the process. Any messenger is only of use if there is something to hear the message and take action. There was reason to expect that the receptor mechanism would be found on the surface of a cell and that the brain was the place to look for such receptors and indeed this was where they first began to be found.

However, over time the story became more and more complex to the extent that it is now recognized that cells in every part of the body have receptors, usually for many different messengers, sometimes acting in combination. Eventually it became apparent that all these cells, all over the body, were not only receiving messages they were also sending them. Peptides, messenger molecules, were being produced everywhere. The brain is not the centre of this process but one among many organs, all of which play a part in regulating physical processes.

To give just a little flavour of what this interaction means, here is an extract from Candace Pert's book "Molecules of Emotion".

Molecules of Emotion

"To cite just one recent example, Rita Valentino of the University of Pennsylvania has shown that the nucleus of Barrington in the hindbrain, formerly believed to control merely micturition (bladder-emptying), sends axons containing the neuropeptide CRF down through the vagus nerve all the way to the most distant part of the large intestine, near the anus. Rita has proved that sensations of colonic distension (i.e. the feeling of needing to poop) as well as those of genital arousal are carried back to the nucleus of Barrington. From there, there is a short neuronal pathway (called a "projection") that hooks up to the locus coreolus, the nor-epinephrine-containing source of the "pleasure pathway", which is also very high in opiate receptors. The pleasure pathway hooks up to the control area of these bathroom functions, which is located in the front of the brain. Goodness, is it any wonder, based on Rita's neuro-anatomical discoveries, that toilet training is loaded with emotional stuff! Or that people get in to some unusual sexual practices involving bathroom behaviours! Clearly the classical psychologists had grossly underestimated the complexity and scope of the neurochemistry and neuroanatomy of the autonomic nervous system. But the limitations of the past are now giving way before our newfound ability to track these fascinating connections.

If we accept the idea that peptides and other informational substances are the biochemicals of emotion, their distribution in the body's nerves has all kinds of significance, which Sigmund Freud, were he alive today, would gleefully point out as the molecular confirmation of his theories. The body is the unconscious mind! Repressed traumas caused by overwhelming emotion can be stored in a body part, thereafter affecting our ability to feel that part or even move it. The new work suggests there are almost infinite pathways for the conscious mind to access – and modify – the unconscious mind and the body, and also provides an explanation for a number of phenomena that the emotional theorists have been considering."

Dr Pert explores the connection between emotions and memory further, going on to note the work on state-dependent memory by Donald Overton, who has shown that memories stored under the influence of an emotion are recalled better when that same emotion is present. This is a feature used by Neuro-linguistic Programming, Emotional Freedom Technique and other methodologies for healing.

The perception that the whole body is active, that it behaves like a hologram in which any part holds information about the whole, that the body is a holistic system in which all organic processes are interrelated, is fundamental to all complementary health and natural-tradition medical systems. The relevance to our spiritual theme is that all of these systems share a core perception that the process is also connected with the spirit - in all senses of that word. They would include the spiritual well-being of the individual, their overall emotional tone. They would include the notion that a spiritual entity exists – spirit in the sense of what might be called a soul. They would include spirit in the sense of a relationship with a wider energy world, a relationship which might be felt with nature, with ancestors, with the land or with the "Divine" whether that be expressed as a supreme being or one of the other formulations that describe that realm.

This consistent linking by healers of all kinds between the holism of bodymind and a greater connectivity is not accidental; it deserves to be taken seriously that all cultures worked with these relationships before the dawn of the scientific age – not out of primitive ignorance, but through observation and deep understanding. The gift Candace Pert brings is to describe some of the mechanics which mediate these relationships. Her sentence in the quote above that "The body is the subconscious mind!" encapsulates what we mean by the word "bodymind". Put another way, the body is mind all over.

When we said earlier that the messenger chemicals are produced everywhere in the body, this does not just mean our organs. One crucial part of the picture is the discovery that these chemicals are found on the cells of the immune system. The cells which are carried in the bloodstream and which detect and destroy disease-producing organisms are as much a part of the communications process as any other. Another crucial part of the picture is that many of the messengers which regulate our processes are integral to the reactions we label as "emotions".

The traditional view was that emotions are some sort of perceptual artifact created by the brain – nothing more than a viewpoint towards the world generated by the mental computer in our head. However we know that our bodies also display these emotional states – we flush with embarrassment, our hearts beat faster with fear and panic. It was assumed that these were nervous system "decisions" but this is quite misleading and leads to a misunderstanding of emotion and its place in our relationship with the world.

We must understand that science finds emotions awkward as they are in the realm of subjective description. The physiological reactions can be measured but the emotional labels that we give to them are subjective and hard to isolate. What one person calls passion may be perceived as anger by his neighbour. You could conjugate these relationships. "I am firm, you are opinionated, he is bloody-minded." Despite this challenge, Charles Darwin was one of the first to be interested in studying emotions. As he observed "...the young and the old of widely different races, both with man and animals, express the same state of mind by the same movements." And elsewhere, "Even cows, when they frisk about from pleasure, throw up their tails in a ridiculous fashion." He interested himself deeply in theorizing how humans and animals display such emotions as fear, anger, disdain, and pleasure and published a book specifically on that subject. It is work that has in most respects been sustained by later scientific research.

In general it is a subject neglected by science since then, except in its more psychological aspects. Pert's work (remember, the title of her book is "Molecules of Emotion") brings this back to the centre of the bodymind. The following passages convey the technical core of this message.

> "In order for the brain not to be overwhelmed by the constant deluge of sensory input, some sort of filtering system must enable us to pay attention to what our

bodymind deems the most important pieces of information and to ignore others….Emotions are constantly regulating what we experience as "reality". The decision about what sensory information travels to your brain and what gets filtered out depends on what signals the receptors are receiving from the peptides. There is a plethora of elegant neurophysiological data suggesting that the nervous system is not capable of taking in everything, but can only scan the outer world for material that it is prepared to find by virtue of its wiring hookups, its own internal hookups and its past experience…..

I knew from my brain mapping over the years that the communicating chemicals were most dense in certain areas of the brain and along sensory pathways…And when we focus on emotions, it suddenly becomes very interesting that the parts of the brain where receptors and peptides are richest are also the parts of the brain that have been implicated in the expression of emotion. I don't remember whether it was Michael or I who said the words first, but both of us had the gut feeling that we were right: 'Maybe these peptides and their receptors are the biochemical basis of emotion"

As their 1985 paper in the Journal of Immunology stated:-

"A major conceptual shift in Neuroscience has been wrought by the realization that brain function is modulated by numerous chemicals in addition to classical neurotransmitters. Many of these informational substances are neuropeptides, originally studied in other contexts as hormones, gut peptides or growth factors. Their number presently exceeds 50 and most, if not all, alter behaviour and mood states, although only endogenous analogs (i.e. man-made equivalents) of psychoactive drugs like morphine, valium and phencyclidine have been well appreciated in this context. We now realize that their signal specificity resides in receptors rather than the close juxtaposition occurring at classical synapses. Precise brain distribution patterns for many neuropeptide receptors have been determined. A number of brain loci, many within emotion-mediating brain areas, are enriched with many types of neuropeptide receptors, suggesting a convergence of information processing at these nodes. Additionally, neuropeptide receptors occur on mobile cells of the immune system; monocytes can chemotax to numerous neuropeptides via processes shown by structure-activity analysis to be mediated by distinct receptors indistinguishable from those found in the brain. Neuropeptides and their receptors thus join the brain, glands and immune system in a network of communication between brain and body, probably representing the biochemical substrate of emotion." (Their emphasis).

Monocytes are immune cells, the ones in the blood-stream which identify foreign substances and destroy them and which also play a part in destroying infected cells in the body. They will "chemotax", moving through chemical influence to sites where neuropeptides are signaling the presence of physiological stress that requires intervention. The biological event and our "feelings" – the way that the biological event affects us emotionally – are linked through the flow of neuropeptides and the way that these chemicals are selectively received by various parts of the brain and body.

In summary then, three previously separated areas of study – neuroscience, endocrinology and immunology, together with their various organs - the brain, the glands and the spleen, bone marrow and lymph nodes – are actually joined together in a multidirectional network of communication, linked by information carriers known as neuropeptides. The emphasis here should be placed on the words "network of communication" as it is the flow of information through the cells, organs and systems of the body which mediates this complex process of regulation, balance and health maintenance.

The view of the organism as an information network takes us away from old, mechanical ways of looking at the body. To the old view of hardwired reflexes and electrical stimulation, with their limited capacity for flexibility and change is added a form of higher intelligence that is running systems and creating behaviour.

The intelligent heart

To give another flavour of this, let's talk about the heart. Traditionally the heart has been written of with deep poetic understanding as the vessel of human love, the seat of courage and a source of wisdom. We feel emotions as much in our heart as anywhere and it was once regarded by many as the seat of the soul. However a female friend recently complained bitterly about the dismissive attitude a science-minded ex-boyfriend had taken to her discussing the heart in these terms. "It's just a pump" he said.

He couldn't be more wrong! The following information is taken from a lecture by Howard Martin and is derived from the research undertaken by Doc Childre's HeartMath Institute. It presents a very different and once again non-mechanical, subtle and complex view of the human body. Of course the heart is a pump but the intuitive truth down the ages is borne out by recognizing all that it does besides.

The heart beat is present in the foetus even before the brain is formed. The idea that the heart is governed by the brain is contradicted by this fact and by the knowledge that it will beat (as it does when transplanted) without a nerve connection to the brain. It is auto-rhythmic, having the source of its beat within itself. It responds to stimuli from the body but is not controlled and particularly not by the brain.

In fact the heart is what people have always known it is – a sensory organ which makes functional decisions and communicates with the brain. This happens in four ways.

1. There is neurological influence. The heart has 40,000 of its own neurons and a distinct nerve pathway through the medulla, the amygdala and limbic system to the neo-cortex. That is, it passes directly through the emotional memory systems to the thalamus and synchronises cortical activity. It sends more information to the brain than it receives – unique among the organs of the body.

2. The pulse of the heart is a wave of energy through the body. The brain synchronises its electrical activity to the pulse of the heart. In effect, the heart rhythm becomes the beat of the body. (It is worth mentioning here that acupuncturists and other practitioners use the subtleties of these pulses as their primary diagnostic tool as they provide a primary readout on the status and balance of the 12 governing energy meridians)

3. It influences biochemically, producing hormones such as atrio-peptide which regulates the stress hormone cortisone. It regulates oxytocin, the chemical messenger that stimulates behaviours of love and maternal caring. It produces the neurotransmitters dopamine and noradrenaline which are neurotransmitters regulating many aspects of brain function including motor activity, sleep, mood, attention and flight-or-fight response.

4. It is the strongest source of bio-electricity, producing 40 times more than the brain (which is the next strongest). This bio-electrical field radiates beyond the body in a toroidal (ring-donut shaped) field that influences

approximately 8-10 feet (3 metres) around. The frequencies of these radiations change with the emotional state of the body. When the body is experiencing what most would describe as negative emotions, this field becomes incoherent. Positive emotional states produce coherence and stability. Aside from anything that we do with our face and gestures, we all broadcast our emotions to those who are close to us. While we cannot cite proof here, we regard it as certain that we can detect each other's fields and that many of us instinctively recognize this additional form of intuitive knowing. In addition it can be shown that the incoherent (negative emotional) states inhibit cortical (thinking) function because they trigger the production of cortisol while coherent states facilitate it because they trigger DHEA, the pre-hormonal natural steroid which is regarded as an anti-aging substance. Put simply, we think more clearly when we are not under stress. That fact may be obvious, but what is less apparent is that it is regulated by the heart through its production of neurotransmitters (i.e. cortisol and DHEA).

The heart rate is highly variable and the changes are happening continuously, second-by second, thus being a further example of a subtle and responsive process. The prompt of many spiritual wisdoms to live with our minds in our hearts is not just a metaphor. It has a real and physiological root.

The types of interactivity we are describing here go beyond the "power of mind over body" concept that is sometimes promoted. We have used the compound noun "bodymind" deliberately. The world has been influenced for almost 400 years by Rene Descartes and his theory of mind-body dualism. In fact we are seeing that the body is mind all over, they are one seamless entity. When we describe either aspect in isolation we are simply changing our angle of view. The power of mind over body enters the whole, influencing at one point in the cycle. Working on the body influences at another point, but it is the same cycle.

How many senses do you have anyway?

In an earlier chapter we discussed the way in which our perceptions are geared to our physical needs and to the history of predators and prey in the way they structure our sense of time. We are accustomed to talk of these physical senses in the way that the song quoted at the head of this chapter does, distinguishing the five described as sight, sound, smell touch and taste.

These five are arbitrary definitions linked more to the appearance of our sense organs than to distinct sensory processes. You might as easily say that you have three sensory systems. One is for detecting vibrations in the electromagnetic spectrum, picking up sound frequencies and some bands of light. Another is a network of chemical sensors for odor and flavour. The third is kinesthetic, detecting movement or variations in temperature against the skin.

The point we are drawing attention to is that our range of perceptions are narrow and incomplete. We all know that dogs hear sounds at frequencies that mean nothing to us. The same dog might also distinguish between two complex molecules with one atom of difference between them, and which we would not detect at all. In the light spectrum bees see flowers quite differently than we do with senses that extend further into the ultra-violet range. Soldiers use night-vision goggles that translate heat radiation (infra-red) onto a screen to make bodies visible in a dark forest. Probably there are creatures which use this frequency range too.

Sensory stimuli are filtered by the processes in the perceptual systems so that we only see what we are accustomed to find relevant. When you are driving there may be lots of information that you are tuning out. Was the person who crossed the road in front of you just now happy or sad? You are unlikely to have noticed.

That filtration is unconscious and happens anyway. But there are experiments that show how a person who is asked to focus on one aspect of a scene will completely miss quite startling events. We have witnessed this in an audience of 250 people with a pre-instructed agenda watching a video clip in which something totally incongruous happens and only about five people laughed. The incongruity was only seen when the clip was repeated and our attention was allowed to open and simply "see" without the instruction toward a specific focus.

These filter processes clearly influence our perception of what is "true" or "real". But both phenomena come after the threshold of information entering our perception. They pale into insignificance when compared with huge gaps like not seeing infra-red, not picking up radio waves, lacking the visual acuity of a buzzard, not hearing the echo-location soundings of a bat.

In consequence, when we talk of a "sixth sense", this is a misleading term of convenience. It is simply a form of information supply which occurs beyond the ones we are focusing on or are normally inclined to be aware of. It is also the case, as observed earlier, that the receiving of this information is processed by the same brain and articulated through the same language channels.

This presents a number of challenges. Intuitive information is a challenge to the person receiving it because it often comes into the consciousness with an appearance which resembles a regular "5-sense" experience but which that individual knows is not coming in the normal way. It is a challenge to that person because it may not arrive clearly and may be more "dream-like" in its symbology, and require some interpretative skill to decode. As Jon has discovered, it is a challenge to teach others to be intuitive because the teacher does not know how the student will function, nor how their internal representation is to be decoded. They have to develop their own knowledge of their unique code.

Not all intuitive information arrives through the regular sensing processes though. Even harder for some people, the information may not come as either pictures or words – it may just be "feelings" or complete "knowings" which then have to be formed into language. This was Jon's experience when detecting the brain tumour. What came first was a sensation, a physiological experience which included screwing up the face as if pain was being felt, but without the actual pain. The emotional body is included in the mediators for intuitive information.

The use of the same brain and language channels, and the even less well-defined kinaesthetic mode just described also challenges science. Even those with prodigious gifts like our quoted medical intuitives cannot tell you anything about the ways in which the information enters their bodymind. If science wanted to construct apparatus to detect and validate the experience, it could not. It's a "black-box system" where we know only what little is visible from the outside and what is reported from "inside". Not only is it impossible to measure the content, science cannot even prove that the communication is (or is not) taking place. It does not even know where on any kind of electro-magnetic spectrum to begin looking. Even worse, if it did know, it is in the nature of the experiences we have described that the intuitives pick up information which is "out there", but that ALL the information is present at the same time. When Mona Lisa Shulz tuned in to Violet, the information for Jon or Juliana or (insert your name here) was equally available to her, but she only got Violet's. What is science able to do with that? It has no apparatus and never will. It just has Mona Lisa.

The intuitive worlds we described in the first two chapters and the neuro-endocrine reality that this chapter portrays share several striking characteristics. They are both occurring inside living humans and are experienced subjectively. They are not susceptible in any meaningful degree to measurement and only in the crudest sense can some aspects be detected by apparatus (for example electro-encephalograph or brain-scan data). They are clearly complex, subtle and deeply meaningful to the person having the experience. They all have to do with an information flow which is part of the relationship between one human and another, and of the connection between one human and the rest of the world.

For all these reasons, it is essential to accept that the only way that we will study these phenomena meaningfully, or create any sort of systematic understanding, is through working with the experiences as they are reported, finding the consistencies that reveal themselves across generations and cultures. We will explore this world next.

Review

In the spiral diagram we have drawn a theme of connection that runs from the level of sub-components of cells to that of the overall human being. This strand shows chemical communication and rhythmic co-ordination. In this chapter we have described forms of each of these. Chemical communication is mediated by messenger molecules. Messages are "read" by the cells, cellular activity is modified and other messages may be sent as a result. These messages can affect almost any aspect of behaviour and some of the resultant changes are experienced by humans as what we label "emotions". This chemical activity brings a means by which all cells in the body can be "aware" of the states of others and of the body as a whole. The emotions affect what we view as "reality" and influence our behaviour and decision-making. In this way, the chemical messengers are one element in our relationship with the world beyond our bodies.

A layer of rhythmic connectedness is provided by the heart, which sends more information to the brain than it receives, and which acts to provide a signal which synchronises electrical activity. The heart also produces chemical messengers and generates electromagnetic fields that radiate beyond the body. These fields reflect the extent of coherence within the body's emotional states and influence cortical activity.

Together, these chemical and rhythmic connections form a significant part of the activity that humans experience as consciousness. As depicted on our rings, they contribute to the internal mediation between matter and energy, and to our information about the world - both ordinary reality and the non-ordinary intuitive experience.

4. I talk to the trees.....

There may be no absolute division of the energetic Universe into isolated or non-communicable parts.

Buckminster Fuller

I talk to the trees, That's why they locked me away

Spike Milligan

Theme

There is a consistent view of the world which is present in the stories both from indigenous cultures and from western individuals who work through a direct internal cognition of information regarding the natural world. In this chapter we present several examples of such experiences in order to illustrate both the consistency of these viewpoints and the ways in which such information is useful to the world. We offer both traditional and modern views of this "shamanistic" experience. Our presentation of intuition, precognition and psycho-kinesis showed that information passes between humans and their world. The shamanistic perspective takes this relationship deeper. According to most spiritual and religious views, human beings have individual spirits. The shaman's relationship engages with a natural world in which there are many kinds of such spiritual entities inhabiting a layer of reality that is unfamiliar to most of us. We also present scientific evidence that plants can demonstrate individual consciousness and connection.

The nature of shamanism

In relation to this chapter, the "Paint your wagon" song parody above from Spike Milligan is more than the simple joke that it appears to be. In even attempting to describe the world of the shaman we immediately encounter problems. Definitions such as that in the Oxford English Dictionary describe a shaman as a priest or witch-doctor who is a member of a class of people claiming to have sole contact with the gods – a definition which might not entirely distinguish a shaman from a Catholic priest. The use of the term "witch-doctor" also carries some very unhelpful images which we may have derived from B-movies which portray hostile and even cannibalistic savages. We need to get well away from such crude depictions. The truth is so much more complex and subtle.

If we are to present God's ecology with any completeness, the shamanistic view is crucial. Shamanistic cultures live in the reality we are attempting to describe. This way of thinking and the approach to life that it engenders is so profoundly different from the one that science frames as to challenge our whole way of thought. Most of us find it very hard to treat these views as having anything to do with reality. Words like "primitive" and "animism" are used; the indigenous people who live this way are presented as child-like, superstitious and naïve.

These descriptions can seem justified when they are applied to cultures which retain superficial remnants of belief systems which have been largely destroyed through contact with the western world and where the true power and deep relationships are no longer living. Where such cultures are surviving, it is difficult for westerners who contact them to cross into their world and very few have made a real attempt, which typically requires years of work as well as openness of mind and spirit. Those who live in these cultures typically do not know our languages and even if they did would not even see the value of communicating a mere description of a deep experience. We are aware of one exception to this, and small glimpses of his articulate and powerful account appear below. We invite you, when you read them, to suspend your disbelief and to make the undoubted effort that is required for most Western readers if we are to see them as equally real with our own experience.

Wikipedia is more helpful than the OED and defines a shaman as "A member of certain tribal societies who acts as a religious medium between the concrete and spirit worlds". This is a more helpful starting point and is amplified by their definition of the culture of shamanism.

Shamanism refers to a range of traditional beliefs and practices concerned with communication with the spirit world, mostly animal spirits. There are many variations in shamanism throughout the world, though there are some beliefs that are shared by all forms of shamanism:

- The spirits can play important roles in people's lives.

- The shamans work with the spirits, seeking assistance or advice for the benefit of the community, or individuals in it.

- The spirits can be either good or bad.

- Most shamans get into a trance by singing, dancing, meditating and drumming. A minority use entheogens (mind-expanding chemicals)

- The songs and dances describe the spirit's journey or the shaman's own personal journey to the other world.

- Many shamans imitate many animals and bird spirits. This happens when the shaman's spirit leaves the body and enters into the supernatural world.

- The shamans can treat illnesses or sickness. The main purpose of shamanism is to understand nature, work with it and heal the sick.

Michael Harner, a leading expert in this field tells us that the word "shaman" in the original Tungus language refers to a person who makes journeys to non-ordinary reality in an altered state of consciousness. Although the term is from Siberia, the practice of shamanism existed on all inhabited continents. He quotes researcher Mircea Eliade who concluded that shamanism underlies all the other spiritual traditions on the planet, and that the most distinctive feature of shamanism, but by no means the only one, was the journey to other worlds in an altered state of consciousness. (More information can be found on www.shamanism.org).

These definitions bring us closer to a realistic frame of reference, but are still highly challenging to the scientific mindset that inhabits our western cultures. The Wikipedia definition assumes the existence of animal spirits though it leaves out plants, which we will be talking about extensively. It is inevitably vague about what the "other world" it refers to might be, and as we have said we are opposed to the view that there is "another world" which is "supernatural". We are seeking to depict an alternative sensing and description of the single world we inhabit. The definition refers to the spirit "leaving the body". None of these are comfortable for our cultural frame of reference. Any of these might be regarded in our system as a defining feature of mental illness.

In consequence, some of the narratives in this chapter need to be read with a fresh mind-set. We hope that by now we have established some of the features of the world which shamans are relating to but we will certainly be pushing the boundaries further with what is to follow. By way of a transition, the first tale we will tell is set firmly in twentieth century technological USA and involves an individual who does not resemble a shaman at all.

This is a story that begins in 1966 concerning Cleve Backster, America's foremost lie detector examiner, and stars a houseplant called *Dracaena massangeana.*

You probably know that a lie detector works by measuring the electrical conductivity of the body by the use of a galvanometer. Backster decided on impulse to attach this device to his pot plant, and see how it responded to being watered. Now if you know anything about electricity you would expect that more water means more current will pass. But the trace on the paper showed a fluctuation that was in the opposite direction - downwards, with a kind of saw-tooth motion that resembles what happens when a human being experiences an emotional stimulus.

He decided to investigate further. When working with humans, police examiners like Backster watch the responses to stress under questioning. One of the most effective ways to get a response in humans is to threaten their well-being. Backster decided to try this on the plant, and dipped its leaf in hot coffee.

Nothing happened. So he thought of a worse threat. He decided to burn the leaf to which the electrodes were attached. The very instant he got the picture of the flame and the action in his mind, the plant responded with a strong upward sweep.

He left the room to get some matches, and found that while he was away, the plant had responded with another upward surge. Reluctantly, he set about burning the leaf, and got a reaction, but less than before. Later he went through the physical motions of pretending he would burn the leaf, and got no reaction at all. The plant seemed to be able to tell the difference between real and pretended intention.

A lot goes on after this as he has other collaborators check his findings on other plants, fruit and vegetables. They confirmed his findings, and he decided to set up a lab for more extensive study. There is a lot of material, and we are going to select just a few more examples.

One time, he was demonstrating his work for a journalist. He hooked a galvanometer to a philodendron, and then interrogated the journalist about his year of birth. Backster named seven years in succession, from 1925 to 1931 to which the reporter was instructed to answer "no" in each case. From the galvanometer chart of plant responses, Backster then selected the correct year of the reporter's birth. That is, the philodendron detected when the "no" was a lie.

To see if the plant would show memory he set up an experiment where six volunteers from his police students drew a piece of paper from a hat. Five were blank, but the other told one of them to totally destroy one of two plants in the room. Each in turn entered the room. No-one but the person with that piece of paper knew who was responsible for the destruction of the plant. This was followed with a kind of identity parade, in which each of the volunteers went in to the room again, with the remaining plant now wired to the galvanometer. The plant showed no reaction to five of them, but the reading went wild when the "culprit" entered the room.

In their book "The Secret Life of Plants" Peter Tompkins and Christopher Bird describe further explorations in which Backster found that the reactions would persist even when a leaf was disconnected from the plant, trimmed to the size of the electrodes or even shredded. As they describe it:-

"The plants reacted not only to threats from human beings, but also to unformulated threats such as the sudden appearance of a dog in the room, or of a person who did not wish them well. Backster was able to demonstrate that the movements of a spider in the same room with a plant wired to his equipment could cause dramatic changes in the recorded pattern generated by the plan just BEFORE the spider started to scuttle away from a human attempting to restrict its movement. "It seems," said Backster" as if each spider's decision to escape was being picked up by the plant, causing a reaction in the leaf."

"At first he considered that his plant's capacity for picking up his intentions must be some form of extrasensory perception; then he quarrelled with the term. ESP is held to mean perception above and beyond varieties of the established five sensory perceptions of touch, sight, sound, smell and taste. As plants give no evidence of eyes, ears, nose or mouth, and as botanists since Darwin's time have never credited then with a nervous system, Backster concluded that the perceiving sense must be more basic. This led him to hypothesise that the five senses in humans might be limiting factors overlaying <u>some kind of primary perception, possibly common to all nature.</u>" (Our emphasis)

The plant subsequently showed a reaction to simple cellular organisms. On one occasion it reacted to Backster mixing jam with his yoghurt, which he believed to be due to the preservative in the jam killing some of the live cells. This belief was later supported by witnessing a similar reaction when boiling water was running down the waste-pipe in the sink and killing bacteria.

Because Backster was interested in this reaction, he invented ways to attach his electrodes to single celled creatures such as amoeba, yeast, blood cells and sperm. All were capable of producing similar results to plants. Sperm cells, for instance, would respond to the presence of their donor. In more recent work, reported in Erwin Laszlo's book "Science and the Akashic field", Backster took cheek-cell swabs from various subjects and took them several miles from their donors. In one of his tests, he showed his subject, a former navy gunner who had been present there, a television program depicting the Japanese attack on Pearl Harbor in 1941. When the face of a navy gunner appeared on the screen, the man's face showed an emotional reaction—and at that precise moment, the lie detector's needle seven and a half miles away jumped, just as it would have had it been attached to the man himself.

Pierre Sauvin, another researcher and electronics hobbyist inspired by Backster's work, was able to construct more subtle detector systems and to connect a philodendron as a control system. He was able to demonstrate in front of live audiences and even under the lighting of an early TV studio that he could make an electric toy train start, stop and reverse at will by using the plant to detect his emotional changes.

There are three clear and simple conclusions to be drawn from these experiments:-

1. There is a consciousness that connects living things, that is constantly active, and engaged in (or at least open for) continuous communication

2.   That consciousness - down to the level of individual cells - is capable of picking up on that connection and identifying other consciousness at an individual level.

3.   Individual plants can have a form of conscious presence.

Note that because the tests were done on plants, there is no need for the double-blind approach to be used – at least for the first conclusion. In theory it is possible that the plant could be responding to the experimenter rather than to the source of the signal - the destructive student policeman or the yoghurt. However in the yoghurt example the effect was not expected. In practice it seems much more likely that conclusion no. 2 is also correct. This is consistent with our observations in other areas and is borne out by all that follows below. Conclusion 3 is particularly significant in regard to the stories that will follow.

These conclusions will come as no great shock if you have been following our thread so far. But note that this is the first time we have been talking explicitly about non-human organisms. The core of this chapter concerns the plant kingdoms, but the reactions with yoghurt and other single-celled organisms indicates that we need to keep our boundaries very open.

Additional supportive evidence has been supplied very recently by research published in the June 2007 issue of Biology letters, by Susan Dudley and Amanda File. They have shown that in the annual plant *Cakile edentula*, allocation of effort to root development increased when groups of strangers shared a common pot, but not when groups of siblings shared a pot. Their results demonstrate that plants can discriminate kin in competitive interactions and indicate that the root interactions may provide the cues for this. It is not stated how they achieve this recognition. Some chemical sensing may be involved (there are other examples where this is believed to be the case).   However, chemical sensing does not seem adequate as an explanation for how plants would tell one human from another, and the kin recognition may well operate through other forms of connection.

The above is our gentle entry into the realm of "plant consciousness", and an introduction to the idea that plants can have a "spirit".   We recognise that we have not so far even attempted to define what it means to describe a human as having a "spirit".   We would prefer not to do so and to allow you to draw your own conclusion and frame it within your own experience. We would simply point out that the language used by others may contain their interpretations. It may not be the only way to describe the experience and human languages may be unclear or even lack the terminology to describe a realm which our culture does not acknowledge. For example to say (as in Wikipedia) that the soul leaves the body implies an entity which moves its geographical location. You may wish to examine this notion in relation to the stories which follow.

The world of the shaman

Malidoma Patrice Somé is a remarkable individual in more ways than one. That he has survived the cultural journey he has undergone speaks of considerable internal resources. His story is extraordinary in presenting a very rare example of a shamanistic world described by one who has been completely immersed in the experience, but who also understands the Western view of reality and can speak directly to us. In his own culture he is initiated as a medicine man and a diviner. In the West he holds three master's degrees and doctorates from the Sorbonne and Brandeis University. His book "Of Water and the Spirit" is a journey of revelation. For Malidoma it is the revelation of his own traditions. For us it is a doorway into a profoundly different way of understanding, experiencing and thinking about the world.

Malidoma's culture – the Dagara people of West Africa – is a shamanistic culture in which many of the tribe (most of the males at least) would be initiated into the experience of the spiritual dimension and in which all accept and understand that frame of reference. It is in that sense quite different from the model of a single priest with unique access that was indicated by the OED. The close relationship with the natural world is embedded in their way of life. As a very young boy he experienced this very directly, but then at the age of four was removed under duress by a Jesuit priest and taken to a Catholic boarding school, which indoctrinated him for the following fifteen years along with other children whom they hoped to turn into a "native" missionary force. As he describes

"At the age of twenty I escaped and went back to my people, but found that I no longer fit into the tribal community. I risked my life to undergo the Dagara initiation and thereby return to my own people. During that month-long ritual, I was integrated back into my own reality as well as I could be. But I never lost my Western education. So I am a man of two worlds, trying to be at home in both of them – a difficult task at best.

When I was twenty-two, my elders came to me and asked me to return to the white man's world, to share with him what I had learned about my own spiritual tradition through my initiation. For me, initiation had eliminated my confusion, helplessness and pain, and opened the door to a powerful understanding of the link between my own life purpose and the will of my ancestors."

Malidoma Somé describes the Dagara world-view as "only one of the endless versions of reality." He goes on to say:-

"in the culture of my people, the Dagara, we have no word for the supernatural. The closest we come to this concept is "Yeilbongura", the "thing that knowledge can't eat". This word suggests that the life and power of certain things depend on their resistance to the kind of categorising knowledge that human beings apply to everything. In Western reality there is a clear split between the spiritual and the material, between religious life and secular life. This concept is alien to the Dagara. For us, as for many indigenous cultures, the supernatural is part of our everyday lives. To a Dagara man or woman, the material is just the spiritual taking on form."

The initial encounter with the spiritual world came quite unexpectedly for Malidoma when he was as a child of less than 4 years old.

"One day something very odd happened. As I was running around madly, I stepped on a rabbit. It dashed out of its hiding place and a wild race ensued. Looking for a place to hide, the rabbit ran straight towards a small forested area in the bush. I rejoiced when I saw the rabbit run in that direction because I often picked the fruits there and knew every corner of that little bush. The rabbit disappeared into the bush like an arrow shot into a pot of butter.

I followed with caution, trying to guess where the rabbit might be hiding. The tall grass put me at a disadvantage. I had to beat my way through while the rabbit slipped along easily. When I turned over the first clump of grass, the rabbit was not there. I checked another part of the bush where I knew there was an animal nest. This nest was an earthen hole dug in a little hill, its opening covered with grass and its inside filled with soft straw. I removed the grass and was ready to leap headlong onto the miserable rabbit, but I never completed the action. All my movements were suspended as if by an electric shock.

Where I had thought there would be a rabbit there was instead a tiny old man as small as the rabbit itself. He sat on an almost invisible chair and held a minuscule cane in his right hand. His head was covered with hair so white and shiny that it seemed unnatural. His beard was long and white too, reaching almost to his chest, and he wore a traditional Dagara mantle, also white.

All around him there was a glow, a shiny rainbow ring, like a round window or a portal into another reality. Although his body filled most of that portal, I could just see there was an immense world inside it.

But what surprised me most was that the laws of nature in that world did not seem to operate like anything I had seen before. The little man's chair was sitting on a steep slope, yet he did not fall over backwards. I noticed there was something like a thin wall that sustained him. He was not leaning against the chair he was sitting on, but against that thin wall even though he still appeared upright in the window.

As my eyes moved from that wall and the world behind it back to the man, I say that his thin legs were bare. His toes were so tiny I could barely see them. Petrified by something that was neither fear not mirth, but felt like a tickling all over my body, I forgot to scream as the man said, "I have been watching you for a long time, ever since your mother started bringing you here. Why do you want to hurt the rabbit, your little brother? What did he do to you, little one?" His tiny mouth was barely moving as he spoke and his voice was very thin.

Confused, I tried to reply "I . . .I …don't know."

"Then be friendly to him from now on. He too likes the freshness of this place. He too has a mother who cares for him. What would his mother say if you hurt him? Now go because your own mother is worried."

While the little man was speaking, I spotted the rabbit, which had been hidden behind him in the magic circle all that time. I moved further into that steep marvellous place, and then disappeared behind a tree. Meanwhile, I heard a cracking sound as if the earth itself were splitting open. No sooner had I heard this than the old man stood up, slung his chair over his shoulder, and walked into the opening as if he had commanded it. The earth closed up on him leaving a gust of fresh breeze in his place. At the same time I hear my mother's voice calling me."

Malidoma tells the story to his mother, who says

71

"Oh, my dear ancestors, my child has just seen a Kontomblé. What else can it be? Don't talk anymore. Let's get out of here. I'll never take you out again."

She was concerned because Malidoma was very young for such an experience and it had significant implications for their relationship if it became known to others. Her reference to a "kontomblé" denotes a spirit who lives in the underworld.

Smart chickens

As an infant, Malidoma had been very close to his grandfather, one of the senior shamans in the tribe who had recently died but whose stories come to his mind regularly. At one point shortly before his kidnapping he is watching chickens in the yard and recalls an incident where his grandfather translates the conversation that chickens are having, and explains that they are about to scatter the millet from a basket where one of the women has painstakingly separated and cleaned it.

Immediately after, Malidoma watches as one of the hens jumps into a basket and causes a fight with the woman that ends with the basket overturned and the contents beyond collection, except by the feasting chickens. In case you should still question why, in a book intending to provide a scientific view of the spiritual world we are telling such stories, the reason is this. The reality we are describing is very alien to most of us. The idea of little spirit men and chickens which communicate is quite fantastic. The journey we are taking requires us to suspend large amounts of culture-engendered disbelief.

Questions are also raised regarding the true nature of what is being described. Is the Kontomblé something solid that one could touch? Do chickens, when they communicate, use a language that resembles ours? Since we are not shamans, we cannot know for sure. Some elements of Malidoma's story are common features when encounters with the spirit world are described – the sense of an altered surrounding reality and the feeling of heat or tickling to the skin. These are cross-cultural elements. But actual descriptions vary a lot, as do the pictures people draw of what they see. It seems probable that the visions are translated into the perceptual systems of our everyday reality and that messages are received as ideas, to which the recipient applies language. There is some indication that the forms are filtered through a culturally derived perception and that the spirit world communicates in a way that resonates with us, whatever form that requires. Indeed there are other reasons we will discuss in later chapters why this is probably so.

These features are not crucial to what we are saying in this book, except that we need to caution those who might be looking for complete consistency to understand that it may be unrealistic to expect this, at least in some aspects. But we need to look underneath at the nature of the world that is being described, and to understand the significance. What is emerging, piece by piece, is a world in which the non-visible aspects which the western world has eliminated from its conceptual framework are potentially more important than all the physical manifestations that we are habituated to.

The authors both have experiences across the boundaries of this alternate reality. We will describe some of Juliana's interactions with it in the next chapter. But neither of us has had the deep shamanic initiations that those like Malidoma Somé describe. It is very difficult to have such experiences and live in the world of TV and mobile phones. In consequence it calls for a great deal of trust for us to even hear these stories as a form of "truth", to not label them as fantasy, hoax or insanity.

The description that Malidoma Somé gives of his initiation, when he returns to his own culture as a twenty-year-old, takes over one hundred pages. It is a rich account, but he indicates that it is nevertheless incomplete, as there is more that his elders do not allow to be shared. The excerpts we are using merely hint at the reality, but we include them because they are the only examples in this book from someone raised in such a culture. All our other stories come from those who have crossed into such a culture from the West. The final example below occurs during his initiation.

The background to the story is that some of the tribal elders have been unwilling to see him initiated because of the impact of his Westernisation, while for him it is his only way back into connection with his people. The exercise he is engaged in requires him to stare at a yila tree until he "sees something". He is struggling to achieve anything and has just tried to "fake it" bringing a mixture of scorn and derision, which has left him feeling a confusion of aloneness, broken pride, anger and alienation.

"Through my tears, I managed to continue keeping an eye on the tree. Then I finally began speaking to it, as if I had finally discovered that it had a life of its own. I told it all about my discontent and my sadness and how I felt that it had abandoned me to the shame of lying and being laughed at.....

I then spoke to the tree again, not angrily but respectfully. I told her that, after all, it was not her fault I could not see, but mine. I simply lacked the ability. What I really needed to do was to come to terms with my own emptiness and lack of sight, because I knew she would always be there when I needed to use her to take a close look at my own shortcomings and inadequacies.

My words were sincere: I felt them while I said them. My pain had receded somewhat, and I found I could now focus better on the tree. It was around mid-afternoon, but I was not really interested in the time. I had something more important to deal with, for suddenly there was a flash in my spirit like mild lightning, and a cool breeze ran down my spine and into the ground where I had been sitting for the past one and a half days. My entire body felt cool. The sun, the forest, and the elders and I, understood I was in another reality, witnessing a miracle. All the trees around my yila were glowing like fires or breathing lights. I felt weightless, as if I were at the centre of a universe where everything was looking at me as if I were naked, weak, and innocent. Indeed I thought I was dead. I thought that something must have happened while I was trying to reconcile myself to the shame of being caught in a lie.

To substantiate my impression, I thought about the hardships of the day – the baking heat of the sun and my sweat falling into my eyes and burning them like pepper. I had lost all sense of chronology. I told myself that this is what the world looked like when one had first expired. I felt as if I were being quite reasonable. I could still think and respond to sensations around me, but I was no longer experiencing the biting heat of the sun or my restless mind trying to keep busy or ignoring my assignment. Where I was now was just plain real.

When I looked once more at the yila, I became aware that it was not a tree at all. How had I ever seen it as such? I do not know how this transformation occurred. Things were not happening logically, but as if this were a dream. Out of nowhere, in the place where the tree had stood, appeared a tall woman dressed in black from head to foot. She resembled a nun, although her outfit did not seem religious. Her tunic was silky and black as the night. She wore a veil over her face, but I could tell that behind this veil was an extremely beautiful and powerful entity. I could sense the intensity emanating from her, and that intensity exercised an irresistible magnetic pull. To give in to that pull was like drinking water after a day of wandering in the desert.

My body felt like it was floating, as if I were a small child being lulled by a nurturing presence that was trying to calm me by singing soothing lullabies and rocking me rhythmically. I felt as if I was floating weightless in a small body of water. My eyes locked on to the lady in the veil, and the feeling of being drawn toward her increased. For a moment I was overcome with shyness, uneasiness and a feeling of inappropriateness. I had to lower my eyes. When I looked again she had lifted her veil, revealing an unearthly face. She was green, light green. Even her eyes were green, though very small and luminescent. She was smiling and her teeth were the colour of violet and had light emanating from them. The greenness in her had nothing to do with the colour of her skin. She was green from the inside out, as if her body were filled with green fluid. I do not know how I knew this, but this green was the expression of immeasurable love.

Never before had I felt so much love. I felt as if I had missed her all my life and was grateful to heaven for having finally released her back to me. We knew each other, but at the time I could not tell why, when or how. I also could not tell the nature of our love. It was not romantic or filial; it was a love that surpassed all known classifications. Like two lovers who had been apart for an unduly long period of time, we dashed towards each other and flung ourselves into each other's arms.

The sensation of embracing her body blew my body into countless pieces, which became millions of conscious cells, all longing to reunite with the whole that was her. If they could not reunite with her it felt as if they could not live. Each one was adrift and in need of her to anchor itself back in place. There are no words to paint what it felt like to be in the hands of the green lady in the black veil. We exploded into each other in a cosmic contact that sent us floating adrift in the ether in countless intertwined forms. In the course of this baffling experience I felt as if I were moving backward in time and forward in space. ...."

If the depiction above should seem unreal or fantastic to you that would be understandable. Yet it is far from being the most other-worldly experience that Malidoma Somé describes. Here he remains to a significant degree in the world we know. In other experiences the sense of dislocation, of travelling beyond the boundaries of our reality, is much stronger. They are journeys into foreign territory and last for much longer. But all the descriptions have the same dreamlike quality and have in this a resonance to "dreamtime", the phrase used by Australian Aboriginals for their otherworld.

We will save discussions about what "reality" is for a later chapter. For now we would merely note that there are strong philosophical grounds for treating these apparently subjective experiences as equally "real". The use of the word "dream" carries an automatic cultural implication for us. We need to step away from that implication because it is a view created by the very philosophy we are questioning here. It is a habit based on a false assumption and if we remain locked inside that habit, none of the descriptions in this chapter can ever be seen as other than fantasy.

Very few of the writings on this aspect of philosophy have been written by a Western thinker who is capable of direct knowledge of the intuitive, spiritual world. The one exception known to us is Rudolf Steiner, who explores it in depth in his books "Knowledge of Higher Worlds" and "Intuitive thinking as a Spiritual Path". He points out that the supposed differences between "external observation", by which he means the use of our regular senses, is not as different from "internal observation" (the intuitive acceptance of a mental picture) as it is commonly taken to be. As he says, this "makes the error of characterising one percept as a mental picture while naively accepting the percepts of ones own organism as objectively valid facts." He sees both as equally misleading. In his view

> "for a relationship to exist between my organism and an object outside me, it is not at all necessary for something of the object to slip into me or impress itself on my mind like a signet ring on wax. Thus the question 'How do I learn anything from the tree that stands ten paces from me?' is all wrong". It arises from the view that the boundaries of my body are absolute barriers through which news about things filters into me."

Instead he states that we belong to the same world as the things we think of as external. The segment that you think of as "you" is run through by the stream of the same Universal life process.

We will return to this topic, but introduce it now in order to underpin the notion that the dreamlike, esoteric and internally perceived world is worthy of the same possibilities for validity as the world of sight and touch. We are doing all we can to keep solid ground beneath our feet and to avoid dismissing what is unfamiliar to our cultural definition of what can or cannot be "real". This is essential if we are to reach our goal of a single world, not one split in two.

Western shamans

One of the reasons we chose the Yila tree story in particular is that it takes us into the realm of plant spirits, which we will explore further in a short while. First though, we would like to mention briefly the experience of Dr Alberto Villoldo who in his book "Dance of the Four Winds" captures with great clarity the experience of a westerner with scientific background as he comes to terms with this alternate view of reality. Having completed his doctorate, studying psychology, neuronatomy and much besides, he is dissatisfied with the clinical models he has been offered and chooses in 1974 to take some time out to discover the ways in which Peruvian healers understand consciousness.

His account switches back and forth between his time in the West and his encounters with a series of healers, shamans and guides who little by little draw him increasingly deeper in to their world. As such it is a revealing depiction of the transformation that is required in order to release western academe and science and find a way into the shamanistic experience. The book covers ten years of exploration as Dr Villoldo learns such aspects as taking on the consciousness of an animal and the healing capabilities of those who learn to see directly into the energy flows of others. He describes working with a healer who has never heard of acupuncture, but when asked to describe the energy pathways he simply "sees" and unblocks on the body of a patient, draws the lines of the Chinese medicine meridians on Villoldo's skin.

In all the descriptions of the journey into shamanism, it seems that it will require the individual to face the fear of death, to overcome and transcend pain and to confront his own inner demons. The world that Villoldo describes seems to be typical of the Latin American view and as such has a different flavour to Malidoma Somé's Africa. But underneath the cultural differences lie strong senses of correspondence and shared viewpoints.

Alberto Villoldo's experience with an independent perception of the energy meridians links us to the realm of Plant Spirit Medicine as presented by Eliot Cowan in his book of that name. Eliot Cowan started practising herbal medicine from a book when a vet told him that a sick goat on the farm where he was working, was incurable. The herbs the book told him he needed grew on the farm and produced a cure within a few days. Further experiences convinced him that natural healing was his calling, and he found his way towards perhaps the most respected western teacher of Chinese medicine and Acupuncture, J.R. Worsley. Some time after qualifying as an acupuncturist he returned to his interest in herbs, following Worsley's advice that anything that needles could do, herbs could also do, but especially to use local herbs because they would be vastly stronger.

In search of information about the plants local to his Californian home, Eliot found that little was available. European texts didn't cover them and the Native American knowledge was effectively extinct from what he describes as "cultural genocide". Because of this he started to study shamanism and to become acquainted with the Huichol people of Mexico, one of the rare cultures which have survived intact. This has led to a journey which in the decades since has seen Eliot become the first non-native to be fully accredited as a fully initiated Huichol shaman. His contribution in his own culture has been the development of Plant Spirit Medicine as a healing practice, and he trains others in the core elements of all that he knows.

Essentially this system uses the principles of Chinese medicine, with their several millennia of wisdom about the body as a diagnostic base. However, rather than use needles or herbal preparations as the means of applying treatment, it is the spirit of the plant itself which acts as the healing agent. Embedded in this approach is a relationship between plant, healer and client which is at the heart of this chapter.

This is the opening passage of Eliot Cowan's book:-

> "My friend Peter Gorman is walking down a trail in the Amazon jungle. He is on his way back to the village after watching his Matses Indian friend set a trap for wild boar. The Indian takes advantage of the walk to show Peter some medicinal plants growing along the trail. Within a few minutes he has pointed out several dozen species and pantomimed their healing virtues.
>
> Arriving at the village, Peter summons his interpreter and returns to the hunter's hut. He didn't have his notebook on the walk, he explains, and he couldn't possibly remember all that he had been shown. Would the hunter be kind enough to say once again how the herbs were prepared and used.

The hunter-shaman smiles at Peter and then begins to laugh. He invites all his wives and children over to have a good laugh too. When they have all laughed themselves out, he explains, "That was just to introduce you to some of the plants. If you want to actually use a plant yourself, the spirit of the plant must come to you in your dreams. If the spirit of the plant tells you how to prepare it and what it will cure, you can use it. Otherwise it won't work for you. Boy, that was a good one! I've got to remember what you just said!" He laughs again."

This story neatly encapsulates the difference between the shamanistic world and that of pharmaceutical companies, isolating "active ingredients" and processing them into pills. As Eliot puts it, "There is only one active ingredient to plant medicines – friendship. A plant spirit heals a patient as a favour to its friend-in-dreaming, the doctor." Here is one illustration of that relationship.

"People have returned after treatment to tell me stories of "falling in love with the Earth" or "feeling like I'm not alone" or "seeing fairies in my backyard". One of my favourite such stories involves Karen, a woman in her twenties who was suffering from depression as well as a number of spiritual complaints. I had chosen to treat her with the spirit of hummingbird sage, a beautiful plant that grows in the coastal ranges of Southern California, where I was living at the time. In my dream work with the hummingbird sage, the spirit appeared to me as a jolly, muscular little man full of fun and kindness. He was dressed in a pointed cap, a medieval tunic, leggings and shoes with pointy turned-up toes. This was Karen's report after her treatment:

After I left here I felt so tired that I went home and lay down. I was half asleep and had a dream or a daydream or something. It was totally vivid and lifelike. In this dream I felt that someone else was entering my body. I wasn't frightened because I felt he was a very good person, kind and fun-loving. I could see him very clearly. He was short and strong and was wearing funny old-fashioned clothing and shoes with pointy, turned-up toes. I felt he was there to give me something I needed.

That afternoon I felt an urge to go to my special spot in the mountains. There is a certain place that I go; the smell there reminds me of the smell of the sage that grows in Colorado, in the Rockies. I lived in Colorado until my mother died. I don't know why, I guess I am trying to recapture the feeling about life that I used to have when my mother was alive, so I go to this place. The problem is, I never quite manage to get the feeling back. I get a little glimpse of it but then it fades away. But this time, after the treatment, I went to my spot and it worked! I got that wonderful feeling back! In fact it still hasn't left me!

> I asked Karen to draw me a detailed map of her special spot in the mountains. After work I drove up there and hiked to the exact location. There I found one of the largest stands I'd ever seen of the fragrant hummingbird sage."

The relationship being described here is magical, the connectivity of viewpoint and experience sublime. We have progressed so far through an attempt to frame the world of intuition and to show the scientific proof of its fundamental realness. In this chapter we have begun to discover the nature of the world which begins to be revealed when such direct experiencing takes place. We are also at the point of glimpsing the two-way nature of this relationship. Our intuition is not purely a passive process. The natural world has something to say to us if can learn how to hear, and really listen. In the next chapter we will explore some of the practical application of these viewpoints and meet today's Western equivalents of the kontomblé.

Review

Our intention in this chapter was to provide some general evidence for the direct relationship that humans can have with the shamanistic, non-ordinary, inner reality. We showed some modern scientific investigation of communication in plants, but concentrated mainly on illustrating the inner experience that is typical of those whose intuitive journeys take them to direct knowing of a spiritual relationship with the natural worlds.

Such descriptions defy our conventional understanding, both of the capability for connection and discernment that exists in plants and animals, and of the kind of intelligence that is present in animals like chickens that we do not normally credit with it. Various aspects of these experiences illustrate the falsehood, described by Rudolf Steiner, that lies within our habit of seeing nature and ourselves as separate, which is only the case at the level of physical matter but is not true at all in the realm of connected information flow that forms the "spiritual" world.

5. Practical shamanism

The characteristics of conduction in the plant nerve are in every way similar to those in the animal nerve.

> *Jagadis Chunder Bose*

In many respects, plant nervous systems are nearly as sophisticated as our own, and in some plants, nearly as rapid in their actions.

> *Stephen Harrod Buhner*   *Secret teachings of Plants*

We can find nature outside us only if we have first learned to know her within us

> *Rudolf Steiner*   *Philosophy of spiritual activity*

Theme

In this chapter we extend the theme of direct relationship with the world of nature. In particular we will look at the practical applications of this engagement and see something of what can be delivered. Some evidence in these realms is provided by simple outcomes such extraordinary gardens like Findhorn.

The idea of a direct relationship with the natural world extends the principle of intuitive connection that we discussed in our first chapters. It takes it beyond the realm of soliciting information about the world into one of active participation in it. Powerful as the passive mode of intuitive awareness may be, there is greater potential emerging here. We discover that the nature spirits are not just general but specific. They have their own tasks and their own form of identity and can engage with us co-operatively.

Shamanic gardeners

Among the most well-known explorations of this reality, particularly to Europeans, is that which has taken place over the past five decades at Findhorn in the extreme North of Scotland. Their full story is to be found on their website (www.Findhorn.org) from which we quote the following section, which refers to two of the founders, Dorothy MacLean and Peter Caddy.

> Peter decided to grow vegetables. The land in the caravan park was sandy and dry but he persevered. Dorothy discovered she was able to intuitively contact the overlighting spirits of plants - which she called angels, and then devas - who gave her instructions on how to make the most of their fledgling garden. She and Peter translated this guidance into action, and with amazing results. From the barren sandy soil of the Findhorn Bay Caravan Park grew huge plants, herbs and flowers of dozens of kinds, most famously the now-legendary 40-pound cabbages. Word spread, horticultural experts came and were stunned, and the garden at Findhorn became famous.

The following is a Dorothy MacLean's description of the communication that she received when during a meditation, she attempted to make contact with the spirit of a pea plant that she wished to grow.

> "I can speak to you, human. I am entirely directed by my work which is set out and moulded and which I merely bring to fruition, yet you have come straight to my awareness. My work is clear before me – to bring force fields into manifestation regardless of obstacles, and there are many in this man-infested world. While the vegetable kingdom holds no grudge against those it feeds, man takes what he can as a matter of course, giving no thanks. This makes us strangely hostile.
>
> What I would tell you is that as we forge ahead, never deviating from our course for one moment's thought, feeling or action, so could you. Humans generally seem not to know where they are going or why. If they did, what a powerhouse they would be. If they were on the straight course of what is to be done, we could cooperate with them! I have put across my meaning and bid you farewell."

She describes the Devas as follows:-

> The devas hold the archetypal pattern and plan for all forms around us, and they direct the energy needed for materialising them. The physical bodies of minerals, vegetables, animals and humans are all energy brought into form through the work of the devic kingdom.... While the devas might be considered the 'architects' of plant forms, the nature spirits or elementals, such as gnomes and fairies, may be seen as the 'craftsmen', using the blueprint and energy channelled to them by the devas to build up the plant form.

Our modern concept of gnomes and fairies may make it hard to hear the use of these terms in an appropriate way, but the indication is that these energies have more resemblance to Malidoma's "kontomblé" than to the plaster ornament or sentimental Victorian painting we might first think of.

Some readers, particularly in the United States, might have heard more of the Perelandra garden in Virginia, where Machaelle Small Wright has pursued a parallel exploration. Inspired by her reading of Dorothy MacLean and Eileen Caddy, she went in to the woods surrounding her property, announced to them her intention to do in Perelandra what they had done at Findhorn, and invited the nature spirits to help her.

She describes the response as immediate, resulting in a "crowd of voices" speaking to her as soon as she was back at the house and started to meditate. She endorses Dorothy Maclean's view of the Deva's role and in her book "Behaving as if the God in all life mattered" describes it as follows:-

"The word architect has been used by others when describing what devas do - and I also find this to be the most appropriate word. It is the Devic level that draws together the various energies that make up, for example, the carrot. The carrot deva "pulls together" the various energies that determine the size, colour, texture, growing season, nutritional needs, shape, flower and seed processes of the carrot. In essence, the carrot deva is responsible for the carrot's entire physical package. It holds the vision of the carrot in perfection and holds that collection of energy together as it passes from one vibratory level to another on its route to becoming physical. Everything about the carrot on a practical level as well as on the more expanded, universal level, is known by the carrot deva."

Each day I would go into meditation and open my connection with devic level. A deva would come into my awareness and identify itself. I was then given instructions. I was told what seeds to buy. What fertiliser to use. How far apart to plant the seeds. When to thin the plants and how much space to leave between them. Spacing between the rows. Desired amount of sunlight, and so on.

As each Deva came into my awareness. I noticed that there was a slight shift in vibration, but each had its own vibration. After a while I could recognize which Deva was entering my awareness. This led me to develop the ability to call upon specific Devas by aiming my awareness for the Deva's own vibratory pattern. It was as if I was faced with a gigantic telephone system, and I had to learn how to make all the different connections. Then I was able to make calls in as well as receive calls.

(Later in the summer I discovered that all I had to do to connect with a specific deva was to simply request the connection. For example, to connect with the Deva of the Carrot, I only needed to say "I'd like to be connected with the Deva of the Carrot." Immediately I would feel the familiar vibration of the Carrot Deva in my awareness. I knew the connection had been made an we were ready to work together. It couldn't have been more simple.)

One day I felt a very different vibration and found myself connecting to the over-lighting Deva of the garden. This Deva talked about such things as the overall layout of the garden, its timing, its progression and its shape. From it, I was also told to change my gardening methods to the mulch method – a method whereby 6 inches of hay, grass clippings and leaves are kept on the garden at all times. Two years later I was told to switch from the traditional straight rows to a garden of concentric circles.

Machaelle Small Wright also takes a similar view to Dorothy MacLean of what happens after the architecting deva has done its work and the nature spirits take over. This is her description:-

"The job description for nature spirits is "blue-collar workers". The Devas call together the different components of a plant. Once the "package" of energy is formed, Devas then hold the package together as it travels from one level to another, changing and adjusting its vibration as it acclimates to the Earth's density. Once the package reaches the etheric level around Earth, the nature spirits take over. It is the responsibility of the nature spirits, not only to receive the package of energy but to fuse it into its proper form as well. They fuse to a plant its light, its essence, its life pattern.

Devas are universal in dynamic. My Deva of the carrot is the same as your Deva of the carrot. Nature spirits are regional. My nature spirits of Perelandra are not the same as those working around you in your area.

Nature spirits, like Devas, are also bodies of light energy. But because they operate in close proximity to earth and its density, their energy vibration has a denser sensation than the devic vibration does. It is still a very high experience for us to feel. Nature spirits don't feel like energy rocks. They simply feel more dense than that devic energy."

This is just a brief look at the world of nature spirits and devas, which we give in order that you have a feeling for the form and shape that consciousness takes when it is working in nature. Note that there is more than one level involved in this creation. We are trying to amplify the sense of what it can mean for consciousness to be involved in the creation of form and provide a glimpse of the experience which those who have a direct relationship with such energies are likely to describe.

The picture of this world as given by both writers is rich and detailed. They each relate communications from different plant spirits, and the sense of individuality and distinctiveness between one and another. They both give a deep sense of the powerful co-operative relationship that is offered to humans when we begin to listen to and work with the forces of nature. There are many others who have documented similar experiences and the examples we give are simply some of the best known. They are not isolated cases and there are many systems for working with them. The bio-dynamic farming methods which come out of Rudolf Steiner's work in this realm are among the most widely practiced.

Very early in this book we introduced Jon and described the path that brought him to the alternate reality we are exploring. Some readers may have felt that Juliana was conspicuously absent at that point. We have saved her story until now, because Juliana now practices Plant Spirit Medicine, having trained with Eliot Cowan. She also works directly with the nature spirits in our garden. This is a good moment in our narrative for her to describe the path that she has taken, and to hear her personal experience of the relationship with plants that this chapter depicts.

I grew up in an extended east-end London family. I loved to sing and dance and had a great affinity to animals. I also had a sensitivity to atmospheres, undercurrents and emotional situations that meant I often felt unwell or uneasy: when I went into a room filled with people I could often feel ill in some way and yet these symptoms would often seem not to have any physical cause. The doctors could never quite get to the bottom of the matter. I was also frequently aware of 'visitors' at night – beings I could see that others could not that seemed to be trying to communicate with me and who my mum and dad reassured me "were not there".

As a teenager I became increasingly disillusioned with the teachings of the Catholic church that I had grown up with and more and more fascinated with other religions – world religions. I was deeply interested in how people worship and connect to something other than the obvious physical world. In my early twenties I joined an esoteric group and felt I had found the education that I had really needed; we studied the natural energies of the earth, astrology, numerology, plants and their natural cycles, the qualities of crystals, the importance of clearing a space of old stagnant energies and much more. I started to become aware of the energies within the human aura and how to bring healing to others, how to feel the energy fields of trees and plants. I connected to nature spirits, angels and other beneficial beings and developed the ability to see the energy fields of trees and people – colours and shimmering energies. Finally, the sensitivity to atmospheres began to become an asset. A few years later I trained as a psychic and learned how to differentiate between my own and other people's energies, which really helped me to make sense of the impressions I was receiving and to do something constructive with them in the form of healing.

This journey of healing has continued and deepened through various disciplines. I worked for around 7 years as a feng shui/space clearing consultant. This work took me into the homes of others to sense and clear the old energies of the house. During the course of this I encountered many spirits that had become stuck 'between the worlds' and it was my privilege to release them. It became known to me that if someone dies in shock that sometimes the spirit does not move on in the way it needs to and will go back to the place it last lived or to where it had the strongest pull. I had several experiences of 'conversing' with the spirit and finding that they were stuck at a particular time – I would ask them the date and they would generally tell me anything other than the current date I was aware of. A process of explaining to them that they were stuck would then ensue and I would advise them that it was time to move on and ask them to look up. Generally at this point they would see someone that they recognised – a relative or loved one - and feel safe enough to go. My experience of doing this release work was always profoundly joyful as the spirit was freed to move on.

Another awareness that came from this work was that of the land underneath the houses. Most of us do not give any thought to the land that we live on but there were several instances where I was called to a house that had been built on a cemetery or other 'troubled' land. These houses were always chaotic and extremely uncomfortable to live in. This can occur where a housing estate is built for commercial reasons and without any concern for the environmental implications. Our ancient relations would never have built on burial grounds or any other ground that would have been deemed sacred and we have lost that awareness in our modern culture.

In one instance I went to space clear a house that was not selling – it had been on the market for a couple of years and the family were desperate to move on.

It was a nicely decorated modern house with all conveniences so there was no rational reason why it had not sold. However, when I went into the house, I could hardly believe the feeling of whirring in my head and chest and the chaotic and muddled feeling all around the house. The lady of the house told me that they could not get anything done, that things rarely came together for any of the family ever since they had lived there. I discovered that the housing estate had been built on the grounds of an old asylum and that this house would have been very close to the sleeping quarters of the big house. After the space clearing, the atmosphere calmed down, the family sold the house and were able to get on with their lives in a new space.

This and many other experiences led me to become more and more aware and more respectful of the land we live on. I began to connect more with the trees and plants in the gardens and to realise how much more connection was possible between these other species and us as humans. I worked for years with flower essences and the positive healing benefits they bring and then was drawn to the work of Eliot Cowan and plant spirit medicine.

In plant spirit medicine we work in the way that our ancestors would have worked – in harmony with the natural world and in particular with the plant kingdom. We develop deep and respectful relationships with certain plants and pass on their healing qualities to our clients. The levels of possible benefits from plants far surpass the physical level. There is a spiritual level to plants that enables their connectedness to the earth and to the heavenly forces that flood through them constantly to come into our bodies and to help realign us to the natural world. If you think of a tree – it has its roots in the earth where it draws on the minerals and energies of earth and its branches in the heavens, where it is bombarded with the energies of the stars, the planets and the cosmos. For millennia our ancestors revered this earth as their mother and in truth there is no life on this earth without the food we eat that is grown in the soil. Again there is the balance of earth and heaven that combine to give us everything we need for life to grow and sustain. We humans have developed our minds to such an extent that we barely acknowledge the interconnectedness of all things and we have forfeited the awareness of the need for respectful relationships with all the forms of life we find around us.

Herbs and plants have been used for thousands of years and all indigenous cultures will have a form of plant spirit medicine. Many times this will be in the form of a tea or tincture but in the plant spirit medicine I work with no physical substance is given. When I call upon the plant spirit through my personal connection to it, it comes as a friend would come if asked. I choose the plant that most closely resembles the deepest need of my client and the plant spirit will work to deliver the adjustments that are required to bring that person into balance and harmony. It does not always clear up physical symptoms. Often it will but as there is a huge increase in wellbeing as well as a sense of connectedness to life, these symptoms often become less significant even if they remain.

One plant I work with is nettle, that most maligned of plants. This is a tough cookie as we all know when we have tried to get it out of the garden! It will grow anywhere, is a wonderful food for wildlife and supports the overall ecology of a garden. It provides nutrients and alkaloids that enable cross-fertilisation to occur and is known in herbal medicine to be a great tonic and blood cleanser. However, at another level this plant is fantastic to help a person face challenges, to withstand knocks in life and bounce back. I would give this plant to those who at a deep level cannot face challenges, who are fearful and timid and who need to develop inner strength and resilience to go forward in their lives. I have one client who was unable to express his anger and was being trampled on by others. He would have a periodic explosion but most of the time seemed to be unable to let people know what he felt. After a few treatments with nettle he has become adept at speaking his mind and is now letting his emotions be known at the time and not needing to store up an explosion about things that happened months before!

I don't pretend to know about science. That's Jon's department. What I do know is that the world I work in is the same world. Everything that he describes and all the people whom we quote in this book are interleaved in the reality that I have just written of. People's lives change when their energy environment alters. Physical changes happen in the body and emotions shift as a result of the connection with spirit. The connections are seamless; they work through all levels and layers. I have chosen a story which describes this connectedness in a way that depicts the richness and integrity of these connections in all their glory. It also illustrates what is possible when someone can integrate their own experience so as to be in a deep empathic connection at the same time as having a normal conversation.

Modern shamanism – a complete illustration

The passage that follows is taken from Stephen Harrod Buhner's book "The Secret Teachings of Plants".

"The woman who had come to see me was tentative at the door, hesitant. Her eyes were nervous, quick, surrounded by lines of worry. She eddied in at the door like a wisp of smoke, whispered across the room, and hovered lightly in the chair. She was 45 years old, short, thin and wiry. Her skin was pale, washed out, her hair a brown, non-flowing shadow of life. Just there.

She had come because she could not breathe. She had asthma.

I said hello as she sat, began drinking tea, telling me her life in many languages. In words. In the small flutterings of her hands. In intonations, the rise and fall of her voice as she spoke. In the slight shifts of her body, in the tiny patterns of emotion that crossed her face. The *shape* of her body. The clothes she wore.

Her asthma had come on suddenly with no prior history. It had been almost twenty years now. Her medications were many, expensive. Laden with side effects. I responded to her gesturings of communication. Talked with part of my mind

hearing her speak of her life

while another part looked deeper, seeking the path the disease had taken in her, searching for traces of its truth.

Her chest caught my attention, standing forth of its own accord. Beckoning.

My attention centered there and I breathed into it, letting my awareness move deeper, touching its shape. *Feeling* my way. I felt a sadness come over me, an overwhelming urge to cry. And then my chest began to feel tight. The muscles clenched, closed down. I began to hunch over slightly, curl around myself. My chest hollowed and I began to breathe high up, rapidly, in small quick bursts of breathing. My breathing a tiny bird, fluttering against the walls of my chest.

I began to feel afraid then, slightly hysterical.

I calmed myself, breathed more deeply, sat back in my chair, felt a wave of relaxation flow through my muscles. Slowly, one by one, they unclenched.

I let myself care for her then. Sent out a wave of caring from me to her. Let it touch her chest, hold it in the hollow of her caring hands. Waited..waited... waited. Breathing slowly, softly, calmly. Into her chest. Slightly urging it, slowly... slowly...., to relax, to calm down, to breathe. It took a few minutes.

I saw her sink more deeply into the chair, her muscles beginning to relax. Her skin tone was changing, the muscles and the skin itself softening. Her face relaxed. And she took a deep breath. There was a slight wheezing sound.

Then she took another, and deeper, breath. Her chest began to open up slightly, the muscles letting go.

And all the while of course, we were talking. I let my deeper breathing flow into the tone of my voice. As my breathing deepened, slowly my intonation deepened with it. My words, originally dancing and quick, in tune with her breathing, began – patiently – to slow down, deepen and become more calm.

Her eyes softened, grew moist. Slightly unfocused. She began to tear up. Softly. Silently.

A few tears trailed down her cheeks.

My gaze focused on her chest, and I began to embed communication in my talking, telling her chest it was okay. That it could relax, breathe, tell me its secrets.

Her talking began to keep pace with my own, grow slower, more studied, less nervous.

She took a slow, deep breath. Smiled hesitantly. Her skin began to get some colour, to glow a bit. I smiled too, then, and nodded slightly. I let my voice wrap her up, hold her in its arms. Telling her it was good, that she was okay now. Telling her lungs that they could relax.

I let my awareness flow deeper then. Through the surface of her chest, into her lungs.

My lungs seized up. It was hard to breathe. I couldn't get my breath. Some small part of me was afraid. Hysterical. I turned part of my vision, focused it inside of me. Looked around. Saw the frightened part of me and held it in my arms. Soothed it with soft words, my intonations and presence saying more than words ever could. The frightened part of me began to relax, feel better. Not abandoned.

Keeping part of myself touching my own lungs and that frightened place, I turned my attention back to her lungs. Letting myself sink deep within them, I began to *look*.

There was a slight hesitation, like pushing against a mushy blanket of cotton wool. A resistance. I sent my caring into the resistance and deeper, through it, into her lungs. Asked them to let me see. I stayed present, *breathed* into the experience. I enhanced the sense of my caring, looked deeply, focused my seeing, *wanted* to see.

There was a slight hesitation again. Then a sudden movement into a still, quiet centre. And I could *see*, could *feel*, the living reality of her lungs. Their colour was off. Some strange cross between gray and mucusy white. It was old mucus, an unhealthy brownish-yellow glue. My nose wrinkled slightly as the smell came to me. It was barely there, slight, as faint as the whispers of children. A sick smell, my stomach nauseous to its touch.

The surface of her lungs, the cells themselves, were clogged, gunged-up. *Suffocating*. Grayish, not pink. Covered with a blanket of old gummy sludge, a blanket that wove over and into them, through them. The mucus was dead, unliving, not like normal mucus which is thin and watery – a glowing, moving living thing shining out its healthy life.

Hers was dead, unmoving, held in place. Old and unattended. Its life force was gone. The cells of her lungs, the tissue itself, were taking on that deadness, that unhealthy unaliveness. The lungs were slowed down in their function, held back by this *oldness*.

My attention *focused* on the lungs, my seeing alive to every part that had been revealed to me, I reached into her lungs with my caring then. Directed the living, feeling field of my heart to hold them, envelop them. My caring moved deeply within her lungs, interweaving with their tissues, *holding* them, all of us now suspended in a living moment of time. Then, still holding them, still present with them, I turned part of my attention at a slight angle, sent it out into the world. Sent out a request for help, a prayer from my deepest being, my earnest need flowing out through this channel I had opened into the world. At the same time I kept a living channel open through me into the reality of her lungs.

Then I felt the *need* of her lungs and let it flow through me and out, attaching it to my prayer for help so that they flowed together, interweaving with one another, flowing as one earnest need and plea.

I felt that living communication flowing out, its field spreading wide, touching the living reality of the world. I felt the living intelligence then, deeply embedded in its own work, its own living. Then, as it felt my touch upon it, and knew that it was genuine, there was caring behind and within it, it quickened, awakened, *turned* towards me and *saw*. A living flow of energy then came back through the channel I had opened between us, a flow with caring in it. A deep caring and loving came back from the wildness of the world. The world from which all of us have come.

And into my mind flashed an image of skunk cabbage

Powerful, green

Luminescent in wetland forest.

I relaxed my touch then; my concentration softened. My focused awareness let go. And still talking with her with that other part of my mind I came back into the room, and let these new understandings flow into my talking. I began to weave the healing of this plant medicine into her body, into her life.

Later when the talking was done, I gave some of the skunk cabbage tincture to the woman with asthma, put one drop of it on her tongue, and watched as she closed her mouth *closed her eyes* and tasted it. Watched as she let her system absorb it. I saw her breathe deeply, then open her eyes suddenly as it penetrated further into her. Then, I saw the smile that came and watched her body relax, the tension lines smooth out of her face.

I remembered her lungs then and found myself standing once again with them, their living reality before my vision. The colour of the mucus was present once again, its thickness within my awareness.

Holding this in my vision I turned slightly, opened a channel from me out into the world, into that wetland forest, to skunk cabbage. Saw the plant once again before me, her roots gleaming wetly in my vision. Saw and felt the living reality of them, felt once more her medicine.

Let her name arise within me

Then, calling to her, asking her to come with my caring, my prayer went out to her, touched her, and she turned, awakening. Her living reality came into my awareness and flowed down that channel of communication, into this woman's lungs.

Then I gave the woman a full dropper of the tincture. I could see the tendrils of the plant, her roots, their colour matching that of the lungs begin to wriggle into the lung tissue, inserting themselves deep into the woman's cellular tissue, flowing through them. I saw the plant interweaving with her lungs. The power of the plant, the medicine of skunk cabbage, flowed deep into her cells, filled her lungs and the mucus began to thin, the colour of her lungs to change. The mucus became more watery, began to run, to flow. It began to ooze out of the tissues, the cells clearing. And I could see the healing begin, see the plant teach her lungs how to be. I could see the lungs begin to take on the power and strength of the plant.   Then from the Earth came a power older than the human, flowing up through her body and into her lungs. An ancient power, old and deep, dark and silent.   Her body began taking it in like a food that she had long forgotten. Her lungs reached out to it, relaxed into it, settled down into it. The power began to flow up into her lungs and out into the world. The old stagnant thing in her lungs began to flow with it, up and out of her body. The plant a channel, as I had been a channel. And, interwoven with that moving stream was the living teaching, the medicine understanding of this plant, this ally, this living being that people call skunk cabbage.

This story is one small but very whole and powerful illustration of the nature of our possible relationship with the plant kingdom and the strength that we might acquire from restoring a healthy relationship with that kingdom and with the living Earth itself. We see it depicting a modern human entering the world that shaman healers have used for centuries, straddling the boundary between the ordinary and non-ordinary realities.   It is just one example, just one modality of possible energy-based healing, but one that integrates several layers of relationship.   It illustrates the spiritual dimension of the healer, the intuitive nature of the connection, the subtle energetic flow of the healing and the added mediation from the chemical action and more physical presence of the tincture. In this, it summarises and weaves together several aspects of our text so far.

In the next chapter we will look at another modality and see the systematic and scientific depth beneath homeopathy. This will lead us toward further examples of miraculous capabilities in the world of healing before heading into the heart of the biology and the physics through which it all manifests.

Review

Our intention in this chapter was to develop our acquaintance with the shaman's world, mainly through practical illustrations of the ways in which modern practitioners in this field are achieving results, and through extending our view of what "nature spirits" really are. The description of devas presents us with a sense of consciousness, of information about the construction of the living world, being localized and focused within a discrete non-material entity. The work done in co-operation with these beings yields practical results providing one kind of evidence that such views are more than mere fantasy.

In Juliana's abbreviated life-history and in Stephen Harrod Buhner's story we see a continuity of these viewpoints through several facets of our relationship with the world – our land, our buildings and their history – through into the many-layered possibilities of a healing engagement. Juliana's experiential history is a personal journey with unique features. We could have found many different biographies just from among her peers and our own network, all containing the same essence and with deep commonality, but viewed from varied perspectives and descriptive frameworks. This is the texture of our common yet personal human relationship with the world of consciousness and spirit.

6. <u>The science of homeopathy</u>

Two women are on a bus, talking.

First woman: "What happened with that homeopath you were seeing?"

Second woman :"Nothing. She gave me a couple of pills but they didn't do anything."

"So who are you seeing now?"

"Oh – nobody.   A few weeks later the problem just went away."

    Anon: Joke enjoyed by homeopaths

Any sufficiently advanced technology is indistinguishable from magic

    Arthur C Clarke

Magical thinking is the most advanced technology we have.

    Jon Freeman

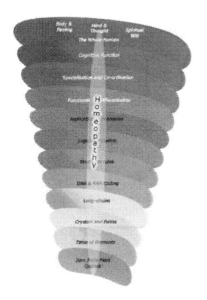

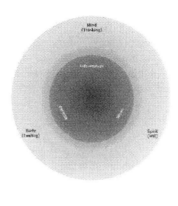

Theme

In this chapter we use homeopathy as an illustration of the scientific method as applied in alternative healing, and show the way in which its systematic study has revealed various aspects of the connected world that we are describing. Homeopathy shows the effects of informational relationships in a very distinct way. It also provides evidence that there are aspects of that information flow which should influence our perception of what happens between one generation of humans and the next, that there is more than simple genetics involved.

There has been laboratory proof of the way in which homeopathy works – proof which has been not simply ignored, but suppressed in a quite unscientific way. This has allowed the myth that homeopathy operates through the "placebo effect" to perpetuate. While the placebo effect tells us something important which science also is unable to explain adequately, it has nothing whatsoever to do with homeopathic effectiveness.

How homeopathy developed

Homeopathy is a science. Many other complementary health practices might say the same, but homeopathy is possibly unique in having developed explicitly according to western scientific methods prior to 1900. This is one reason we will concentrate on it at the expense of other strong contenders such as Chinese medicine and acupuncture which, regardless of their millennia of practice and huge curative history, are more difficult to frame in western terms. The other reason for a focus on homeopathy is that it illustrates perfectly the nature of the universe we are describing and exposes the gaps in the scientism paradigm.

We will use the term medical here to denote the core of pharmacologically and surgically based western Medical practice. This is not to deny that complementary therapies are also medical – it is simply a narrative convenience.

A convention has developed among the medical and scientism advocates in their references to homeopathy. That convention is to dismiss its practice in a very simple way. They note that its principle is to use remedies prepared in such a way that potentially there may be not one single molecule of the original substance from which the remedy derives, present in the pill taken by the patient. By this simple logic, Medicine takes the right to attribute all experiences to the "placebo" effect. What they mean by this is that the patient "imagines themselves better" because they are made to feel good. We will show that the notion and implications of the placebo effect are important, but not applicable to homeopathic treatment.

This convention has been present for so long and is so entrenched that it is largely taken for granted that no further study of its theory or history is necessary, creating a conspiracy of ignorance. Such trials as are undertaken are not conclusive. Often this is for methodological reasons we will examine below. On Page 167 of the "God Delusion" Professor Dawkins echoes the conventional viewpoint, which he repeats regularly in hostile TV polemics and one suspects, as with all his co-conspirators, that he has not been willing to look any further. In most cases we simply disagree with his views of science. In this instance it is fair to accuse him of inadequate research.

At this point let us remind ourselves of what the fundamental principles of science are supposed to be. A simple view is that science is the search for one kind of truth about the universe. Scientists might say that this method is the only way to determine truth. Such truth would be based on a straightforward set of processes.

- Observe the nature of the world with detailed care.

- To the greatest possible extent, undertake such observations in such a way that they can be measured and repeated by others under the same conditions.

- Try, when measuring and compiling the data, to avoid interfering with the subject under examination in such a way as to distort the events observed.

- From these observations attempt to formulate theories which would explain the relationships of cause and effect that determine what is seen.

For example: "I release an object at height. It falls to the ground. Therefore there is a force which operates on objects. I will name it 'gravity'." This is the background to the image of Newton's stroke of genius under the apple tree.

Theories can develop to greater complexity such that we can then measure and determine mathematically just how strong earthly gravity is, how quickly a falling object will accelerate towards the ground, and what the effect might be of resistance to that motion from the air such that feathers fall more slowly. Further theories might then develop regarding why it is that the Earth exhibits a property such as gravity and explanations would appear for the observed motions of the planets.

Depending on the phenomena observed, we would then repeat the observations under controlled conditions in order to test the theory and determine as completely as possible the boundaries of the theory. Is it always true? Under what circumstances does that theory vary, and how?

At the core, this is what science is – an attempt to create systematic processes for describing the observed world in a way which can be labeled as "truth". The process is simple in theory but due to the great complexity of the world the practice is not easy. Science has grown because a theory (e.g. Newtonian gravitational mechanics) was insufficient to explain why light bends and does not always travel in straight lines so that it is distorted when under the influence of gravity from large objects in the universe. A new theory is required and Einstein finds curves in space-time (don't worry – we don't need to understand that here).

The example above illustrates the requirement for science to change when new facts emerge. There is a linguistic misunderstanding over the phrase "the exception proves the rule" because we hear the modern meaning of the word "proves" as "shows it to be true". The original meaning of "prove" was "test". Thus, if a new and exceptional fact emerges (e.g. we notice conditions under which light bends) we test if the rules of Newtonian mechanics still apply. Depending on circumstances, we must either find a bigger theory in which our current theory is seen as a local approximation, or we have to throw the theory out and find a better one.

Forgive us if we are labouring this point. To do so would be insulting to scientists in particular were it not for the tendency through history for them to behave in fallibly human ways or to be influenced by political and economic forces. Ask Galileo. Science has regularly experienced the cycle of influence when a new fact emerges that does not fit with previous accepted theory. The fact in question is then denied by scientific authority. There is then a prolonged period of struggle (sometimes ending with the death of a particular authority figure) after which the fact is admitted and a new theory becomes authoritative. This has been neatly summed up by Schopenhauer who said :-

"All Truth passes through three stages.

It is ridiculed

It is violently opposed

It is seen as self-evident",

which brings us back to homeopathy, whose current scientific credibility, continues to lie between ridicule and opposition. Homeopaths must yearn for the day when the Earth will revolve around the sun.

Homeopathy's Galileo is Dr Samuel Hahnemann who was a physician and expert in pharmacology born in 1755, one of whose medical successes was to live to the age of 88. Hahnemann was by any standards a remarkable man, who was fluent in seven languages, and the initial prompting for his research came when he was translating the work of an English doctor, William Cullen, into German.

He was unconvinced by a statement of Cullen's regarding the reasons behind the effectiveness of Cinchona bark as a treatment for malaria. In order to find out more about its properties, he took repeated doses of the substance, up to the point where its toxic effects began to show. What he noticed was that the toxic effects were fever, chills, and other malaria-like symptoms. From this he theorised that rather than being due to astringent properties, which Cinchona bark shared with other substances that were ineffective against malaria, the reason for its effectiveness was that the symptoms produced by the bark were similar to those of the disease. He set out to test this hypothesis systematically.

His method was scientific but since one observation does not make a science, Hahnemann spent the next six years, with the assistance of a small group of followers, testing the observation on a wide range of substances and conditions, using his family too as subjects. At the end of the process he published his findings in a medical journal. He immediately met with opposition, both from physicians, and from apothecaries. The latter were upset at the potential damage to their businesses, because Hahnemann recommended only one medicine at a time, and in small quantities, so were not disposed to comply with his prescriptions. When Hahnemann found that homeopathic medicines were not being prepared correctly by apothecaries, or that they were taking it on themselves to prescribe different medicines, he began to do the preparation himself. This was unlawful, and resulted in his being charged, and forced to leave his home in Leipzig.

It is perhaps helpful to see homeopathy against the background of its day, when treatments were very coarse - bloodletting and the use of leeches being among the common techniques. It is recorded that in 1833, 41 million leeches were imported into France. Orthodox medicine also used preparations from arsenic, lead and mercury - all poisons, as well as strong herbal purgatives. But despite this it was homeopathy that was labeled as "devilish", "cultish", or "quackery".

Like cures like

The first principle discovered by Hahnemann, and the foundation of homeopathy, stemmed from the initial observation, and can be summarised as follows:-

- Every pharmacologically active substance produces symptoms in a healthy, sensitive individual which are characteristic of that substance.

- Each disease has a characteristic set of symptoms.

- An illness can be cured by administering to a patient a small, homeopathically prepared dose of the same substance which, during trials, produced symptoms similar to the illness in healthy individuals.

His approach to treatment represented a dramatic move away from the established method. Allopaths (conventional medics) establish the existence of a particular disease, clarify its symptoms, and then test the effectiveness of various medicines on it by the use of substances that oppose the symptom(s), a principle of "opposite suffering". An illness accompanied by fever and diarrhoea, for example, would call for the combined use of substances that calm the fever and others that normally constipate, and so in a crude way, a total balance would be found by using a number of appropriate medicines together.

Homeopaths tried the opposite approach: first build a repertory of substances for medicinal use, they said, by giving them to healthy volunteers, and carefully noting the symptoms produced. Then use small quantities of the substance which produces the correct combination of symptoms as the single medicinal agent for those with disease conditions, a principle of "similar suffering". To use a substance which potentially produces, rather than suppresses the symptoms seems at first counter-intuitive, but was found to work in practice. A simple example of the principle that "like cures like", would be that if you were suffering from the particular type of cold symptoms combining streaming and burning nose, watering eyes and bouts of sneezing, the remedy to be used would be derived from onions, which as any cook knows, produces the same symptoms. Likewise Allium Cepa, the remedy referred to, is used to combat hay-fever with similar presenting symptoms. The cause of those symptoms is not necessarily relevant. The fact that one may be caused by a viral or bacterial pathogen, and the other by an airborne irritant does not matter, because the body is seen to mobilise the appropriate curative resources when its energy is stimulated by the remedy to fully engage.

Returning to Hahnemann, in the six years of work before publication, many examples of this process were collected. In doing so he set a further fundamental principle in the development of the science of homeopathy; it should be based on detailed observation, extensive trials, and systematic testing of theoretical and philosophical ideas, through careful experimentation. This tradition thus meets the criteria described earlier for a scientific process and continues to the present day.

Homeopathy was successful, and spread rapidly. It was taken to America in 1825, and expanded so rapidly that in 1844 the first national medical association was formed, by Homeopaths. Two years later the American Medical Association was started with the specific intent of slowing the growth of homeopathy. The AMA specifically excluded homeopaths from membership, and expelled members who admitted any contact with it (which in many states was a precursor to loss of license to practice).

Nevertheless, the rapid spread of the science had the beneficial consequence that there were many practitioners, and a vast body of growing validation of its effectiveness. A second effect of this growth in numbers was that many practitioners were formulating, sharing and testing new theories (as too was Hahnemann, who remained active throughout his long life). As a result the body of information and experience as well as the recognised range of effective remedies, increased steadily. We want to stress here, that the point of this chapter is not to compare levels of homeopathic effectiveness with that of modern medicine. It is not a question of which is better. Our point is firstly to show that the principles discovered by Hahnemann and his followers were real and scientific and that there are sound reasons why homeopathy is effective. It is secondly to show the implications that this has for current scientific thinking.

Less is more

Having established the first principle, Hahnemann's second line of investigation was to determine what amount of the "similar" agent would be required to bring about the best curative effect. Some of the patterns in disease resemble the actions of seriously dangerous toxins. For example the sickness and diarrhoea that occur with food poisoning are sometimes like the effects of arsenical poisoning. It is obviously desirable that only the smallest quantities of arsenic would be used in treatment.

This line of research led to the second counter-intuitive finding. Just as it was better not to suppress the symptom with an opposite, Hahnemann discovered that the less of a substance he administered, the more effective would be the cure. His second axiom for treatment is the Law of the Minimal Dose. This states that the effective dose for a disorder is the minimum amount necessary to produce a response. The process by which a homeopathic remedy is prepared is known as potentisation, and involves a sequence of progressive dilution and a rhythmic shaking, termed succussion. In a typical method, one part of the source substance is added to 9 parts of water and shaken rhythmically. This is known as a 1x (decimal) dilution, or 1 part in 10. One part of this is then taken and added to another 9 parts of water, again succussed, to give a 2x dilution, or 1 part in 100.

These dilutions can be repeated a large number of times. A typical UK health-store remedy might be 6x (or 1 part in a million). But it might also be 6c, a centessimal (1 to 100) preparation where the original substance is diluted to one in a billion levels. Practitioners often use dilutions down to one in a trillion and well beyond. While the toxicity of such medicines is obviously very low, the dilutions quickly approach levels where it is doubtful whether a single molecule of the original substance remains. This is the cause for the chemical reality which underlies the "placebo effect" dismissal.

There is more to reveal about the findings of homeopathy and its scientific implications, but it would be good to get the "placebo" issue thoroughly out of the way. While it might be apparent to an open-minded reader that the founding processes are so detailed as to make the placebo theory inadequate, there are many more facts which support the case for homeopathic effectiveness.

The placebo myth

One simple fact giving lie to any psychosomatic effects is that homeopathy works with infants and animals. The numbers of parents who have experienced the almost miraculous effects of chamomile in homeopathic potencies in calming their teething infants probably amounts by now to millions. This could be enough on its own, but it is far from being an isolated example.

Jon has practiced homeopathy as an amateur for over 20 years now with friends, family and pets. In his early days he visited with friends whose small cat had suffered for days with worsening symptoms of sneezing, runny nose and wheezing. Cat-lovers will know that this can be quite serious – more so than a human cold – and the hosts (you can't "own" a cat) were getting worried. They gave permission that evening for Jon to experiment, despite his never previously having treated any animal. A few remedies were placed in the cat's food and water and by the following morning all symptoms had vanished.

If this was a one-off occurrence it could be regarded as coincidence, but it is not and there are homeopaths who specialize in veterinary practice. What it emphatically cannot be ascribed to is a placebo effect. It is even less appropriate than with infants to apply such a term.

There is strong epidemiological evidence too. In 1830 cholera, a disease that had never been seen before in Europe, was having devastating effects all across it. Nowadays it would be controlled by hygiene and by preventing diarrhoea and dehydration but even now if cholera occurs in an unprepared community, case-fatality rates may be as high as 50% according to World Health

Organisation figures -- usually because there are no facilities for treatment, or because treatment is given too late. In 1832, two hundred and fifteen deaths occurred in Sunderland alone, and by the summer of that year the disease had taken toll of some eight hundred lives in nearby Newcastle-upon-Tyne. From North-East England the disease quickly spread to Southern Scotland causing three thousand one hundred and sixty-six deaths in Glasgow. In April the disease appeared in Hull and in Liverpool where one thousand five hundred and twenty-three deaths occurred. Leeds, Bristol, and Manchester were also soon afflicted as well as many other towns and sea-ports, the disease being especially rampant amid the shacks and hovels of the new industrial districts.

At the same time the Russian Consul General reported results from homeopathic treatment practised at two locations. Of 70 cases, all were cured. In 1849 Cholera had reached America, and an outbreak in Cincinatti was treated similarly, with a 97% cure rate in a sample of 1116 patients. In 1854, cholera broke out again in London. At the London Hospital where homeopathy was used, returns gave 61 cases of cholera with 10 deaths (83% cured), and 341 cases of choleraic diarrhoea with one death (99% cured). In contrast the neighbouring Middlesex Hospital received 231 cases of cholera and 47 cases of choleraic diarrhœa. Of the cholera patients treated conventionally 123 died, a fatality rate of 53.2 per cent.

When doctors could not cure the disease they attempted to treat the wound to their professional pride. The homeopathic cases were excluded from statistics presented to parliament due to the claim that they would give "an unjustifiable sanction to an empirical practice alike opposed to the maintenance of truth and to the progress of science". (Evidence of the Medical committee to the Parliamentary Board of Health).

The same year in Naples, a Dr Rubini treated 225 cholera cases without a single death. At this time the success of allopathic medicine was generally no better than one in three patients cured. Similar effectiveness was reported later in the century, for treatment of a Yellow fever epidemic in the Southern USA.

We said earlier that the effectiveness of homeopathy against cholera was important in itself, and not as a comparison with antibiotics, or any modern medical procedure. The importance is that you cannot conceivably achieve a 90% cure rate for as hostile a disease as Cholera with a placebo effect, or other treatments would have been able to do so as well. It is clearly quite ludicrous to dismiss homeopathic results in this way. There has to be a better explanation and indeed there is one, which takes us back to the theory.

Small doses stimulate

In conventional pharmacology, one of the basic tools is the Dose-Response curve. This graph illustrates one of the rules of thumb in drug use: that an increased dose of drug will give an increased effect. But this applies only at higher dosages. One of the very earliest laws of pharmacology, known as the Arndt-Schulz Law also expresses the homeopathic effect. Formulated by Arndt in 1888, the law states that for every substance, small doses stimulate, moderate doses inhibit, and large doses kill. Allopathic medicines, with their emphasis on moderate drug doses, work in the inhibitory part of the scale, and are used to suppress symptoms. Homeopathic medicine, on the other hand, begins at the stimulatory end of the curve, and moves to smaller and smaller dose ranges. Its emphasis is on the stimulation of the body's natural response mechanisms.

But although the basis is there in pharmacological theory, we must go beyond pharmacological action to understand the homeopathic effect. Since there is often insufficient substance to have a pharmacological effect, the action has to be taking place at some kind of "energetic" or "informational" level. We accept the statement from critics that there may not be a molecule of the source substance present. It is clear that the effectiveness of homeopathy does not lie in chemical action or conventional pharmacology. Equally clearly, it has great capability to be selective and specific about the effectiveness of different substances, or their actions would not be so precisely targeted. This is the first of our observations regarding the validation that homeopathic theory gives to the transmission of a healing effect through a medium which is purely "energetic" or "informational". We will add more definition to these terms shortly.

By now you will hopefully be recognizing the fundamental reason for our earlier focus on scientific principle.

- Something is happening in homeopathy that is scientifically backed by volumes of systematic evidence gathering but which does not fit with existing medical theory.

- Since the existing theory is failing some tests of evidence the theoretical model needs either to expand or to be replaced.

- In order to develop a more comprehensive theory further investigation is required into the data and the underlying principles of similarity and minimum dosage

Fortunately there is more evidence for us to look at. Unfortunately medicine and science are in a state of denial (ridicule and opposition) around this too. They have cause to do so because the evidence strikes at the very roots of the errors which we listed in our introduction. But the alternative theories which emerge from this evidence are very exciting indeed.

Suppression doesn't work

As we delve more deeply into what homeopathy has discovered, the evidence throws up yet more challenges to scientific theories, and in some very interesting ways. We are going to have to abbreviate a lot more of the theory to get to this. There is so much of value regarding the way in which healing works, and we can only encourage you to read of it elsewhere (the work of Deepak Chopra being one excellent example).

We referred above to the choice allopathic medicine makes to cure by suppression of symptoms. Most alternative and holistic approaches are fundamentally opposite to this. There is a basic respect for the actions of the body - an assumption that if the body produces fever, it is because it needs to do so. This approach is inclined towards supporting the body in its natural response and views suppression as likely to drive fundamental causes of ill health deeper into the body, bringing worse trouble later on. In homeopathy the use of a substance that shares the underlying symptomatic signature (similar suffering) is designed to propel the symptom(s) to completion.

Examples of the ill effects of suppression form a very strong part of homeopathic case lore. A whole strand of investigation in homeopathy relates to the situation where actions that were taken to suppress a disease result in the later appearance of another symptom pattern. These new symptoms can then be alleviated by applying the treatment appropriate not to the new symptoms, but to the disease that was originally suppressed. This is shown to be effective no matter how long before the current problem it may have occurred, or how absent those original symptoms may be.

A typical example of this which occurred frequently during the 19th century, when the development of homeopathy was at its height and when venereal disease was also very common, arose from the treatments used to suppress Gonorrhea. The case we use to illustrate this dates back to 1875, when the eminent homeopath concerned was treating a man of 60 for an obstinate case of rheumatism. This patient was walking with a cane, wrapped in a muffler, thin, bent and aged in appearance, and his condition had persisted for several months. Unable to shift the problem with remedies conforming to the current symptoms, the homeopath recalled the correspondence that had frequently been observed by him and his colleagues, between arthritic conditions and earlier treatments to suppress gonorrhea. His insight was to treat the patient with the remedy derived from that disease. The case notes describe that the patient returned ten days later feeling well, and that within the month he had ceased use of the cane and muffler. His weight subsequently increased from 140 pounds to his previously healthy 212 pounds.

Although this example illustrates powerfully why homeopaths and other alternative practitioners are so concerned to bring disease out of the body, rather than push it deeper in by suppressing symptoms, that is still not the main point of the story. There is a further and even more remarkable stage to go yet. It was also consistently observed by homeopaths that the effect we have just described could span the generations. That is, an individual could present the symptoms of rheumatic disease, and that this could be cured by the gonorrheal remedy, even though the case of suppressive treatment had occurred in a parent. What this means is that there is experience in homeopathy that the energy pattern relating to a disease can pass from generation to generation, and that the inheritance can be treated. This observation has huge significance. For the avoidance of any doubt we must stress that according to accepted theories this inheritance cannot occur by way of the genes and has no known alternative scientific explanation. It clearly needs one. We will examine this area extensively when we get to grips with the true mechanics of genetic processes.

Energy sickness down the generations

In fact this understanding is one of the basic strands of homeopathic science, which recognises that there are certain diseases, such as Tuberculosis, Gonorrhea and Syphilis which have widespread influence through inheritance. That is, they are so embedded energetically and informationally in the human race that their influence may be detected several generations beyond the last known experience of the disease in the person's lineage. A modern homeopath might rarely encounter a patient who knows the last time tuberculosis or syphilis occurred in his or her family, but it is nevertheless frequently an element in that individuals "make-up". Homeopaths call such an energetic lineage a "miasm". Treatment of miasms is a strong part of a practitioner's armoury, deeply validated by practical experience.

So now we have a second instance whereby some sort of energy is perceived as being transferred, without any known mechanism. It is not being suggested that the miasm is passed via the DNA, or that it has been incorporated into the genes. So just as in some way, the energy of a substance can be put into the fluid that is used to impregnate a homeopathic tablet, the energy of a disease can be passed - perhaps in the cytoplasm of a sperm or egg cell - from one generation to the next. The implications of this fact (and I repeat that homeopaths have been healing people on this principle for a very long time) are profound. This means of transmission implies the strong influence of a vibrational or information-carrying energy component in the disease, and on its passage between generations. We cannot over-emphasise the significance of this fact. In case minds are beginning to wilt in face of the apparent improbability of the facts being described, we also have to repeat the statement that these facts have been repeatedly validated through systematic observation by multiple practitioners across several continents and over very many decades.

The laboratory evidence

Clearly some aspects of these effects are not suitable for laboratory examination. We cannot deliberately infect patients with gonorrhea and then manipulate their treatments for the purposes of measurement, still less monitor the effects on their children. But there is scientific evidence in the laboratory of a means for this transmission to take place. It was discovered by Jacques Benveniste, when he was director of the French National Institute of Health and Medical Research and specialist in immunology. The evidence demonstrates a phenomenon known as "molecular memory". This is akin to a kind of subtle electromagnetic language, whereby the "sound" of one molecule could be recorded by another, like a tape-recorded sound. Benveniste's research was first reported in the magazine "Nature" (Vol. 333, No. 6176, pp. 816-818, 30th June, 1988). Benveniste had taken a substance which typically produces the chemical activity associated with allergic reactions when mixed in a test-tube, with a blood serum preparation. He diluted the substance tenfold, and repeated the experiment. He continued this process repeatedly, and as with homeopathy, progressed way beyond the level where any molecule of the substance remained. In effect his solution was just distilled water, containing in theory, 1 part of the original antibody to 10^{120} parts of water. (10 followed by 120 zeroes - a trillion multiplied by a trillion repeated ten times). The effect on the blood serum persisted regardless.

This experiment was replicated in Jerusalem, Toronto and Milan with the same results, and his paper was signed by twelve other researchers. This should have been hailed as revolutionary and groundbreaking. Even now it should be seen as hugely significant for scientific theory. At the very least its results give considerable credence to all that Hahnemann and his followers had discovered in practice, but the implications go much further – right through medicine and biology. Instead of hailing the research the medical and scientific establishment treated the results as a problem, one reminiscent of an anonymous poem which runs "Last night when walking up the stair, I met a man who wasn't there. He wasn't there again today - I wish, I wish he'd go away." This is very much the response that Benveniste's work has met with.

The poem's last line may also be substituted with "I think he's from the CIA". It can be risky to challenge authority, and the attacks on Benveniste in the years since have been outstanding in their abusiveness, including Nature's choice to send its editor and two "fraudbusters" to Benveniste's laboratories. One of these was the noted stage magician James Randi, an arch-skeptic whose name appears regularly as a "debunker" of alternatives and who was reported to have taped information to the ceiling "to prevent tampering". Benveniste complained that the process was unprofessional, accused the team of poor controls and of using one week's work to wipe out the activities of five years research in his and five other laboratories. The results Benveniste obtained in their presence were mixed, and inconclusive, with the first three trials providing some confirmation, but a further four showing nothing.

There are many subsequent failures to replicate the original work but there was a notable success in 2004 when Madeleine Ennis, who claimed to have begun as a skeptic published a study which stated "it has been shown that high dilutions of histamine may indeed exert an effect on basophil activity". (Inflammation Research 2004: 53; 181-188). Such mixed evidence is unhelpful but who knows what happens with such subtle energies, especially in such an environment as the chaotic Nature investigation and under such stress and hostility. If there is a relationship between thought and energy such as we are suggesting, then confusion is exactly what you would expect from this scenario. One clear result was that Benveniste was hounded from the scientific fraternity. He died in 2004 following heart surgery.

English researcher Cyril Smith has also demonstrated the ability of water to store electromagnetic frequencies, and French physicist Michel Schiff likewise participated in replications of the experiments and in his book "the Memory of Water", acknowledges that the water memory effect does seem to occur. Despite the totally central role of water both biologically, and at a planetary level, there remain many properties of water that are not understood. Those who want to know more might care to look into the work of Viktor Schauberger. A further source of wonder comes from those such as Masaro Emotu, who has photographed the Benveniste effect. You can see examples at www.hado.net .

As far as homeopathy is concerned, we repeat once again that the effects we are describing are consistent, and have been repeatedly observed for over a century. It is frustrating to continue to read material that speaks of homeopathy as unvalidated. This is completely untrue, it is simply that the evidence is being ignored or misrepresented, and the mythology passed on in medical schools. The consistency and volume of evidence inside the homeopathic world has been developed over two centuries and could only be denied by those who have not actually read it. People's lives and health are at stake, because we are not making full use of the healing techniques that are at humanity's disposal. We feel it appropriate to issue a challenge to science and medicine: put the same degree of funding and constructive open-minded effort into the investigation of the theories described here, and refrain from attack until an adequate alternative explanation is on offer. Such would be a genuinely scientific response.

Our explanation follows a pattern that will now be familiar to readers. We are giving consistent evidence that there are phenomena occurring which could take place only through some kind of transmission of information. That information has to be specific enough to convey the characteristics of a molecule even when that molecule is chemically absent. It has to be specific enough to convey the characteristics of a disease pattern (or at least of the triggers it provides to the body) such that the "picture" of suppressed gonorrhea, or the "picture" of family tuberculosis can travel down the generations. This requires an informational content that is both complex and subtle. That it persists at all speaks of its power. That it is so hard to detect the mechanism speaks of something that is not visible to our normal processes of investigation. In these features it corresponds deeply with the nature of a spiritual reality, of a pervading consciousness. This is our explanation, it is the one which is consistent with the other phenomena described in this book and the one which corresponds with the varied aspects of human experience usually described as "spiritual".

Why science often can't find the evidence

A typical example of the debate over homeopathy recently took place on the BBC "Today" program, (23/05/07). On one side was Ray Tallis, a Professor of Geriatric medicine who is attempting to persuade UK NHS Trusts to abandon their co-operation with homeopaths. On the other was Peter Fisher, the Clinical Director of the Royal Homeopathic Hospital. Ray Tallis claimed that the "authoritative reviews" of published studies on the efficacy of homeopathy conclude that there is no proof of any benefit. He further described homeopathy as an example of "magical thinking" because the basis on which remedies operate is "impossible". In contradiction to this, Peter Fisher cited other reviews showing value from Homeopathy, in particular citing the views of the major health insurers in Germany – the "Krankenkasse" – that homeopathy is adding benefit and proving cost-effective.

This debate exemplified the prejudices and lack of understanding we have just examined, but we must to deal explicitly with the issue of "experimental evidence" and of adequate design. Scientific experiments aim to isolate phenomena. They therefore work best in simple scenarios and are well suited to a situation such as that pertaining to drug-testing. In such tests a set of people with a single condition are tested against a single pharmacological substance. Usually this is conducted in such a way that some people get the drug, some a placebo, and that neither subject nor experimenter know who is getting what. This is known as double-blind placebo control.

Homeopathic remedies are not drugs. They are informational stimuli which promote reactions of self-healing by the body. They are not selected by homeopaths on the basis of correspondence to a disease diagnosis, but on the symptom pattern. One disease may manifest with different patterns in different individuals and be treated with different remedies. Also, homeopaths would often not administer just one remedy because they are treating the individual holistically over a period of time. This means they would be administering other remedies which support the patient constitutionally or which deal with the underlying conditions that are seen, based on personal and family history, as antecedents to the currently presenting symptoms.

This complex and holistic approach does not fit the experimental methodology that medicine currently regards as scientific. In fact it is notable that when discussing the evidence, the anti-homeopathy camp cites those studies which show positive benefit as being those which have the greatest weaknesses in methodology.

This sets up a situation where it is likely to be very difficult, or even impossible, for homeopathic medicine to be evaluated on anything like a level playing-field. Science is making the rules, and the homeopathic approach does not fit those rules. It goes to the heart of the case we are making – that the scientific model breaks down in these areas.

It is also appropriate to take more note of the issue of "placebo effect". The homeopathic effect is distinct from a placebo result because it is highly specific in the information that it carries. But since the effect is mediated through the bodymind response to the remedy stimulus, there is no way in which to distinguish it from a placebo effect. They look the same from the outside, just as from the ground it appears as if the sun orbits the earth. The evidence comes from cumulative health improvement and there is no means by which to demonstrate beyond doubt that the patient could not have healed spontaneously.

In the complementary medical world, all healing is self-healing. That's the whole idea! It's a model of health creation, not of disease control.

The mere existence of the placebo effect speaks volumes regarding the relationship of mind and body in health and healing. It goes to the heart of the very relationships which complementary medicines work with and which science would like to convince us do not exist. Conventional medicine cannot explain the placebo effect – it has no model adequate to accomplish this. The perverse consequence of this is that rather than investigating an obviously powerful phenomenon, science works hard to eliminate it from all research. The recent advances in neuro-endocrine immunology have been showing science the way out of this cul-de-sac, but to date these advances are under the same pressures as homeopathy and the medical community as a whole has yet to embrace them fully.

The writer who conceived the idea of communications satellites, Dr Arthur C. Clarke notably said "Any sufficiently advanced technology is indistinguishable from magic". From our point of view, homeopathy is a technology which is in advance of scientific understanding – it is inevitable that they will label it as magic. But the use of the word "magic" in public debate is more corrosive because it is intended to imply naivety and gullibility on the part of homeopaths and patients. It is a subtle but deep insult.

As we have pointed out, there are experiments which show the "molecular memory" effect in water. We believe that these were done reliably by Jacques Benveniste and reproduced by several others, despite being extremely subtle. The work of Candace Pert and others described earlier underpins many of the relationships that are involved within the body (or bodymind). Generations of homeopaths, complementary practitioners and their patients, work daily with the evidence in systematic ways which conform to scientific principles, even if not to scientific "knowledge". They are not gullible or deluded and it is time that they ceased to be treated as such.

But there is one more aspect to the experimental evidence which we must address. You are by now becoming familiar with the connected world we are describing, one in which energy and information are communicated at all levels, through all types of organisms. You know of our view and of the evidence that the human mind has the capability to be a receiver and a transmitter, and that the homeopathic effect, like a hands-on healing, can be passed directly.

The implication of this for scientific experimentation is profound, and for the kinds of trials required to "prove" homeopathy it is catastrophic to scientific methodology. If the remedy can be transmitted to the patient by pure energy means, which includes the fact that the homeopath has it in his or her mind and might transmit it directly, there is no such thing as a placebo or a double-blind trial since all patients are receiving the remedy (at least in some measure). Equally, if the experiment is being run under conditions where actively hostile skeptics are involved, the energy effects from their thinking can also interfere with the outcomes. This could explain why those who initially replicated the Benveniste experiments were successful, and why later researchers with a less open mind-set were unable to achieve results.

Lastly, practitioners know that the engagement of the patient with their healing process contributes to its effectiveness. To describe this as a part of the placebo effect grossly oversimplifies the relationship and goes against the whole thread of neuro-endocrine immunology described earlier. The bodymind relationship is too subtle and complex for this. The patient is not a mechanical object. Any good doctor knows this. It is the pharmacological approach which drives the scientific model. This is not the place and we are not the people to lead discussions about conspiracy theories. But we would be naïve not to recognise that drug companies are there, that they are influential in research funding and wield enormous influence with huge amounts of money at stake. At the very least this has to be seen as creating massive inertia and pressure against the changes we are promoting.

Science is a powerful tool and its experimental methodology is very valuable in sifting truth and understanding underlying mechanisms. But in the area under discussion it is not effective. For sure, we need to apply scientific understanding and analysis and to be systematic about our observations, which homeopathy does, and is. But the experimental tool is too primitive. The observer cannot be separated and the variables cannot be controlled. We would not use a chainsaw for brain surgery and we must recognise that there never will be an effective double-blind placebo trial proof for homeopathic healing. It's an inappropriate methodology. The healing processes described in the next chapter present even greater difficulty to science. They also take us back into the heart of the spiritual debate.

Review

The evidence from homeopathy fits centrally with all that we are saying. Homeopathy demonstrates:-

- A scientific and systematic gathering of evidence

- Epidemiological proof of effectiveness of remedies

- Consistent and specific relationship between substances and the conditions that they treat

- Transmission of a healing that is neither pharmacological nor a placebo effect

- Evidence of the passage of disease-related information across generations, not mediated by the genes

- The weakness of experimental approaches when dealing with alternative healing

- Dubious standards of scientific objectivity applied to its evaluation

The implications of these facts support the case that we are making for the types of connection and information carrying that we see as central to the science of spirituality and add another element to this consistent picture.

7. <u>The routine of miraculous healing</u>

Sensorially disconnected from their theoretically evolved information, scientists discern no need on their part to suggest any educational reforms to correct the misconceiving that science has tolerated for half a millennium.

Buckminster Fuller

The mystery of life isn't a problem to solve but a reality to experience

Frank Herbert

Theme

It is common for our collective view of healing to be contaminated by incredulity. Many of us have been conditioned by science to regard energy healing, spiritual healing and many kinds of alternative therapy with disbelief. In this chapter we will attempt to create a new perspective on both what might be seen as a miracle and what should be regarded as ordinary. We will use some examples from direct personal knowledge and others from clinical observations in order to illustrate many remarkable features of healing and to complete the foundation of evidence that our science is required to explain.

The miracle of human existence

Humans have a patchy perception of the miraculous. Take, for example, the famous physics equation $E=MC^2$. It doesn't look that impressive, and perhaps the demonstration of its raw power – a Hiroshima-style unleashing of the energy locked up in a small ball of matter – has negative connotations that you do not want to think about.

Underneath that fact and the associated image lies the truth that your body encapsulates the raw power of a tiny sun. When, in the early stages of creation of the universe, inconceivable amounts of energy were formed into matter, every atom that was created in effect locked up a little piece of it. Each atom was forged in the centre of a star. Eventually some of that matter found its way to be Jon, Juliana or you. If the energy inside your body were to be released, it would free up a larger power than Hiroshima. That portion of creation, that piece of something like a primeval sun, is inside you.

Alternatively, take a look at biology. The human body is the most exquisite miracle of organisation. Everything about it is extraordinary. Take a look at what our biological systems are able to do:-

- Starting from one single cell, we build an organism composed of trillions of cells.

- The new-born arrives with some capability of function and behaviour, e.g. nipple rooting response, suckling mechanism, eliminative functions, breathing.

- The organism will grow over two decades, in a co-ordinated way, at a largely predetermined rate typical for our species.

- Every one of those trillions of cells has a specific function, and is in its correct location.

- Each of those cells has sub-components concerned with individual internal functions

- Every one of those cells will take in nutrients, expel waste materials and regulate its environment

- Every one of those cells, when exhausted, is capable of producing its replacement

- The organism is capable of responding to malfunction of its own replication process, and deal with unhealthy cells. A cell, if damaged, will make it possible for the body to recycle its materials.

- The cells will work together to function as organs.

- Each organ will function within the context of the body, regulating its activity as required and in harmony with other organs.

- The body will consume energy as required, converting it into activity, or new tissue.

- The body will dispose of toxic by-products of its metabolism.

- The body will respond to environmental variability such as heat and cold to maintain temperature stability. It will regulate water balance, salt balance, oxygen supply and more.

- It further regulates these factors in relation to demands for activity, including the substantial changes required by emergency responses which range from peak instant performance to long-term endurance under deprivation.

- It will repair damaged tissue or broken bone, responding to injury with incredible rapidity

- It will resist and repel the attacks of viral, bacterial and fungal parasites, and cleanse the body from a vast range of environmental toxicity

- It will reproduce whole organisms to replace itself and perpetuate the species, carrying its immature offspring within its body and nourishing it there for nine months.

- It will display a variety of skills - intellectual, social and physical, in mastering and ordering its external environment

All the above are scientific facts. They are "everyday miracles" and we will revisit this list in more depth. The things that we are familiar with no longer seem miraculous. Both the physics and the biology above are very hard to grasp. For most of us it is quite a stretch to visualise oneself as containing the energy of an atom bomb, or hold the image of 50,000,000,000,000 cells. Our day-to-day senses just don't go there. Part of our challenge in this book is to help you see a number of equally miraculous features of our world as likewise equally mundane, to take your senses towards places that they probably don't ever go. We faced this credibility gap in the discussion of shamanism. We face it again here in relation to "miraculous" spiritual healing.

In the previous chapter we described the systematic validation that homeopathic science has given to a particular form of connectedness. That connectedness has characteristics of being able to transfer defined energy signatures, to convey information from a substance to the human body systems and to transfer similar types of information across generations, independent of a genetic mechanism. We also referred to experiments which have shown that these energy signatures can be proved in the laboratory to imprint on a carrying medium such as water.

We focused strongly on homeopathy because of its systematic approach, one which maps as closely to an experimental methodology as is ethical when our subject is the health of a living human. In this chapter we will widen the examination of other modes of healing in order to broaden our understanding of this energy and these relationships. We have used the expression "energy signature" as a term of convenience. It is vague; in much the same way that "magnetic field" is vague. What can we do to create a richer description (and perhaps even have it be equally acceptable as a scientific term)?

In keeping with some earlier chapters the first approach is illustrative. We will switch back into personal stories in order to provide some pictures which help the presentation of theory that follows. As previously we recognise that a few anecdotes do not make a science. At the same time we remind readers that to see these as "miracle stories" places them in the realms of the extraordinary when they are in fact examples of widespread and frequently reported phenomena. The limited extent to which these are validated by a body of conventional scientific investigation is a symptom of their wide exclusion from research. It is easy for scientism to present an argument that it is up to us to prove that the phenomena exist, not for science to prove they do not. This is logically correct. However there is also a duty on science not to exclude from consideration the evidence that is available and to fund the appropriate research into effects that are reported across all continents and cultures.

The next three stories come from personal experience. In chapter 1 we wrote of the training in intuition and to Jon's first experience of a psychic event. The founder of the training which gave rise to that experience also led courses in hands-on energy healing. This story begins with Jose Silva's 1983 healing course in London.

The timing of the course coincided with the rise in awareness of AIDS and two students in particular were acquainted with people who were ill or who had died from this disease. They called on others present to form a group to use their new skills to help with this rising crisis.

A protocol was designed which involved three visits per day by three group members together to the client. When visits started, "Peter" was in hospital, unable to leave his bed. His family had been summoned from Switzerland with the prognosis that he had about 4 days to live and the priest had given the last rites. His weight was down below 100 lbs, not much for a man of 6ft 2ins – even a lean one.

Over the first week, the visits proceeded regularly with sessions of approximately 40 minutes of "hands-off" energy healing accompanied by meditative music and guided visualisation. Peter was visibly improving. Jon was not in the first "wave" of healing sessions. By the time he first saw him one week later Peter was already reported as more alert, and had some colour. He was receiving a lot of attention, a total of nearly two hours per day. This improvement continued, and after three weeks, he walked to the bathroom. After five weeks, he left hospital. He was still fit and healthy and apparently pronounced by his specialist to be free from any trace of HIV infection when Jon last saw him about 6 months later.

It is worth noting also, that during the first session that Jon participated in, Peter reported at the end of the treatment that he had felt a physical change take place in his mouth and that all the symptoms of oral thrush he had been experiencing had simply disappeared. It never returned. This specific relief of an individual disease pattern was a unique occurrence, but is mentioned to show both how rapidly a change can occur and that on this particular occasion the connection between healing and the presence of the healing team was quite specific. Because it was Jon's first time, the Candida healing was jokingly attributed to him (he claims no such impact), but for some time the more camp members of the group took pleasure in calling him "Candy".

This case was admittedly an isolated success. Only a couple of other clients were able to receive the same treatment regime, without similar results. Before long the group disbanded despite the success, largely because the time and effort required was too demanding for all concerned. Members were covering two different hospitals and a personal home; travelling from all around London at personal expense was plainly not viable. We would perhaps not tell the story if the healing had been less dramatic and also had it not been documented throughout by dramatic changes in the T-cell count by which immune system damage in HIV patients is monitored. Even though this was too demanding on a volunteer group, how much might be achieved by one which was funded and even resident in a hospital? A case like this begs for scientific research since such treatment would still be hugely cost-effective compared with any currently available alternatives. Note too, that the healers concerned were recently trained and none would have claimed any special gifts.

A second story once again has connections with homeopathy, but with a distinctive twist. It concerns a time when our young son was an infant of about 1-year old. He was sitting contentedly on Jon's lap during a meeting. Exciting things were being discussed and at one point in the meeting Jon jumped up to cheer, raising his arms (and son) above his head.

There was no reaction at the time, but sometime after midnight, the baby woke suddenly and began to cry – howling with distress. For ten minutes both parents sat with him, trying to figure out the cause for such a sudden eruption. Jon was scanning for symptoms and thinking about potential homeopathic remedies when a flash of insight took his attention back to the meeting. In the space of two seconds, the thoughts went through his mind – meeting – shock – find shock remedy - and he reached for his kit. By the time he had opened his bag, the crying had stopped, as abruptly as it started and the baby was sleeping again.

Sceptical readers – especially those who have raised children - will know that events like this can sometimes be hard to explain. It would be easy to dismiss what happened and Jon has questioned this himself over the 15 years since, but the experience was too strong to ignore. That two seconds during which the recognition of the cause and the treatment took place was such that experientially there was no doubt of the sense of connectedness and that the application of the "remedy" had taken place through a direct engagement. The energy required to treat the condition had been applied through direct connectedness and not through a prepared pill.

One more example is appropriate concerning the same infant son earlier in his life before he was on solids and when he had never experienced bottle-feeding. Juliana had contracted a severe gastric upset, possibly from food poisoning, as we were in a hotel attending a convention. The result was that she was mostly too ill to breast-feed and when she did manage it the milk caused our son to vomit. But by chance, a friend at the convention had recently weaned her son and was still producing some milk so was recommended as a wet-nurse.

This worked well, but by the evening our son developed a quite strong fever, which was very unusual for him. We consulted a very experienced homeopath who was also present and he advised that the wet-nurse showed strong indications of carrying the miasm that comes with family history of tuberculosis. As we discussed in the last chapter, such disease "imprints" are carried and maintained through the generations.

At this point things get even more "alternative". No-one at the convention carried the required remedy, which is not a part of any first-aid kit. Since the fever was not going down at all, we adopted a radical strategy. We decided to use hands-on healing to "program" the remedy into water, by consciously attuning to the nature of the remedy – its "signature" and consciously visualising the energy going into the glass container. The drops were then given directly to the child. Within an hour the fever was clearly subsiding and he was asleep. By the morning he was completely normal.

The picture we are attempting to paint with these stories is of a quite seamless connection which runs between individuals whether this be through the physicality of a substance like breast-milk or through the connection of "thought energy", as when the shock remedy was recognised. That connection also runs between individuals and other substances as shown when the energy imprint of a remedy is transferred by thought alone. Even more, it indicates that the miasmic effect referred to in the previous chapter can communicate not just between generations, but between one individual and another. (Note though that there may perhaps be some indication of susceptibility to the energy on our son's part.)

In the case of the AIDS healing it is not possible to be specific about how healing was brought about. However, we would point out that no touch was involved (at the time this was discouraged both because of uncertainties and caution around transmission and because of the risk of dislodging the various tubes keeping Peter alive). The effect is not one of mere soothing. It should also be noted that during the first week he was not very conscious and even when awake, although he had accepted the offer of this treatment, was quite negative, resigned and dismissive of any likely success. At that stage this could not be regarded as an example of positive thinking.

From the Silva healer's point of view, the method of delivering healing is through visualisation. Simple techniques are used to achieve a space of mental and physical relaxation (technically intended to increase the proportion of alpha-wave rhythms in the brain). The mind is then engaged in a way that pictures the existence of healing energy and its transmission from their hands to the client.. Each healer uses their own image. As an example, Jon's at that time was to imagine the silver lining in the clouds as a source of energy and to imagine it being pulled down as a pillar that enters the body between the shoulder blades and leaves through the hands. There is an assumption which applies to most such healing practices (such as Reiki) that the client's body will make the best usage of the energy supplied. Unlike homeopathy, where the apparent power derives from the very specific stimulus provided by a very small quantity of remedy, hands-on healing is typically intended to deliver a lot of energy. Typically healers may well experience a lot of tingling or heat in their hands, though this is not essential.

We don't ask or expect anyone to take the above as scientific proof. The fact that an experienced homeopath identified the relationship between the constitutional history of the wet-nurse and a disease-pattern in a child is not a scientific validation of anything, just an opinion. Since so little study has been performed in the areas we will cover, this is to be expected and we would argue that the cause of this lies in scientific thought-structures and scientific funding processes.

Others have presented volumes of evidence concerning many other healing methodologies. We will have to focus our attention elsewhere. However, we would not want you to think that the examples above are the only personal ones we could have given and we could find countless others of our direct acquaintance who would bear witness to similar events. Such miracles are genuinely everyday events which have been testified to by many people. They are meant as an encouragement to open-mindedness so that the scientific model we are about to present can be better understood.

Mind over matter

One of the most articulate, knowledgeable and respected writers in this field is Deepak Chopra. An American of Indian extraction, he qualified in conventional medicine. His cultural background also led him into profound exploration of the traditional ayurvedic healing system and into the meditative spiritual practices that are also strongly associated with that tradition. His blend of East and West informs all that he writes. Among his many books, Quantum Healing is the one we point to as most directly relevant to our text.

Deepak Chopra goes into great depth regarding the extent to which mind, emotion and physical form are intertwined. It is a book full of revelations and insights. All of it deserves to be included here, and in its absence, we are merely going to attempt to represent one of its points.

One thing that he reveals, is the extent to which the mental process can influence body chemistry. A simple but graphic example he cites is the case of Timmy, a boy with Multiple Personality Disorder (MPD). MPD is a strange syndrome in which a single body exhibits two or more personalities. In the case given by Psychiatrist Daniel Goleman, one of Timmy's personalities is allergic to orange juice, and breaks into hives when he drinks it. If Timmy's "normal" personality returns while he is in the middle of the allergic reaction, the itching stops right away, and the blisters begin to subside. On the other hand, if "normal" Timmy drinks the juice, and the other personality appears while he is still digesting it then, and not until then, the allergic reaction will break out. You probably think of allergies as being a direct biochemical response to a purely physical cause, especially if you are a hay-fever sufferer, but this response is totally at odds with that way of thinking.

This feature of bodymind can be worked with. In 1971, Dr Carl Simonton was inspired by his experience of the Silva Method, to try out a process of visualisation with one of his patients, a 61-year-old man with advanced throat cancer. The man was encouraged to enhance his radiation therapy by visualising his cancer, and choosing an image which appealed to him, showing the attack of his immune system on the cancer cells. The man chose to see the white blood cells of the immune system like a blizzard of snow, covering the black lump of his tumour. This process was repeated a few times per day. He had fewer side-effects than expected from the radiation, and after two months, the tumour was gone.

It is an unfortunate and puzzling truth that although there were other successes from this methodology, and the Silva network had many stories of such reversals in cancer and also in arthritis, the statistical success rates from Simonton's research and others of a similar kind are quite poor. Nevertheless, we include it, because it reveals that a process akin to that which occurs spontaneously in Timmy, has the potential to be instigated by conscious choice. In both cases, the mind is shown as having a direct impact on processes otherwise seen as "biological" and "unconscious".

In coming chapters we will encounter the part of body "intelligence" which is continually active, cleansing, balancing, repairing, nourishing and protecting. Many scientists still choose to conceive of this intelligence as no more than the result of a chemical accident (or series of them) that happened to produce life. That point of view is hard to refute - you either choose to believe it or you don't. But when we are dealing with conscious intelligence, we need to be rather more careful in our consideration.

It is ironic, considering that each of us lives with an experience of consciousness all of our lives, that we have almost no idea what consciousness really is. As we discussed before, some scientists view consciousness as purely an effect, a description that we overlay on a biochemical process. It is clear that we share the view of others that it is a crucial feature of humanity, and one for which a specific explanation is required. As we said in the introduction, far from seeing consciousness as a side-effect, we see it as the prime cause and the simplest explanation that is consistent with the facts.

You might view this choice as being just as deep a personal decision, and one taken with as little hard evidence either way as whether you have chosen to believe in God. It may almost be the same choice. For one person, the glories and intricacies of the natural world are clear evidence of a creative intelligence at work. For others the same data are evidence of the spontaneous, random occurrence of the most miraculous, self-sustaining chemical reaction imaginable. In one, the question "why are we here?" yields simply "chance". In the other, a creative consciousness is involved.

The difficulty in distinguishing between these two viewpoints lies partly in the fact that consciousness cannot be located. It is indistinguishable from the physical activity which generates it, or which provides our evidence of it. As Dr Chopra points out, the implication of Timmy's allergic reaction through one of his personalities, is that the white cells await the arrival of the orange-juice, and then a decision is made whether to react. For this to be the case, the "intelligence" (Dr Chopra's word) has to be in the cell. "Moreover", he says

"its intelligence is wrapped up in every molecule, not just doled out to a special one like DNA, for the antibody and the orange juice meet end-to-end with very ordinary atoms of Carbon, Hydrogen and Oxygen. To say that molecules make decidecisions defies current physical science - it is as if salt sometimes feels like being salty and sometimes not."

We will close this chapter on the miraculous with one more story – just to ensure that we are stretching your credibility to the maximum. We might hesitate to include this one had we not both witnessed it first hand.

In Essex UK there is a healer called Stephen Turoff. He has been widely reported on in recent years, both in print and on television and there is a full autobiography available. Stephen works as a "psychic surgeon". He describes himself as being a channel for a long-dead German physician, and working under his control "like a puppet". (Kindred Spirit, June 1996). His capabilities too are beyond belief, such as treating a man unable to walk for three years due to a brain tumour, who stepped out of his wheelchair and walked. Another story is of a woman with a heart complaint, whose doctor had taken X-rays and warned that the heart could fail at any time. After treatment by Stephen Turoff, that same Doctor reacted with shock to follow-up X-rays, not just because the patient's heart was fine, but because it appeared to be a quite different heart. We know personally several people who have received treatment from Stephen, and some of these had clearly benefited.

In one case we both observed an operation on Juliana's mother, a lady then in her late seventies who walked into the treatment room with the aid of a stick. The operation dealt with long-term severe back pain by removing a sliver of bone from her spine. We were about five feet away with a clear view. We could hear the scrape as the bone was cut. The operation took place at high speed, and the patient was back on her feet ten minutes from the start, with a small line marking where the incision had been, and no bleeding. For the duration of a one-hour journey home she was uncomfortable and recovering from the shock.

When she got home, she had been in the lounge for a few minutes when she noticed a small piece of litter on the carpet. She bent over to pick it up – bending from her back. She was clearly quite unaware that she was doing anything out of the ordinary, but our jaws dropped. Just hours before she would have been quite unable to do this. It was very apparent that her mobility was considerably improved, and this sustained in the following months. There is no doubt in our minds that Stephen Turoff is genuine. You could fake the operation with conjuring tricks, but you cannot fake results like that, which is perhaps why his waiting room always has very long queues.

Stephen Turoff was an "ordinary" man in every sense, except that he grew up with a strong sense of a personal connection with God. He had practiced "laying-on-of hands" healing for fifteen years prior to "Dr Kahn's" intervention in his life, and though he called from deep within to make his connection manifest in his work, he had no idea that he would do what he now does. Could something like that happen to you? Can you envisage creating such a connection with the "source"? If you could, what would you like to be able to do? What connections would you like to make with the "resonances" which would enable you to do it?

We do not see it as being of consequence here to know what Dr. Kahn is or whether he is real or imaginary. The fact that Stephen Turoff is able to attune himself, and to use energies and resonances in the way that he does, is all that matters. It is of little importance what he thinks, or feels, or visualises in order to achieve that. We emphasise this point, because in our view the power is with the individual. Stephen Turoff sees it this way too. When asked how he does what he does, he now says "because I am God". Then he says "and so are you". If you ask him "Why can't I......?" he will likewise say "because you do not know yet that you are God". Given his track record, who has the authority to disagree? His successes testify to the potential for great powers in each of us.

We have indicated that our core purpose with this book is to place a scientific context around stories of this kind and to give corroboration that supports that science. This chapter has strayed as far into personal anecdotes as we are willing to allow, but we would not have wanted to leave out the very experiences which have led us to our viewpoint. We now need to return to that core agenda and describe just what kind of physical organism experiences these things and how it functions. We must gain some understanding of the physics that makes this universe possible and provide a scientific model for how both that universe and we humans come to be. It is a picture by turns exciting, complex, multi-layered, wonderful and rich. Beyond the complexity we will draw out some simpler patterns which make deep sense of it all. Underneath the miracles that happen we will find a deeply miraculous and connected world.

Review

There is much in the world that we are accustomed to, take for granted and do not think of as miraculous. There are other aspects to the world which we are in the habit of treating as extraordinary which might well be regarded as mundane if more of us had the training or the personal beliefs that empower them.

The examples quoted continue to hammer home the thread of connection, that information can pass at the material level (through pills or breast-milk) but equally well without physical contact, as when hands-on healing, or visualisation are involved. Energy healing can have almost instant results, and equally be used over a longer period in the most serious of conditions. Within the body, psychological information at the level of personality is shown to dramatically affect physiological response, to an extent where it appears that each cell is affected by the psychological change, and the consciousness appears to be present in, or influencing the cell directly. The most capable of healers are capable of delving into this reality in order to firstly diagnose a condition and then to "operate" surgically on it, without any blood loss and with instant healing of the wound and no scarring. The healer we witnessed is performing such operations hundreds of times per year, with widely attested results.

Section 2 : Our biology

What was your face before you were born

When the heart bursts into flame

history completely disappears

and lightning strikes the ocean

in each cell

There before origins

when the double helix

is struck like a tuning fork

there is a hum

on which the universe is strung

Stephen and Ondrea Levine   *Embracing the beloved*

8. <u>Simplexity and the taming power of the small</u>

All life is an experiment

Oliver Wendell Holmes

A single group of atoms existing only in one copy produces orderly events, marvelously tuned in with each other and with the environment according to most subtle laws... we are here obviously faced with events whose regular and lawful unfolding is guided by a 'mechanism' entirely different from the 'probability mechanism' of physics

Erwin Schrödinger   *What is life?*

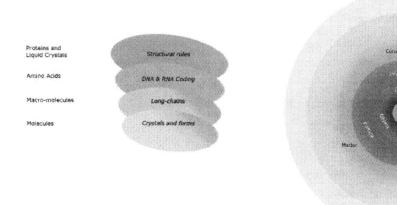

Theme

Questions such as "who are we?" and "Where did we come from?" seem to require answers at the high level, derived from our perceptions of ourselves as whole organisms in relation to our external world. In this section as a whole we explore a contrasting viewpoint, that in order to understand who we are we also need to see what is inside – the origin of life in single cells and how those cells function together in trillion-celled creatures. We have to understand how the apparent simplicity of a single being which perceives itself as one conscious entity emerges from huge underlying complexity.

The section's first chapter explores the concepts we are working with. We look at some of the core ideas and questions, the extremes of scale, the types of evidence available in order to create a high-level map of the territory, a helicopter view of the journey that we are about to take. We have several strands to weave:-

Knowing who we are requires knowing where we came from (evolution)

This must be integrated with understanding how we "work" (living functionality)

Knowing how we work connects to how we were "made" (individual development and growth)

The way I am made both resembles and differs from the way that my father was made and this change is a tiny reflection of the way in which planetary life changes over long time-scales. We come full-circle to evolution, and the question of where we came from.

None of this happens in isolation. Every thread in this tapestry occurs in relation to an environment. Each cell relates to what is outside it. Groups of cells such as organs function in relation to the bodies they are part of. Each organism relates to its surroundings. Groups of organisms function together in eco-systems where they are in relation with each other, with the physical surroundings of the planet (geology, climate) and with the change in both. The change may be daily cycles, seasonal changes or alterations in climate or the development and extinction of other species.

The answers to questions such as who we are and how we came to be must incorporate all of these layers and must understand how they form a whole. It is a significant task.

Simplexity

In order to provide an adequate picture of the biological realm we will need to go further into the depths of the science than in any other section. The detail provides the keys to our understanding. We have borrowed the word "simplexity" from Jack Stewart and Ian Cohen, whose thinking has influenced this section strongly. We are attempting to show how an entity that we think of as a single part – a human being – emerges from the complex detail which forms it. While is not crucial that you understand every piece of the detail it is essential to be aware of their existence and to have a grasp of the number of levels and relationships involved. So please bear with us, and don't give up if some parts are more technical than you would prefer.

Our chapter heading "The taming power of the small" is also borrowed, and is the name of a hexagram in the I-Ching. We use the phrase to encapsulate the way in which this big organism is managed through microscopic events. The behaviour of single cells and the co-ordination of information flow via activity below the level of those cells are central to the coherence of that big organism and to its way of relating to the environment. Little changes have big consequences. As Anita Roddick observed, the power of the small is only overlooked by someone who has never attempted sleep with a mosquito in their room.

Everything pertaining to the human spiritual experience is mediated through our incarnation. Whatever anyone may imagine or conjecture regarding the existence of a soul independent of the body, the fact that we are beings of flesh, blood and bone and that we have and describe all our experience through nervous system, sensory apparatus and cognitive interpretation puts biology right at the centre of our narrative. We encountered some of this truth in Chapter 3, but the endocrine system is just one among many layers. We will examine several other layers to this relationship in order to show where and how spirit and biological matter meet.

The genetic strand

In the past 160 years the scientific world has been rightly excited, first by Darwin's insights into evolution and more recently by the discovery of how DNA works. This excitement, however justified it may be, has led to exaggeration of what is known and proven. Some of the images have been further distorted by simplistic or inaccurate film or TV plots. The underlying scientific work has been phenomenal and the complexity of the picture is indeed widespread in the scientific literature, but the public presentation has been misleading, or even unconsciously oriented to exclude our view of consciousness and spirituality.

As Richard Dawkins says of himself in his preface to "The Blind Watchmaker" his book is "….not a dispassionate scientific treatise. ….."I may not always be right, but I care passionately about what is true and I never say anything that I do not believe to be right." Although we would not dispute the honesty of his intention there is a risk involved – one that we potentially share. Beliefs are dangerous as soon as they begin to lead people into stating as truth things that are unproven or half proven and to a spurious certainty which leads people into perceptual filtering where evidence is ignored or avoided because it does not fit the belief. We are about to show the ways in which science has gone down this route, with Dr Dawkins among those leading the charge and taking the Western world along with his powerful and articulate presentation. We need to open up this narrowed presentation and re-introduce some uncertainties.

Uncertainty 1. In the face of a story which refers to "genes" as if these are always simple discrete units determining identifiable "characteristics" in an organism, we will have to present the full tale of the way that organisms develop, and show how misleading that simple story truly is.

Uncertainty 2. Beyond the supposed relationship between "genes" and "characteristics" we have been led (or at least allowed) to believe that DNA and chromosomes determine everything about the organism. They are presented as a full and complete instruction set that is in total control. There is no flexibility in this model of how an organism develops, nor any responsiveness to the environment. This is simply not accurate.

DNA is represented as a "code", one which decodes itself as it constructs organisms. Just what can codes do, and how are they "decoded"? How do the features of codes really work, and what does this mean for the relationship between developing cells or developing organisms and their environment?

Uncertainty 3. Cells are presented as if they are just blobs of jelly and their functioning is easily overlooked. This is far from reality and, since we are composed entirely of huge numbers of cells, the real story of how they interact with each other, and mediate our interaction with the corporate cellular environment is key to how we function.

What are the processes of life in the sense of the second-by-second functioning of a complex organism, and what do they tell us about the nature of life and its organisation? We will need to include in our answers the way in which physics affects biology and show some aspects which have been seriously neglected.

Uncertainty 4. The other function of genetic material is to guide the process of inheritance from one generation to the next. The core of the Darwinist fundamentalism which Richard Dawkins champions is that all life evolved to its current state without any kind of guidance system. This suggests a wonderfully complex but ultimately mechanical relationship. On one hand we have random and spontaneous change through re-combination or mutation of genetic instructions. On the other we have the process of natural selection, by which some of those changes will result in organisms that are more successful than others in reproducing. We are not about to repeat any of the arguments that Dr. Dawkins has so eloquently demolished. Nevertheless we will raise some questions around the absolute absence of guidance in the fundamentalist viewpoint. Here the core question is not about whether Darwin was right. It is about the boundaries within which he was right. Evolution is presented as both entirely random and entirely mediated by changes to chromosomal DNA. To what extent are these presentations open to question?

Uncertainty 5. The thread of Dr Dawkins' arguments over decades extends beyond the pure science of how evolution takes place. His argument is not purely in favour of fundamentalist Darwinism, it is also against a primary alternative, the existence of a "designer" in any form. His view that no designer is required is a strong platform on which he builds a different argument – that "God", in the sense of a single creative being, does not exist. This has then extended into an exclusion of any kind of spiritual component to life. These are so strongly bound in his presentations that they have come to seem almost as if they are the same thing. We need to disconnect the two. Rejecting the biblical Yahweh, and eliminating all possibility of a "Divine" realm are two different things, a difference which is quite crucial.

In our previous chapters we have presented evidence which needs to be encompassed within the scientific model. We have described Cleve Backster's experiments (Ch.4, P.70) which demonstrate the presence of consciousness in plants. We have quoted the understandings from Malidoma Somé, Eliot Cowan and others which depict the presence of some form of spiritual being within the plant kingdom. We have shown how others like the Findhorn gardeners have worked with these beings in a way which influenced the development of plants – the 8Kg cabbage phenomenon. In our chapter on homeopathy we showed the evidence of disease suppression in one generation being carried somehow to the next. Where does all this evidence find space within the biological model?

We look at other theories which indicate that there is a missing element in the picture of consciousness and attempt to fill crucial gaps in our understanding. We will summarize and draw together the strands in a way which shows the potential for non-visible energies to play a part in all of these processes; we will show the ways in which such subtle and small influences have the potential to drive larger and more visible events.

The size of the task

Thus we embark on such a discussion of genetics, development, inheritance and evolution with some trepidation as we attempt to cover scientific evidence which ranges from the microscopic investigation of molecular-level events to the grandest scale of evolutionary evidence, based on several billion years of organisms living on planet Earth. Throughout we will keep in mind our core questions, those which have driven both religious and scientific thinking for millennia.

Who and what are we?

How did we come to be?

What, if anything, lies behind our existence?

The science of genetics is now central to the answers that the scientific model offers and it comes at a particular place and time in the development of thought.

In mathematics, early insights came from the Greeks. Beginning with Pythagoras about 600 years BC, they began to discover the way that space is ordered. Early models of the cosmos, which can be seen in the construction of astrolabes, viewed the sun and planets as moving in circles, because that was the most elegant way they could imagine it to be. It was a model that humanity found helpful for over 1500 years. Similarly, the shapes of platonic solids, the cube, the octahedron could be seen mirrored in the fundamental structure of matter, like a crystal of salt. God's universe was ordered by the harmony of the spheres and the unbreakable relationships of numbers. These discoveries travelled into the Arab world and were central to Moslem culture and art through the European dark ages, as well as to architecture in the use of oriental sacred geometry.

These mathematical relationships are timeless, or perhaps for all time. The art in Moslem temples, however beautiful and glorious, is regular and patterned. Pictures have no perspective. Music is linear without structural depth. It is only in the centuries leading to the renaissance that this begins to change as Moslem culture and mathematics re-emerges into Northern Europe. Art acquires a sense of three-dimensional perspective and astronomy shifts its viewpoint with Copernicus' revolutionary perception (1543) that the Earth is not at the centre of the universe, but rather revolves around the sun and Kepler's recognition (1609 and 1618) that planets move in ellipses. Mathematically these insights involve a new understanding. Perspective recognises the laws governing the way to map three dimensions on to a two-dimensional surface. Elliptical motion brings the fourth dimension - time - into the mathematical models of the cosmos and this develops further with the invention by Newton and Leibnitz of what we now call calculus.

Biology lagged behind physics and it took a further 400 years before it made the shift from a static view to the dynamic one. The biblical model of biology is that God made everything and that all creatures were here by the seventh day. Biological science was about cataloguing species and labelling organs, with some recognition of cyclical change where everything comes back round the same. Time only really enters biology properly with Darwin.

It is hard to overstate Darwin's genius. Much of the material now viewed as evidence has only been gathered since his time, and examined in the light of his vision. "On the origin of species by means of natural selection" was published in 1859. His brilliance was to look at a snapshot of nature in time, a small portion of all the species in existence, and recognise some core truths answering the fundamental questions we ask in this arena, questions which mirror those above.

How did all these different living organisms come to be on the planet?

Why is one creature different from another and how do those differences arise?

Where do we (humans) come from and what is our relationship with the rest of creation?

Since there is a creation, is there a creator?

Bear in mind that the mechanics of inheritance were not known until later. At the level of individual characteristics this was revealed by the work of Gregor Mendel, published in 1865 but barely recognised for decades after. His understanding of "hereditary factors" paved the way for modern genetics. The molecular chemistry that underlies this activity begins to be understood with the discovery of chromosomes by Flemming (1882) and the sequences and combinations of nucleic acids in a strand of DNA in 1953. Darwin could not have had any knowledge of how the biological development of the individual organism takes place, nor of the mechanisms by which one generation is related to the next.

So Darwin's insight, which has driven scientific understanding for almost 160 years was a huge and brilliant step. In place of a static catalogue of living organisms, pre-determined in six days by the Old Testament God and with humankind his finest creation, came a moving picture that unfolded over time. Species change. In time they differentiate, and features are accentuated or lost according to how well they enable the members of that species to survive and reproduce in their environment. That environment is itself changing in relation to climate, geology and alterations in other species.

The question is not whether Darwin is right or wrong. It is about the boundaries to this insight and about some of the slants within it. Both Darwin and his contemporary Alfred Russell Wallace, who independently formulated similar views, were strongly influenced by their intellectual culture. We know more now than they did. Darwinism has acquired its own form of fundamentalism, which takes the principles that Darwin put forward and argues that they are complete and that nothing more is required to explain everything we see in either the development of an organism or the evolution of life. We intend to show that this fundamentalist view is unsustainable, and is imprisoning biological science as well as spiritual understanding.

Echoing the two core questions of who we are and how we came to be here are two strands to our story. These are the biological mechanics of what we are and the evolution over time of who we are. Both are huge subjects to cover and they are linked as closely as the two strands of a DNA double-helix. We will try to keep the strands clear, but we cannot separate them entirely. While doing so we cannot help but meet the even deeper question of the possible existence of a creator or of an underlying "plan" or inevitable logic that drives the process towards higher complexity in function, behaviour and mental capability? Within all these, and central to the theme of this book is the question of whether there is thread in this tapestry that has any relationship with a "spiritual" view of the world?

The scientific challenges

An anonymous humorist once said of Christopher Columbus that when he left for America he didn't know where he was going, when he arrived he didn't know where he was and when he returned he didn't know where he had been. A voyage into the evolutionary record is not much better. Some of the work done by those who specialise in this area is amazing and brilliant, but their successes come in the face of major evidential challenges. So much has to be inferred, conjectured and tested against this limited information.

A few billion years of organic life have left relatively few visible traces. Those we have are patchy and sporadic, such as fossil remains. Whole categories of creatures have come and gone (e.g. dinosaurs) and it is certain that many species left no trace at all, particularly aquatic ones which end up as mud. Even where evidence exists, we see mainly the hard-tissue remnants (e.g. bones and teeth) and quite obviously the organism is dead. We do not see how it grows, or witness it move, breathe, eat etc. Our picture of the environment in which it lived is also threadbare.

Our picture of the timing of any supposed events is equally fragmented. We know an organism existed but not necessarily when it first existed, what the true geographic boundaries to its existence were or when it became extinct. Note too that the geography and geology themselves have changed continuously over the millennia involved.

Many of the conclusions reached about genetics and evolution also require considerable understanding of how to classify the remnants. In human taxonomy (the branch of science which catalogues these classifications) debates have ranged over decades regarding the precise significance of a few bones – whether they represent something pre-human, late-ape, or just where in-between they belong. As stated by researcher J Shreeve, 'Fossils are fickle. Bones will sing any song you want to hear'. If you would like an example, web-search the virulent debate over "Toumai", but expect to find more heat than light. Such complexities of classification, affecting the entire historical record, reduce the sharpness of focus on even the patchwork of material that we do have. Investigators are presented with a big challenge if they are to draw reliable conclusions in this area.

But since evolution works through genetics, our first challenge is to understand what is claimed to be known about genes and genetics as distinct from what is really known. Here the challenge is not lack of evidence, but the opposite – vast volumes of intricate detail which we must slice through to reveal the crucial features. Fortunately there is a clear if complex pattern discernable beneath the detail. As this is revealed, so too will be the areas which are relevant to our theme of a relationship with the world of subtle energies and information content that underpin our notions of consciousness and spirituality. We will find the non-physical mind, and meet what Gilbert Ryle called "The Ghost in the Machine" and what we think of as the spirit of the matter.

Life as a lottery

People like Richard Dawkins and Stephen Jay Gould have written whole series of books delving with passion and erudition into aspects of these issues. In attempting to cover our central "spirituality" question in a few chapters we will have to cut to the chase. We will abbreviate, summarise and inevitably over-simplify some parts of the discussion. This is a risky business. Professor Dawkins in particular is ruthlessly scathing when demolishing opponents who over-simplify.

We agree with much of what is said by Gould, Dawkins and other scientists who have developed and extended the understanding of evolution and genetics based on the Darwinist model. We are not about to argue for the view that there is an external creator as literally depicted in Genesis. We acknowledge that it is possible for complexity to emerge through subtle change and selective pressure, and that the existence of wonderful design (e.g. the eye) does not imply the existence of a designer as such. The central questions we address are the nature of the subtle change involved and precisely how, when and through what mechanisms the environment influences that change.

As stated above, the conventional view from Richard Dawkins, Stephen Jay Gould and other campaigners is that random change, together with selective pressures on survival to the next generation for genes (and / or the species that contain them) is a sufficient explanation for all of life's wonder and diversity and that nothing more is required. The image that Dawkins borrows from Paley of the "Blind Watchmaker" encapsulates some of the wonder that such a wonderfully complex tapestry could indeed arise through a purity of chance, chemistry and eons of time. The detail of his writing demolishes, one after another, the arguments that there has to have been a creator, or indeed any natural law that drives gene selection or evolution in a pre-destined direction. If nothing more is required then it is against scientific principle to add anything. This model of Darwinism is made to appear so complete that it is very hard to challenge.

Nevertheless we must challenge it. The evidence does demand that we add something. And even if it is only 0.1% incomplete, the fundamental difference is as significant as when you walk into your living room at night and switch the light on. Physically the only thing that has changed is a small amount of moving energy in a section of wire – everything else is as it was. But life with the light on is very different. Our search is for something that lies in between a creator god and utter randomness. Fortunately that is a big space to play in, and it starts in the cell.

The complexity of cells

The science of genetics is looking to explain several related aspects of biological existence. The "what we are" aspect is about the mechanics for controlling and managing a complex organism. The "how do we come to be" has two perspectives. One is the development of individual organisms. This is a lot to explain when you consider that each of us started from one single cell. The other is our evolution, and the introduction of changes to that development over the generations.

Let us break into some of that complexity. Multi-celled organisms are a miracle of existence and it helps to be aware of all the things that we and other creatures can do biologically. At the start of Chapter 7 (P.123) we listed the many miraculous things which our biological systems are able to accomplish. We refer you back to this list and ask that you continue to keep it in mind.

Just as miraculous, and maybe more surprising is that when you compare a multi-celled organism with a single-celled creature, or compare it with one of its own constituent cells, the list you get is not much different. As Dr Bruce Lipton puts it in "The Biology of Belief":-

> "Each eukaryote (nucleus-containing cell) possesses the functional equivalent of our nervous system, digestive system, respiratory system, excretory system, endocrine system, muscle and skeletal systems, circulatory system, integument (skin), reproductive system and even a primitive immune system, which utilises a family of antibody-like "ubiquitin" proteins".

As above, so below. Cells are not blobs. We hesitate to use the word "intelligence" here as it can so easily be taken to mean we are saying that individual cells think. But it is hard to find a good substitute. There is deep capability akin to intelligence built in to anything that shows such functional complexity and that manages itself in relation to its environment to such a degree. Perhaps, like the complexity of the eye, it could arise randomly. Or perhaps there are other factors.

We are accustomed to looking at whole organisms, and we need to remember that organisms may co-ordinate many cells together for a purpose, but nothing happens that is not facilitated by cell-level activity. As throughout our story, it is necessary to grasp many different scales simultaneously. One helpful perspective is to see where cells came from.

Back to the very basics

Here again we ask the basic question "What is life?" but in a more specific sense than before. What we mean here is – at what point does "life" become recognisable as distinct from the background of what we see as non-living material existence? Our normal descriptions don't attribute life to lumps of coal, but they do so to algae and bacteria.

As best we know, this planet started as a ball of molten material which cooled and eventually formed a ball of rock with an atmosphere. This is not the atmosphere we are familiar with, having no oxygen, but quantities of methane and ammonia. An experiment by Stanley. L. Miller and Harold Urey in 1953 showed that a flask containing such an atmosphere, and having electric current passed through it in a way that simulated the lightning storms believed to have existed at the time, would start to form carbon-based organic compounds and eventually amino acids of the kind that are required to make proteins and which are the basic prerequisites for cellular life.

So where and how would we define the transition from amino-acid slop to a living organism? The chain of evidence is extremely thin, and the next stage that we believe we are capable of recognising is the presence of fossils in 3-billion year old rocks, which look similar to what we know now as bacteria. To reach this distinguishable state requires the object in question to show itself as having a boundary. That boundary is the cell membrane. It is this which defines an object that is capable of organising itself in distinction from its environment. The most primitive form of life, we suggest, is first recognisable when there is some sort of autonomous entity. The cell membrane is more than a marker in space though. It is not like a plastic bag containing the cell's "jelly"; it is an active component of the living process and the means by which the cell maintains its autonomy. This is the boundary at which environmental influences on the cell take place.

What we are saying is that this relationship between organism and environment is not just as old as life itself, but rather is the definer of life itself at its most basic, and that the relationship is facilitated by the cell membrane. The membrane is so thin that it is barely visible, seven millionths of a millimetre thin, and can only be detected using an electron microscope. But functionally it is highly complex and contains a multitude of molecules called phospholipids.

These form a barrier to the passage of molecules in and out of the cell. Within the barrier are a further set of molecules, the Integrated Membrane Proteins (IMP's) which are its gatekeepers, controlling what may pass through the phospholipid barrier. They are classified as being of two kinds. There are receptors, which detect environmental signals – the equivalent of sense organs- and there are effectors which control the behaviour of the cell – such things as motility, shape, synthesis of molecules and supply of cellular energy.

In your school biology you may possibly have studied the amoeba. As one of the simplest creatures it is a favourite topic. It is a single-celled organism which is common in ponds and is an easy study both because of its size – some are as large as half a centimetre and because of its visible "behaviour" as one of the most primitive predators. Typical foods are smaller single-cell organisms such as paramecium. The way the amoeba catches its prey is to alter its shape. Its membrane extends either side of the prey, and then extends further around behind, under and over the prey until they meet up in three dimensions. These extensions are known as *pseudopodia* (pseudo-feet) though for us an analogy is more like putting our arms around an object and hugging it. However, during the process, the amoeba does not touch the prey until after it has completed its encircling.

To do this, the amoeba first has to sense its prey, detecting it chemically. It then has to respond to this detection by extending – not towards the chemical it senses nor away from it, but at an angle to it. The membrane has to continue to sense the position of the prey as it extends, so the surface has detectors all along such that can always maintain the distance appropriate to the size of the target. If it gets too close, the paramecium could take avoiding action using its cilia (tiny hairs) for propulsion. There is no brain or nervous system involved in this activity yet the sensing and movement are as if guided. The "intelligence" of this primitive cell is built-in to its membrane detection receptors and to the internal effector structures which change its shape. There are good pictures of this process to be found on http://www.microscopy-uk.org.uk .

This is just one example of the capability of a simple one-celled creature and shows what is possible with a combination of receptor and effector proteins. It is typical of cell function in all organisms and all happens independently from the genes. The genes are necessary to build a new cell and for it to reproduce itself, but the cell can function in all other ways even if the nucleus, which contains the instructions for reproduction, is removed. But even when the genetic nucleus is present, its activity is controlled by the effector proteins which determine how to "read" the code according to environmental signals picked up by the membrane's receptors.

We have no way of knowing how many IMP's were present in the earliest cells. This cannot be discerned from a fossil. But evolution is a process by which the "intelligence", or functional complexity of the cell increases by the incorporation of larger numbers of proteins into the membrane over time, eventually reaching the thousands and even hundreds of thousands. There is a limit to how many IMP's can be fitted into one cell membrane. Eventually, life could only improve further by forming units of more than one cell.

In its earliest stages, single cells used messenger molecules to "co-operate". This is the type of process which allows slime mould amoebas to co-ordinate when they live as separate cells, and control when they come together to form a group to produce new spores. It is assumed, in the absence of any evidence, to be the beginning of a process which leads eventually to genuinely multi-celled creatures. That is to say, that the first multi-cellular life forms communicated chemically. You may recognise in this, the likely seed of the neuro-endocrine communication system Candace Pert describes (Chapter 4).

Through this history, or something like it, we have reached the point where individual cells exist, where there is life on the planet, and there is potential for cells to group together into more complex multi-celled organisms. Now we can start in earnest to look at the ways that genes are involved in development and change.

Review

We set out in this chapter to introduce the central issues in our examination of humans as biological beings, and to indicate the areas in which we will explore the potential for a spiritual dimension to the way that life came about, the process of evolution, the growth of form in the developing organism and to the relationship between organisms and their environment.

We indicated that this would need our understanding of small scale detail such as cell function alongside large-scale events such as 4 billion years of evolution. We indicated some of the claimed certainties in the conventional explanation and the areas in which we believe that doubt should be applied. As a first step we have looked at the many functions that cells perform, how the cell responds to its environment, and where the first cells came from, as a prelude to exploring the genetic mechanisms that guide these processes.

9. Genes and characteristics

All of life is an experiment. The more experiments you make, the better

Ralph Waldo Emerson

The most heinous offense a scientist as a scientist can commit is to declare to be true that which is not so; if a scientist cannot interpret the phenomenon he is studying, it is a binding obligation upon him to make it possible for another to do so.

Sir Peter Medawar.   *The limits of Science*

Theme

We have indicated elements of life that genetics are intended to explain:-

What are you? How do we explain similarities and differences from other humans.

How did you develop from that first single cell?

How did it come about that life exists at all and that so many different species exist together on the Earth?

At the centre of the answers, science gives us the gene and provides us with a model of how it delivers what we are asking for. In the last chapter we indicated that we would need to unpick some of the certainties that genetic science claims to have achieved in answering these questions. The first spurious certainty lies in the implication that there is a simple relationship, where one gene determines one identifiable characteristic in the organism. We will show that this does not stack up and that the knowledge that would substantiate it is a long way from being complete.

The second appearance of certainty is given to the developmental process itself and the way that science encourages us to draw over-simplified conclusions about how the genetic coding system delivers outcomes. We will see that the story is much more interesting than that, and that genes simply cannot explain everything – indeed that there is much about the process that has not been adequately explained at all.

These two uncertainties drive significant gaps into the story that genetics has presented to us. We start with a refresher of what that model says about the genetic part of the answer.

The conventional view

The instruction book to make a human being is contained in the first, single egg-cell. It is contained in strands of a chemical known as DNA. The strands are tightly wound, packaged in a set of predefined units known as chromosomes, of which there are 23 pairs. The pairing system enables each new organism to inherit half of its chromosomes from the father through a sperm, and half from the mother via the egg.

The long chains of DNA, coiled up tightly in the chromosome package, consist of two linked strands, and these strands are capable of separating. It is usual to imagine this process as being like cutting a ladder down the middle of each rung. DNA is an unusual chemical, because each side of the "rung" is a particular type of component, called a base. There are four types of bases, and they only connect with each other in specific pairings. This means that by assembling bases, one by one, to match up to the free half-rung, the other half of a ladder could be re-manufactured exactly as before. That is, a strand can split, leaving two halves, each of which can be re-matched, and the result is that you

have two DNA strands, each identical to the original. In this way, when a cell divides to create a copy of itself all 46 chromosomes split, attracting new bases to complete themselves. One of the new sets of chromosomes then becomes the nucleus of the new cell, and one remains with the original. (A chromosome is one tightly coiled, very long DNA strand-pair).

The base-pairs enable genetic material to replicate, and while that is a remarkable achievement it is only the means to an end. There is no point in creating copies of something meaningless. The bases themselves form a code. There are chemical messengers capable of reading that code and using it as an instruction set for the manufacture of other chemicals. The chemicals that are made (proteins) will be all that is required to create a functioning body. There will be proteins to make a transparent lens for the centre of your eye, and proteins to make hard enamel for the surface of your teeth. The instruction set is phenomenally clever, since the same set of instructions – the same original nucleus from a single fertilized egg - will make a liver cell or a brain cell, and put it in the right place in your body. It will wait 6-7 years and produce a new set of front teeth. It will wait another 6 or 7, and then cause the body to change, growing facial hair or breasts, widening hips or shoulders as appropriate for the different sexes. A 3D animation video describing the human genome project can be found on "Youtube" and is much more illuminating than any graphics that we could insert here.

The key elements in this theory are:-

There is a chemical code which controls the process by which cells replicate and organisms develop

Sequences of those chemicals can be identified and are called "genes"

Those sequences are associated with particular outcomes in the body, or characteristics, leading to the idea that you can have "a gene for cancer" or that there is a gene responsible for being left-handed or for Mozart's genius

Everything about our development is dictated by our genes, by the sequence of chemicals contained in our chromosomes.

We need to unpick this theory and find just how much of it is proven, and how much is a combination of conjecture, scientific over-simplification and tabloid tosh.

So what's a gene?

In the above paragraphs we would have liked to avoid the word "gene". Linguistically the word has complex roots, at the core being the Latin genere to engender, but being closely related to "general", to "genesis" and to "genus" (stock or race) and possibly to "genuine" (as in authentic to its stock). Francis Galton, a cousin of Darwin, was particularly interested in the inheritance of "genius" (extraordinary inventive capacity), though perhaps had more influence in his idea to use fingerprints in identification of criminals. But what actually IS a gene?

For a word in such common usage it is remarkably hard to find a definition. Many books simply use it without giving one. Wikipedia has the brief "a unit of heredity" and the longer "A gene is a hereditary unit consisting of DNA that occupies a spot on a chromosome and determines a characteristic in an organism", which is similar to that given in the Concise Oxford Dictionary. Part of the trouble with the science we are discussing, is that this pervasive lack of definition causes much confusion. Identifying what is a "unit" is less obvious than it might sound. The simple link between "a unit of DNA" and "a characteristic" is more an exception than a rule.

Science, as well as Hollywood (Jurassic Park for example), is responsible for creating, and allowing a myth. The CD that you play on your stereo contains the code for a piece of music, but it requires a CD-player. Genes do not operate in isolation either. So far, children require mothers to grow in (or at least eggs, in the Jurassic instance). Test tube babies are not born out of test tubes, merely fertilised there. Science implies a fixed, deterministic development. That is, you have a set of genes; the codes they contain say how you will develop and who you will be. That supposedly is that, the whole story.

Another image that is often used is "genetic blueprint". But the architects' drawings of your house conveyed little of how it finally looked and said nothing about how it got built. The engineers drawing of your car has no fuel in it. So even though we used the expression "instruction set" earlier and may use such metaphors elsewhere, we need to make clear that there are limits to their accuracy. The areas where they break down are crucial to our whole understanding of the fit between the scientific building-blocks, and the energy-systems of the complementary world.

The description of replication and development above involves a good deal of "shorthand". The relationship between a chemical sequence of DNA and a characteristic in the organism it produces is complex. Sometimes scientists may pinpoint a unit of heredity, especially with simple organisms, and identify simple processes which they have discovered how to alter (to make tomatoes which are slower to break down and rot, for instance). But more often they won't know, since much of development inevitably involves multiple processes, and many different strands of DNA, possibly on different chromosomes. It may be far from obvious where or what a "gene" is, in any physically definable sense. It is a convenient but misleading abbreviation to designate a notional portion of the DNA which corresponds with a characteristic.

Often what scientists see of gene expression is dictated by what goes wrong, for example what happens if the "clotting" mechanism for blood is absent, as in haemophilia? A few diseases which can be traced to a specific locus in the DNA sequence seem to validate this form of thinking. Cystic Fybrosis is one example. But such examples encourage stupidity and misrepresentation in the press of the "we have found a gene for cancer" kind. If only it could be that simple! As Dr Bruce Lipton puts it:

> "..single-gene disorders affect less than two percent of the population; the vast majority of people come into the world with genes that should enable them to lead a happy and healthy life. The diseases that are today's scourges – diabetes, heart disease and cancer – short-circuit a happy and healthy life. These diseases however are not the result of a single gene, but of complex interactions among multiple genes and environmental factors."

In fact, the suggestion that there is a simple relationship between a "gene" and a "characteristic" is at best a metaphor and at worst a dogmatic assumption that is quite erroneous and always was. We would like to use a childish joke to illustrate this thinking.

Did you know beetles have their ears on their legs?

No, how do you know that?

When I pulled the legs off mine and told it to jump, it couldn't hear me. (Boom

boom!)

In practice there would be many potential "genes" for deafness - one that fails to form the auditory nerve, one that fails to form a tympanic membrane (ear-drum) or the small bones of the cochlea, one that blocks the ear canal with excessive wax, or another that stops the canal from forming at all. In that sense, there is no gene for "hearing" or equally, there are many genes for it. The relationship between genes and characteristics is opaque.

There are abundant examples to illustrate the complexity of isolating (or failing to isolate) a genetic cause for something observed in the individual. The attempt to understand how homosexuality arises makes a great example for the obvious reason that such a preference appears to operate counter to the expected evolutionary drive towards reproduction. Clearly a feature such as this does not bode well for competition to produce offspring. The Wikipedia article on this subject makes it clear how complex the relationships may possibly be both in the context of genetic pathways and in the potential relationship with both social and maternal factors. Whatever the genetic cause of homosexuality, it would have to be a side-effect of something with adaptive advantage.

The other side of this question would be to ask "Is homosexuality a characteristic"? Do we have a definition of what a characteristic is? Is that something "simple" like eye-colour, or more complex like sporting prowess. Is the gene for baseball the same as the gene for tennis? Is the liking for olives a characteristic? If so, is there a gene for it? It all sounds rather fuzzy and that is because the question is close to unanswerable except for a minority of quite specific instances where the characteristic is clear and the link has been found.

The "usual story" tells us that the gene package determines what develops in the organism in which it is present. This story is further undermined by some "genes" which do not affect the organism itself. An example of this occurs in snails, whose shells are formed in spirals. Viewed from the rear, they coil either clockwise or counter-clockwise. It might be expected that this is coded for by some gene, and that this could be detected in the organism itself. There is a gene (or genetic factor) and it can be detected, but it is not in the organism. The gene is in the parent. That is, there appears to be a gene which says "this organism's offspring will (or will not) coil clockwise". The effect of the gene is delayed by one generation. You can equally well describe the gene as being "the tendency to produced clockwise children".

The way that this comes about is highly significant. When the snail is developing, it does so according to the "package" of material that it receives from the parent. That is more than its chromosomal DNA. Just as a human foetus grows in a whole maternal environment, a bird's egg does not just merely contain the genes for a new generation. It includes a whole growth medium, and in a less obvious way snails' eggs contain other materials besides DNA. In the mother's ovaries, even before they are fertilised, the eggs are accompanied by pre-packed messenger RNA and proteins. Accordingly, when development starts, this predetermined package and not the chromosomal DNA dictates the direction of shell formation.

The origins of pre-determined elements and the balance between such fixed features and the flexibility of environmental influence is critical to our understanding of the subtlety in these relationships. We will return to it several times. Before doing so it will help us to understand some more of the metaphor that is contained in such expressions as "instruction set". This too is not as simple as it seems.

Builders, blueprints and codes

Any code is capable of being used in more than one way. You can use an alphabet code to construct the German or Italian language as easily as English. In either of those languages, you could write instructions for baking a Christmas cake, the rules for football or a description of the Taj Mahal. You could write in the present tense, or in a historical past tense, or you could write of imaginary things that will happen in the future. You could also use the alphabet as an encryption for itself. A simple version of this would be where each letter is used to stand for the one prior to it in alphabetical sequence - B stands for A, X instead of W. KVTU MJLF UIJT. (Go on, try it!)

It is entirely possible and even quite likely that the genetic "alphabet" of bases in the DNA strand could be used for more than the encoding of proteins. In Douglas Hofstadter's book, "Gödel Escher Bach", he devotes several pages to the postulation and exploration of a made-up game which he calls Typographical Genetics. In this he shows how it would easily be possible for a further level of code to be in place, which would determine how strings of genetic material could be cut up, moved in sequence, switched around, deleted and reassembled. With this level of coding, it is entirely possible to construct a set of instructions that tell a sentence to copy itself. This is therefore the kind of mechanism that would be necessary to trigger a cell to reproduce itself. It might also be the type of mechanism that would be required to control timing. Simple versions of this type of process can be modelled in computer programs which can be made to produce self-replicating code - and even some which are to a limited degree self-repairing. The human genome project, having completed the basic code sequences, is now investigating this "fifth base" aspect, the higher-level phenomenon of control.

If you look at a strand of chemical it is far from obvious where the clock is, or even could be. So how might control of timing be done? What would it take to construct mechanisms such that a six-year-old loses and replaces her front teeth, but not her molars? What is needed to instruct a 14-year-old boy to grow facial hair but not grow breasts, expand his voice-box, widen his shoulders but not his pelvic girdle? The process has to stop as well as start - what determines when these events are deemed to be complete? Why do we continue to grow only until we have reached a certain size, and not indefinitely throughout our life-span? Equally, why do we eventually cease to replenish, shrink, age and die? The last question may be different than the rest, since one possibility is that ageing processes happen because of cumulative maintenance failures, rather than as part of an intentional "program". But the others seem to be purposeful, ordered, largely consistent throughout our species and well-controlled.

In simple terms, what would be required is that certain instructions would be dormant until turned on by other sets of instructions. This is rather like ensuring that in the genetics of house building, the roof-truss genes do not operate before the wall-erection genes have completed. This at least would provide a mechanism for establishing an order of events. In the case of sexual differentiation we do know something of how this works, and that the presence or absence of hormones like testosterone is a trigger. But that doesn't mean we know how the genes achieve this. This kind of mechanism could also be used to delay the production of an enzyme, which would then be fed back into the system. Such a chemical device is capable of performing the function of a molecular clock. Moreover, since delayed feedback in systems generally produces oscillations, it would be likely that the body processes that we see would have an element of cyclical operation about them. There are in fact many of these. We have mentioned some of the longer-term ones, but a typical and important short-term cycle, is that which operates in the mitochondrion (a sub-component of the cell) to produce the energy which powers the cell. Called the Krebs cycle, tricarboxylic or citric acid cycle, it lasts approximately four minutes. As we will see later, there are much shorter ones.

What we are encountering is the fact that genetics is immensely more complex than a blueprint, or an architects' drawing, or the "instruction set" that we called it earlier. It appears that the very first cell supplies the drawing, but it also supplies the mechanical shovels that dig the foundations, the concrete that is poured in, the bricks, beams, window-panes and roof-tiles, plus bricklayers, hod-carriers, plasterers and electricians. And if that was not enough, they also tell each operative what to do, brick by brick, joist by joist, year by year, under variable environmental conditions.

In the light of what we will discover to be a limited number of genes, it is clear that a lot is dependent on these control and timing sequences. But these too cannot be separated out easily. Maybe the hod-carrier is effectively a part of the roof-tile - an extra piece of chemical designed to ensure that the chemical it is attached to cannot be used until it is in the right place. This makes the decoding of genes potentially very difficult. To distinguish control from function requires almost arbitrary lines to be drawn. And if the hod-carrier is a determinant from outside the DNA strand, it is just as hard to show where it is and how the triggering occurs.

This detail is not yet present in scientific knowledge.

Codes require code-readers

There is yet another whole area of further complexity in organism development. As stated earlier, a code is of no use without a decoding machine. The compact disc conveys nothing to you when you lick it, however hard you try. Pressing it to your forehead, staring intensely and rubbing it with a finger don't work either. You have to put it in the CD drawer of a computer or player, and activate the software which decodes its bit-patterns.

With the snail example, we indicated that development involved an interaction between the instructions supplied in the cell nucleus and other factors supplied by the mother in the egg's environment. This is far from being the only effect that is environmental. In a laboratory, much effort is expended in establishing and controlling the conditions for a reaction to take place. Any cook knows that the temperature of the oven can often be critical. Too hot, and the outside browns before the inside is cooked. Too cool and the dish dries out, or fails to develop the structure it needs, like a soggy sponge cake. Home wine-makers know that they have to give the yeast in their fermentations the right temperature, without which they are inert, or killed, or produce flavour-spoiling by-products.

In the living world, organisms may have to cope with much variability. For instance there is good evidence that there are large proportions of additional DNA in egg-laying creatures which enable the egg to respond to differences in temperature that are encountered during the developmental process. But these sequences are believed to be redundant or missing in mammals, where the temperature of the growing-medium is well-regulated by the host-organism. A frog embryo may well be capable of coping with temperatures from zero to 20 centigrade (32 - 80F), the potential variation from dawn to peak daytime in a spring pond. In comparison an in-vitro human embryo will not cope with variations much above 1 degree C.

Thus in some circumstances the genetic process works to reduce the effect of the environment - to make the outcome the same, even though the conditions are widely varying. But the opposite also occurs. There are other areas where the developmental process responds to the environment with variation. One example of this occurs in insects, some of which will breed earlier in their lives when food-surpluses are present. Amazingly, some will even breed while still in the larval stage, rather than wait for adulthood. So there is a degree of flexibility supplied even within the genetic instruction set. Cell activity is not fixed. It is capable of responding to environmental conditions, and will produce some enzymes only if those conditions demand them.

This is not new knowledge. In the work which won Jacques Monod and Francois Jacob the 1965 Nobel prize, they showed that some strains of a bacteria, which in one environment normally lacked the enzyme to metabolise the sugar galactose, would proceed to manufacture the required enzymes when exposed to it. The indications are that this flexibility is carried in the DNA, and that there are mechanisms there for manufacture of repressor proteins and detector proteins. With these the cell can detect the presence of a substance, or in its absence, suppress what would be uneconomical activity. This type of mechanism clearly confers adaptability to a variety of conditions upon its owner, and such mechanisms are found to be widespread among micro-organisms. But it also indicates very clearly that the genes do not simply dictate outcomes. There is interaction with the environment and "choices" are made.

A rather different example of this occurs as trees develop, where root growth will be inhibited if the tree is not subject to wind. In enclosed environments like the Eden project or the Biosphere, growers were obliged to shake the trunks of saplings regularly to ensure that the trees were stimulated to produce adequate root systems. When you think about it, this is quite a subtle mechanism involving not a one-off "switch" but a progressive series of responses over time.

All of this gives us added cause to regard with great caution the notion of a blueprint, or a program, or an architects' drawing (even one complete with builders). What was passed down to the developing organism involves a degree of responsiveness to conditions that surround the development process. As well as deciding whether to hang the doors inward or outward-opening, the builder's mates construct thick doors for cold climates, and ventilated doors for hot ones. The code is subject to interpretation.

One classic demonstration of this feature was made as long as 100 years ago, in H. Driesch's experiments with sea-urchin embryos. An assortment of variations was shown. The removal of one of the first two cells in the developing embryo gave rise, not to half a sea-urchin, but to a complete one of smaller than normal size. Similarly, if two embryos at this stage were fused, a giant, but still correctly-formed organism developed. Since that time, similar experiments have shown that a dragonfly embryo will form complete, but reduced in size, if the egg is tied around the middle. We will need to look in more detail at how form is determined.

We simply don't have enough genes

Cumulatively the above examples show several levels at which the description of the connection between "gene" and a "characteristic" misleadingly implies a close-coupled and simple chemical cause-and-effect. But perhaps the biggest nail in the coffin of close-coupling finally came from the Human Genome project – a global scientific co-operation to create a catalogue of all human genes. The assumption had been that the connection between gene and characteristic was mediated by proteins. There are about 100,000 different proteins that make up our bodies. In addition there were assumed to be perhaps 20,000 genes which orchestrate the activity of the protein-encoding genes and address the problems, such as timing, that we have just described, so science expected a minimum of 120,000 genes to be found and present in the final map.

In what he describes as a "cosmic joke" on the scale of the discovery that the earth was not flat after all, geneticists experienced a huge shock at the outcome. To quote again from Dr Lipton:-

"...contrary to their expectations of over 120,000 genes, they found that the entire human genome consists of approximately 25,000 genes. (Pennisi 2003; Pearson 2003; Goodman 2003) More than 80 percent of the presumed and required DNA does not exist! .....Now that the Human Genome Project has toppled the one-gene for one protein concept, our current theories of how life works have to be scrapped.....**There simply are not enough genes to account for the complexity of human life or of human disease**." (*our emphasis.*)

He goes on to detail how fruit flies have 15,000 genes, a nematode worm 24,000 and that rodents and humans have roughly comparable numbers of genes. In the face of this knowledge it is obvious that we have to look beyond the sequences of DNA themselves for an explanation of how outcomes are determined.

Epigenetics and environmental influences

While it may be difficult to draw the line between control and function, builder and brick, science is beginning to rise to the challenge. In the last decade or so, the science of epigenetics has come into being, specifically to look at the phenomenon of "control above genetics". Their research has established that DNA blueprints passed down through genes are not set solid and do not dictate our destiny. Environmental influences, including nutrition, stress and emotions can modify the expression of those genes, as we have indicated.

Only half of the contents of a cell nucleus are DNA. The other half, largely ignored in the stampede toward genome decoding, is made up of regulatory proteins. These are turning out to be just as crucial to our heredity as the DNA.

In the chromosome, these proteins cover the DNA strands. Like a tattoo under a shirt-sleeve, the code under its sheath of regulatory proteins cannot be read. However, proteins can change shape under the influence of environmental signals, giving access to the gene for copying.

From half a century of assumed genetic determinism, science is moving towards an understanding that DNA does not have primacy. There is a sophisticated interplay of blueprint and environment, just as our earlier examples indicated should be expected. It is like the distinction between the hardware of your TV set and the programs which are transmitted through it. You can change what the TV set shows by switching channels. Equally, you can change what the program displays on the screen by altering colour and contrast settings. The two are interdependent.

This relationship has been proven conclusively by an experiment with mice. A particular strain of mice carries the "agouti" gene which causes them to develop yellow coats and obesity, with a predisposition to other diseases. The scientists experimented by giving genetically identical mice different diets. One group was fed on a diet of methyl-rich food supplements such as vitamin B12, folic acid and choline. These supplements were able to attach to the gene's DNA and cause the regulatory protein to bind in such a way that the agouti gene would not activate. There were no yellow coats and no obesity. You can see a picture of the results on the American Society of Microbiology website.

Just how do environmental factors influence cellular development? There are a few known mechanisms by which small changes can have impact at the level of the individual cell. We include the following as indicators of the potential for this. In one experiment, Japanese researchers used drugs to damage the insulin-producing cells of the pancreas in laboratory rats. These rats, when they bred, produced offspring in which diabetes was inclined to occur spontaneously. That is, a specific change in the organ of a parent could be seen to have an effect on the production of genetic material. (Note from earlier discussions that this does not necessarily act through the chromosomal DNA.)

In another, Andrew Maniotis experimented with the effects of mechanical force on the external cellular membrane and showed that the force could transmit to the nucleus and produce a mutation. Further work by Michael Lieber showed that other external stresses from the environment such as heat and radiation could also trigger such mutagenic and potentially adaptive response. Other experiments have shown that when plants and insects are subjected to toxic substances, they often mutate in such a way as to confer increased resistance. In another area of study, researchers at the Renssaeler Institute have shown that external chemical and mechanical factors influence the ways in which developing stem-cells differentiate and become osteogenic (that is, bone-producing).

To these examples we should also add the recognition from the work of Barbara McClintock, and later by Temin and Engels, that large proportions of DNA are indeed not directly genes (in the sense of sequences that code for proteins) but transposable elements and that these move around in response to stress on the organism, a further indication that changes can be generated non-randomly in the genetic material.

As well as influence on the development of the cell, there can be environmental influences on the proteins themselves. Dr Judyth Sassoon gives the following description:-

> "Proteins are long chains of chemical units called amino acids, strung together in the order specified by DNA and then folded up into active conformations. They are the molecular components that accomplish almost all the essential tasks in living cells. For example, proteins catch other molecules and build them into cellular structures or take them apart and extract their energy. They also carry atoms to precise locations inside or outside the cell. They are able to behave, in the metaphorical sense, as "pumps" or "motors" or form receptors that trap specific molecules.
>
> They can even act as "antennae" that conduct electrical charge. In order to perform their particular tasks, proteins must have the correct shape and the way they are folded in space determines whether they are active or not. Most biology textbooks declare that protein folding is due almost entirely to the chemical sequence of its component amino acids, also known as the primary structure."

She quotes a standard biochemistry text that states that a protein's primary chemical structure dictates its three dimensional structure and goes on to say:-

"This is a very misleading statement because it lays all the emphasis on the protein's intrinsic chemistry and does not stress the importance of the "proper conditions". Yet every biochemist knows that proteins in different environments behave differently. .... External forces clearly play a very significant role in determining correct protein conformation and activity."

She then describes an experimental process with lysozomes from egg-white. She describes the crucial part played in this by water and the factors affecting solubility, drawing the following conclusion :-

"There is, in fact, a mass of scientific literature indicating that protein structures are dependent upon their relationship with water, but this fundamental detail is rarely stated explicitly enough. ....It is clear that the forces giving rise to protein structures in nature are, in actuality, external. Biochemists lay so much emphasis on the chemistry of the amino acid sequence because they consider the external environment to be fixed and the sequence to be the only variable between proteins. This way of thinking is totally in accord with the tendency of modern science to limit and simplify nature and completely obscures the essential relationship between biological systems and their surroundings." (*Our emphasis*)

The private life of the cell

In Chapter 8 we took a brief look at the process by which organic life developed – from the first amino acids which gave rise to protein formation and to the first cell, surrounded by its membrane. We then saw how important the cell membrane is, not just as a bag that holds the cell together, but as an active chemical process through which receptor proteins detect the environment and effector proteins cause change.

Within this we need to recognise that a small number of proteins are doing a much greater number of jobs. Proteins are therefore being used for multiple purposes throughout the body and a linear (A causes B causes C) model of the biochemistry is inaccurate and over-simplified. This is also why pharmaceutical medicines inevitably have effects other than those which they are designed for. A causes B and D, which cause E, F, G and H, which may well feed back into A and C. And so on. Pharmaceutically the only target may have been B.

In our earlier description we referred with deliberate over-simplification to the cell's "jelly". In fact what is contained within the membrane is far from jelly-like. Be it ever so tiny, the cell contains various structures (organelles) with specific functions separated by a further membrane (the reticulum). This membrane allows us to distinguish organelles such as Lysosomes, Golgi apparatus, the ribosomes which mediate much of the protein decoding and transcription process, and the mitochondria. Fortunately we do not need to know about all of these, but it is worthwhile to discuss mitochondria, the cellular power-pack which we referred to above when mentioning the Krebs cycle.

According to a widely accepted theory put forward by Lynn Margulis, all eukaryotic cells (ones which have a nucleus) are descended from early bacteria and result from an event (or probably several events) perhaps two billion years ago where different bacteria combined their material, forming a co-operative unit. This may have come about by bacteria with stronger "electric motors" invading slower cells. Over time what perhaps began as a competitive or parasitic process evolved into a co-operative one where both parts survived together with mutual benefit. The theme of co-operation is important and will re-emerge regularly. The organelles and structures described above may well have been incorporated over many millennia, or even eons as it is apparent that the additional complexity facilitated many more design possibilities, including that of multi-celled organisms.

Mitochondria contain their own complement of DNA (referred to as mtDNA) and they replicate independently of the cell chromosomal DNA. (In plants this is also true of chloroplasts). For a while it was believed that all mitochondrial DNA passes only through the egg. Richard Dawkins states ("Blind Watchmaker", P176) that "Sperms are too small to contain mitochondria so mitochondria passes exclusively down the female line. .... Incidentally, this means that we can use mitochondria to trace our ancestry strictly down the female line" More recently in "River out of Eden" he modifies this view to state "Sperms are too small to contain more than a few mitochondria ... these mitochondria are cast away with the tail when the sperm head is absorbed in the egg at fertilisation." Of course he is entitled to modify his view, but this so-far unproven belief system (that the sperm's tail is discarded and no male mtDNA present afterwards) has led to an entire evolutionary hypothesis ("mitochondrial eve") which is used to justify the statement that all human life originated in Africa and that there were several subsequent bifurcations in human inheritance which can be traced through the human population. This may as a result be an over-simplification.

That particular debate while interesting, is not crucial to our argument. But we point to the mtDNA issue as an indicator that there is much more passing from generation to generation than chromosomal DNA. And potentially, even if it turns out that much, most or even all of this non-chromosomal material comes from the mother, it supports our case for looking beyond the chromosomes for some elements of inheritance. Take note also that some of it may indeed be more stable over generations than the chromosomal DNA if it has not undergone sexual splitting and recombination. As we will see, the balance of stability and opportunity for change is important in the evolutionary process.

You may recall how we noted earlier that homeopathy shows the potential for non-genetic information to be passed from one generation to the next and also the indirect influencing of the spiral direction in a snail-shell. The non-chromosomal material is one of the places where such factors might be carried through.

We are saying not only that the cell is home to other parts of the material which governs human development but that each cell has a life of its own. Beings live and replicate but they do so through their individual cells. The IMP's, the receptor and effector proteins are the means of regulating the cell's individual life. They are also a means for one cell to sense and communicate to another, though they are not the only means, as we shall see later.

We want to remind you that we are telling three parallel and interlinked stories, all mediated by "genetics". We have mainly focussed on the genetic role in building the organism, from one cell to many through replication, a process which includes their differentiation into functional units such as organs. Another function of living cells is that once built, each is a "photocopier" producing a replacement for itself within the body when needed. These aspects of first building and then maintaining stability are the way in which the organism "becomes". We must progress our narrative now towards "being". Now the organism is keeping itself alive and "doing stuff" which in most cases will eventually include reproducing itself. From there we can lead towards the long-term developmental process for the species as it deals with environmental change.

Just how does the cell relate to its environment? Crudely speaking, the ability to manage that relationship is critical to an organism's survival. Can it find an energy source? Can it avoid toxicity or attack? Can it find the right conditions to reproduce? We can see much of this in our own behaviour or that of other multi-celled creatures, but how do single-celled organisms do this? How do our own cells? Bear in mind that your lungs or liver only do what they do through the activity of the individual cells they are composed of.

If an organism is to locate an energy source or avoid attack it first has to sense it. In chapter 8 we briefly described the amoeba, its ability to sense food chemically and for the effector proteins to then bring about a change of shape, moving to surround its prey. A single-celled organism is taking in chemicals to consume for itself, or passing waste-product from its metabolism back out into its environment. Inside our bodies, individual cells do this too, but they are also co-operating with other cells so that not only their own internal environment is managed, but the collective environment too. Waste carbon dioxide, like oxygen, travels through the blood to be exchanged in the lungs. Other waste products may ultimately be excreted via the kidneys or passed into the bowel.

Thus within our bodies, cells are maintaining themselves and they are also maintaining us. But in addition to that environmental regulation they are also working together to create our "behaviour". Collectively they allow us to walk, talk, eat, and have sex. There is collective "doing stuff". The power of these big cellular collectives greatly exceeds that which the cells possess individually.

We are not used to thinking about the way in which trillions of cells achieve this collectivisation. We are accustomed to imagine that decisions are made in our brains and that muscles act to carry them out. We are led to believe that our brains work out what to do and then we do it. But if you have been following our story through the "mind all over" aspects of neuro-endocrine function and you have grasped the scale of chemical activity at the cell boundary, perhaps it is apparent to you that much more is happening besides our mental process. You may think that it is your brain which tells your lungs that it is time to breathe, but there are multiple control systems working together.

Small indications

People, scientists included, like simplicity. This is often a good thing and brings the most elegant solutions. However it sometimes leads us all into over-simplification. When we are faced with such monumental complexity and intricate detail it becomes more than the average mind can handle. We struggle to comprehend that we have tens of trillions of cells in our bodies. How do we grasp that 20-30 million of our skin cells replaced themselves in the time it took to read this sentence?

Science compensates in two ways. The first is through specialisation. The rule for specialisation is that a person knows more and more about less and less until they eventually know everything about nothing at all. Joking aside, the risk (and in our view the reality) is that many scientists cannot see the forest because they are looking at one leaf on a tree. The second way of compensating is that they resort to crude models. Even when they are as complex and brilliantly argued as a Stephen Jay Gould opus, those models are still unable to encompass in full the implications that arise from a process as subtle as a single protein change in a single cell.

As authors we face here the opposite risk to specialisation. We are generalists looking at the big picture. We know less and less about more and more until we finally know nothing at all about everything. The subtlety can also be lost in this way. The picture is painted with big brush strokes. We are attempting to cover a huge canvas without losing the resolution of a 600 dots per inch ink-jet and we ask for you to hold these two perspectives with us simultaneously.

The case we are making is for the presence of consciousness; you cannot get more subtle than this. We are talking about influences at the finest grain of detail, and yet with powerful implications. We will meet this problem of scale again when we talk about quantum physics and deal with the deep paradoxes that it presents us with. It is not critical that you understand the detail of everything that is being presented here. We are not intentionally glossing over anything, and yet we have to feel our way towards the answer, pixel by pixel.

What we have to show is a paradoxical combination – the subtlety of very small and non-visible changes combined with the potential for them to influence larger outcomes. This could happen in several ways.

- A small change in one area could "ripple" quickly through a system and become visible.

- A single small change could be a trigger for other processes which would unfold over an extended time-frame.

- A multitude of small changes happening in the same or similar ways could accumulate and have a large impact over time.

Space restricts the depth of analysis we can give to this area, and we thoroughly recommend Dr Bruce Lipton's very entertaining full text. We are now part of the way in our journey through genetics and evolution. We have shown the need for greater recognition of environmental influence but we have not yet shown all of the ways in which this relationship with the environment is mediated and we still have only described a small portion of the processes which make life actually work. Beyond that we still have to examine the process of change over long time-scales and address the dogma that the mechanisms for it all arose entirely as a result of random chance and competition to survive. And we have yet to bring in the possible areas in which consciousness or spirituality may play a part. These will be the tasks of our next two chapters.

Review

In this chapter we have addressed the impression that science has given of a simple one-to-one relationship between genes and characteristics and shown that:-

The chemical "code" is only part of the means by which development is accomplished

The notion of "genes" is poorly defined, and that there are too few of them to manage the processes for which they are claimed to be responsible.

The outcomes are complex and most often cannot be related to a single gene – indeed, most of the mechanisms have yet to be understood.

There are complex relationships with the environment and intricate controls of sequence and timing that are still not known in detail and sometimes clearly not managed by the DNA code

The current idea of what "genes" are and what they do is an oversimplification and the way they are typically presented should not be accepted as a full picture.

We have indicated the great complexity of a genetic code, both in relation to its capability to achieve several different functions and its capacity to extend that control over long developmental time-scales. This provides a platform for greater understanding of the way in which genes are influenced by the environment, and for the flexibility that would required for any of that environmental influence to be derived from a layer of information in the realm of consciousness.

We have touched upon the complexity of the cell and the part played in reproduction by other parts than the cell nucleus. We have also given indications of the relationship between activity in individual cells and the overall workings of a multi-celled creature. With these aspect we have the beginnings of a deepened understanding of how coherence may be brought about.

10. <u>The rhythm of life</u>

The hostess at a dinner party introduced the distinguished-looking gentleman at the table. "I would like you to meet Professor Feinstein. He is a world expert on crocodiles." "My dear lady," responds the Professor, "I fear you exaggerate my knowledge. I am only an expert on the crocodile's eyelids."

Anon

A tiny spark and a gentle breath can produce a forest fire

Anon

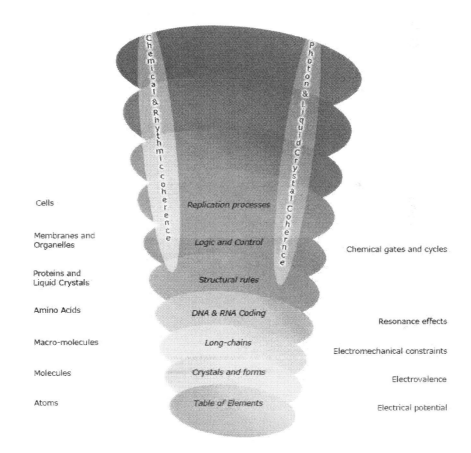

Theme

In this chapter we carry forward our journey into uncertainties and build on the image of cells managing their individual integrity and interacting with their environments. We can now examine further the way in which this process of interaction is then extended into a systematic, coherent and co-ordinated relationship. This co-ordination encompasses billions or trillions of cells, all working together with a mix of differentiated function (lungs, kidneys, blood-cells muscles etc.) that nevertheless function as a unified whole. We will see that this requires several layers of connection, viewing the body as a biological computer and as a system exhibiting the qualities of laser-light focus through organically derived coherence processes. These are added to the body rhythms synchronised by our beating heart and the decision-making capacities of our brains.

Quantum Biology and Coherence

The ability for a human body composed of 50+ trillion cells to function as one single entity is another daily miracle. Don't forget that this functionality runs all the way from the basics of heartbeat, breathing and digestion to the sophistications of peak athletic co-ordination, consummate musicianship, poetry and intellectual achievement. We continue to ask fundamental questions about life, many of which are built in to the related words we are employing – organ, organic, organism, organelle (within the cell) and above all - organisation. Where does the organisation come from, and how does it work?

When it comes to scale, you can't get smaller than the quantum level. We were tempted to place the chapter on quantum physics earlier in our story in order that some terms used here would have a deeper context. Instead we will attempt to indicate the flavour of the quantum world, and expand on that later. Quanta are the stuff of the universe which are even smaller than atoms, and which make up just about everything. Put another way, different atoms are composed of different combinations of quanta. We are talking of electrons, protons, neutrons and many others. Their behaviour is weird, in some ways unpredictable and still not entirely understood.

When matter was originally created, the forces in the core of stars caused increasing densities of matter to form over billions of years, from small atoms with a small nucleus and one or two electrons like Hydrogen and Helium to bigger ones like Iron with 26 electrons or Gold with 79. This has its own place in the spiral of evolution, potentially its own spiral with a layer to represent each of the electron shells, but all this is abbreviated to a single band in our overview diagram.

Underlying this quantum unpredictability, and beneath their role in coalescing into stable material forms there are properties which cause the behaviour of one quantum to be related to another, and to bring about forms of "coherence". To have the feeling for this we would ask you to recall a film you may have seen showing large shoals of fish which respond to the presence of a predator with a seemingly instantaneous collective shift of direction. (Some bird species , when in flocks, behave in a similar way that might also be familiar to you.) That is, coherence provides the possibility for large numbers of potentially free events to be co-ordinated in such a way as to act together. This coherence is a somewhat paradoxical state which maximises local freedom at the same time as facilitating global cohesion.

Jumping in with a more fulsome description, here is an extract from an article by Dr Mae-Wan Ho. This description is at the molecular rather than the quantum level, but illustrates the concept, as well as showing that coherence is significant at many levels of existence. (A fuller text can be viewed on www.i-sis.org.uk and complete references downloaded by becoming a member.)

> "The macromolecules, associated with lots of water, are in a dynamic liquid crystalline state, where all the molecules are macroscopically aligned to form a continuum that links up through the whole body, permeating through the connective tissues, the extracellular matrix, and into the interior of every single cell. And all the molecules, including the water, are moving coherently together as a whole.
>
> The liquid crystalline continuum enables every single molecule to communicate with every other. The water, constituting some 70 percent by weight of the organism, is also the most important for forming the liquid crystalline matrix, for intercommunication and for the macromolecules to function at all.

Coherence is a term that was developed in association with superconductivity and laser light rather than living systems. If you have seen a neon or fluorescent light you have experienced the way in which an atom can be stimulated by energy to emit light (photons). Normally these photons are emitted in a scattered way in all directions. In contrast, if you have seen a laser light-show you will have seen that the light from a laser stays together in a beam, does not scatter, and can travel for long distances maintaining this visibly coherent direction."

In a laser, the atoms or molecules of a crystal, such as ruby or garnet -- or of a gas, liquid, or other substance -- are excited in what is called the *laser cavity* so that more of them are at higher energy levels than are at lower energy levels. Reflective surfaces at both ends of the cavity permit energy to reflect back and forth, building up in each passage and raising the energy level.

In a ruby laser, light from a flash lamp surrounding the ruby, in what is called "optical pumping", excites the molecules in the ruby rod, and they bounce back and forth between two mirrors until something happens called a "phase shift". When this happens, the photons become coherent (vibrating in phase with each other) at which point coherent light escapes from the cavity. For a simple image of phase, think of an army marching in time and of the way that they have to break step in order not to set up vibrations that will crack bridges when they cross. That is, they deliberately shift to being out of phase. An alternative image would be Busby Berkeley choreography or the difference between successful synchro-swimming and splashing around.

Self-organising systems

Another way of describing coherence is in the capacity of a system to be self-organising. As the laser shows, a system does not need to be an organic life to show self-organisation. We are used to thinking of chemical reactions as irreversible processes. Iron rusts, but rust does not turn to iron. But there are reactions which run counter to this expectation, and one example is known as "the chemical clock". (Please refer to Plate 3, after page 42.)

There are certain kinds of chemical reactions which change colour. Picture then, a reaction which changes colour between two different states, in a cycle which is regular, and which also displays beautiful spiralling structures. This involves a reaction which can be reversed, and reversed again. It also requires that the whole mass of chemicals is performing this cycle in a co-ordinated way. You don't have a soupy, undifferentiated mixture, the way that you do when cream mixes into coffee. Rather, it is as if the colour of your coffee were to switch from brown to cream, and back to brown. There are billions of molecules, operating as one "unit". Instead of an apparently random and disorganised state, we have a form of order - an order which contains some self-organising principle. (For the sake of accuracy we should point out that the "soupy" state does eventually occur, but the cycle continues for as long as fresh ingredients are being added to the mixture.) Another example is more purely in the realm of physics, and concerns what happens when we heat a layer of liquid that is sandwiched between two sheets of glass. One might expect that when we apply heat all the molecules of the liquid would become more energised, and show greater and more random movement. It is not to be expected then, that what happens is the appearance of a honeycomb pattern, made up of hexagonal cells of convecting liquid. That this happens, was discovered nearly one hundred years ago, but its significance in regard to dynamic, non-equilibrium states, was not seen until much later. Here again, the phenomenon of self-organisation applies only while energy continues to be supplied. Without heat, the liquid reverts to an unstructured state. (Bear in mind that there is always new energy being introduced to a live body.)

Both of these examples exhibit the same phenomenon of self-organising "communication". In the liquid honeycombs, a hexagonal cell is the width of millions of molecules, but all those millions become co-ordinated in the process. In the chemical clock (also known as the Belousov-Zhabotinsky reaction), the distances involved are even greater, but the molecules appear to "know" when to turn red, and when to turn blue. They work together in an apparently instantaneous series of changes, or phase-shifts.

How can we prove coherence?

We are not aware of any experiment yet which conclusively demonstrates a similar co-ordination in the human body. Indeed, it may prove quite hard to show this in a complex living system. You might ask how an experimental design would isolate the variables concerned? It would certainly be a challenge. Consequently we must look at what might constitute the necessary evidence.

We referred earlier to the existence of cycles of activity in the body and used the example of the Krebs cycle to illustrate one with a time-period measured in minutes. In practice, living systems have a multiplicity of cycles within cycles and you can work through biology down to events of energy-exchange which, represent an electronic vibration that has a period of femto-seconds (1/1,000,000,000,000,000 of a second).

As a result, we have to build our picture of the mechanisms which could maintain coherence in small stages and at different levels, and once again we will skim the surface of the material. A very full and comprehensive technical view of both the physics and the biology that we are summarising here is presented in Dr Mae-Wan Ho's book "The Rainbow and the Worm", which we would recommend particularly to those who really want a much deeper picture of the science.

What then are the elements that would demonstrate coherence? What would indicate that there is a co-ordination and organisation taking place across our trillions of cells that would be akin to the almost instantaneous change of the molecules in a B-Z reaction? What mechanisms would we expect to see?

By way of answer, and as Dr. Ho suggests, the components we are looking for might include:

1. Maintenance of order over long range and at high speed

2. Rapid and efficient energy transduction

3. High sensitivity to external cues and triggers

4. Symmetrical coupling of energy transfer

5. Populations functioning together without "noise" (a term communications engineers use to denote the energy fluctuations which are not part of the intended signal – like radios before FM.)

Let's look at these briefly, one by one.

1. Order   We used the image earlier of the shoal of fish changing direction. When required (particularly in emergency) organisms can mobilise great amounts of energy in an instant, and nerve communication to muscles is incredibly fast. Yet it appears that the muscle responds in advance of the nerve signals for enhanced co-ordination being received. This suggests that there is a

system of communication which sends emergency messages simultaneously to all organs, including those not directly connected with the nerve network. It acts at a speed which appears to rule out conventional nerve mechanisms.

There are indications that there are electro-dynamic signals involved. It has been shown that Daphnia emit light and that the rate of emission is related to their distance from each other. Such a mechanism would enable collective behaviour such as the fish shoals described and could also take place cell-to-cell in a multi-celled organism. Fritz Popp, a quantum physicist turned biophysicist and a pioneer in the investigation of photon communication, has shown direct communication between separated containers of luminescent bacteria, which synchronise their light flashing when there is no light barrier between them.

There are numerous examples of phase-locked oscillations within organisms, one such being the way insect wing-beats are governed. Similarly patterns have been detected in brain-wave activity which shows rapid coherent changes across large areas. The pacemaker cells of the heart and the insulin-secretion cells of the pancreas likewise show synchronised electrical activity.

2. Energy transduction Muscle activity in mammals is highly efficient. Outside of living organisms, chemical reactions lose 70% of the energy available (or supplied), which would cause mammals to overheat very rapidly. Muscle contraction is triggered by an instant of electrical discharge at the point where the nerve meets the muscle-cell membrane; within a millisecond calcium ions are released to trigger contraction of the entire cell. In a typical muscle contraction, all the cells, often numbered in billions, are executing such contractions together and the chemical energy, which is stored in a molecule called Adenosine TriPhosphate (ATP) is converted into mechanical energy. Thousands of billions (Dr. Ho uses the figure of 10^{19}) of molecules are utilised rapidly and co-ordinated over distances ranging from the microscopic to the length of a long muscle (e.g. calf or thigh). This energy is supplied at close to 100% efficiency

3. Sensitivity to cues The eye is highly sensitive, and in some species can detect a single quantum of light falling on the retina. The signal that this triggers in the nerve contains perhaps a million times more energy through a molecular cascade. The muscular activity described above mobilises vastly more energy than the nerve impulse. Another aspect of sensitivity would be the

ability of the cell, or groups of cells, to respond to very weak electromagnetic signals. Think of the way in which a radio, when tuned to the right frequency, can pick up a radio station and deliver the co-ordinated information that it contains. Irena Cosic has shown that groups of proteins which share the same function also share a periodicity in electronic potential and exhibit a form of common recognition of an electromagnetic frequency. That is, there are fluctuations which are co-ordinated in response to electromagnetic signals. Such an effect would create a crucial relationship between communication of information and organisation of energy and function.

4. Coupled symmetry The process in the body that creates ATP (above) from ADP (which has one phosphate group less) is reversible. We just described the release of energy. But when energy is supplied (e.g. from food) the ADP adds a phosphate group and becomes ATP. So there is a repeatable cycle of energy store and release. This is just one example from many where the body has chemical cycles which fulfil the criterion of symmetrical coupling.

5. Noiseless communication The examples such as pacemaker cells in the heart given under point 1 show noiseless functioning, but this can also be demonstrated at the molecular level where high-speed ultra-sensitive instruments indicate that the contractions in fine muscle activity (such as the beating of cilia in mussels) show synchronised quantal behaviour with little or no fluctuation.

The Liquid Crystal bio-computer

We appreciate that we are piling one level of detail upon another, and adopting multiple modes of description for the observations of bodily activity. While we are sorry if this is potentially confusing, we are only describing what is actually there. This is how nature works, building layer upon layer. It is complex, it is multi-layered and it does involve many different processes taking place at small and large scales of activity from the quantum to the cell to the organism. Please allow us therefore to introduce one more layer.

It is quite common for people to draw analogies between a brain and a computer. It is more of a surprise for someone to present the whole body as resembling one. This is not as far-fetched as it might sound, and the reason for that lies in "liquid crystals". You will have come across these in a laptop display, and some flat screen TV's and monitors, but they have properties beyond display technologies.

Bruce Lipton tells the story very entertainingly of the moment over 20 years ago when he had insight into the role of liquid crystals in cells. A crystal is a structure where molecules are arranged in regular and repeated patterns. We are accustomed to diamonds or table salt as crystals which are solid, but fluid molecules can also adopt regular and repeated patterns. Even though they are flowing they retain their organisation. They can alter their shape and yet maintain integrity, and this is just what the phospholipid molecules that make up cell membranes do.

We described earlier the receptor and effector proteins that may be conducted across the membrane. Bruce Lipton perceived that the fact that the membrane conducts some things and not others made it a semiconductor. He further perceived that effector proteins formed gates and channels in the membrane and arrived at the description "The membrane is a liquid crystal semiconductor with gates and channels." He then recognised this as just the description that was used in describing the microprocessor chip inside a computer.

He also describes how 12 years later, in 1997 B. A Cornell and colleagues isolated a cell membrane and placed a piece of gold foil under it. They then flooded the space between with an electrolyte solution. When stimulated by an electrical signal, the membrane's receptors opened up and allowed the electrolyte solution across the membrane. Through the foil, the electrical signal could be picked up and displayed on a screen as a digital readout. This device demonstrated that the membrane can function like a chip. As a result there is a potential for levels of interrelationship between cells that would be the equivalent of multi-processor computing. Nature did it first!

Dr Mae-Wan Ho follows a parallel train of thought in her recognition of a potential relationship between the liquid crystal continuum and consciousness. Her suggestion is that it is not appropriate to locate consciousness as a property of the brain, but that it has to be seen as throughout the entire liquid crystalline continuum of the body. Further than this, she describes the importance of connective tissues in bringing this about.

The connective tissues include the extra-cellular matrix that surrounds all cells, along with skin, bones, cartilage, tendons, veins, arteries, air-passages and more. These tissues are also liquid crystalline in nature and are ideal for mediating the rapid intercommunication that would be required for the efficient energy transduction that enables coherent behaviour across the whole organism. This is facilitated by the properties of collagen, which is a protein that provides an ordered network that can orient itself in response to electrical signals and in addition binds water molecules in such a way as to support rapid jump-conduction of protons.

Jump-conduction of protons is faster than electrical conduction in the nerves. As a result, the connective tissue of the body provides a superior intercommunication system to that the nervous system offers by itself. The collagens also supply an element of structural stability which enables tissues to retain memory of previous events. This adds a further element to the bio-computer, that it has processing (the yes/no of the membrane gate), rapid connectivity, a form of input (senses), output (change and behaviour) and now, memory.

Phase-shifts and pumped systems in the body

When discussing lasers and coherence, we referred to the process of "pumping" which is applied to the photon emissions within the laser crystal and the eventual jump, or phase-shift, into coherence.

Herbert Frohlich, a solid-state physicist, has suggested that the dense packing of dielectric molecules in living organisms could lead to the condensed-matter conditions where metabolic pumping could result in a build-up to collective modes of vibration. Taken together with the rapid energy transfer features of the connective tissue and also with the jump-conduction of protons, there is potential for the conditions that facilitate phase-shift and coherence to occur.

We will return to this area in our discussion of physics, but for now would merely note that other researchers have supported this conclusion. Additionally, there is work which demonstrates the greater degree of coherence present in healthy people compared with cardiac patients, and also showing the coherence associated with varied forms of meditation.

We said that this chapter would concentrate on the processes which enable life as we know it, especially the kind of life which large multi-celled organisms exhibit. We also said that we would indicate how the facts we see would create a space in which consciousness could become an active part of the picture.

What is beginning to reveal itself, is a combination of necessary factors which would enable this to occur. We are seeing:-

sensitivity to external conditions

the possibility that such sensitivity includes detection of subtle electro-magnetic or other low-energy changes

the capability for such low-energy changes to affect low-level processes in the cell

the existence of a mechanism or mechanisms that would propagate a low-level change throughout the organism

In the previous chapter we painted the picture of flexibility in the mechanisms which manage the building of cells and of multi-celled creatures. In this chapter we have begun to view those cells firstly as individual units with their own mechanisms for maintaining their integrity and balance, and then as a set of co-ordinated components which communicate with each other and work together. There are several aspects to this co-ordination – electrical, electromagnetic, bio-computer, liquid crystal continuum and laser-like phase coherence. Many of these are not understood in detail, and the balances and interplay even less clear. When they eventually emerge, these details will be fascinating but are not essential at this stage. The overall picture is sufficient to indicate that there are several ways in which individual organisms are sensitive to very small changes of energy and can co-ordinate their responses to those changes. Such mechanisms are also sufficient to provide physiological mechanisms which are capable of explaining many features of life that we are describing – intuition, and energy-healing for example. The only reason that we do not have such explanations is that the research is yet to be done.

This is merely a beginning, but it is a gateway to a scientific picture which can explain some of the relationships that were evidenced in Section 1. We will explore these connections more in the context of physics. In the meantime, we should take a look at evolution and the fourth uncertainty that we set out to address in this section. We are returning to the theme of fundamentalist

Darwinism in order to complete this discussion. We will present the evidence against a completely random universe, and the flaws in a purely competitive view of evolution. Into this we will weave a potential for consciousness to enter the relationship between the long-term development of life, species differentiation and the emergence of ecological balance.

Review

In this chapter we set out to show how individual cell function could extend into a systematic, coherent and co-ordinated relationship that encompasses billions or trillions of cells, all working together with a mix of differentiated function (lungs, kidneys, blood-cells, muscles etc.) that nevertheless function as a unified whole.

We looked at the phenomenon of coherence to understand what might demonstrate our body's ability to demonstrate laser-like organisation and found several features that indicate this. We found evidence of systems in the body to be self-organising and saw mechanisms which would contribute to this, jump conduction of protons, the liquid crystal membrane "biocomputer" and metabolic pumping of the sort required to bring about phase-shift.

In all of these we say the level of sensitivity to small energy triggers which would enable us to detect very small changes in the non-visible world and for them to affect our function, in the way required for examples of energy healing such as homeopathy.

11. Not staggering, but dancing

To be properly expressed, a thing must proceed from within, moved by its form

Meister Eckhart

"...[The] place of the embryonic formative process is a field (in the usage of physicists) the boundaries of which, in general, do not coincide with those of the embryo but surpass them. Embryogenesis, in other words, comes to pass inside the fields. ... Thus what is given to us as a living system would consist of the visible embryo (or egg, respectively) and a field."

Gurwitsch, A.G.   *The Theory of the Biological Field.*

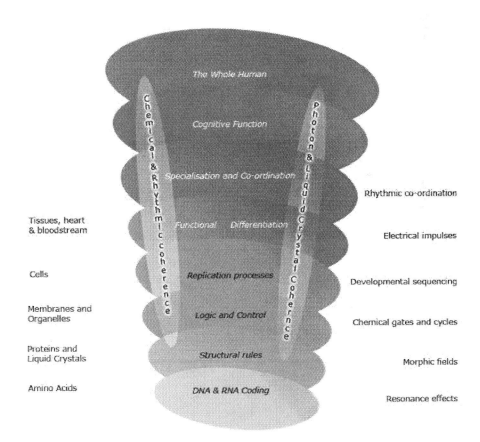

Theme

We reach the conclusion of our journey through biology in which we have been exploring the themes of who we are and how we came to be. We now return to the theme of how multiple species on the Earth have come into being, how and why their differences arose, and what is the driving force for increasing complexity of form and behaviour.

Here we encounter the crucial issue of whether the absolute purity of proposed randomness as championed by the Darwinian fundamentalists is justified. We look for whether there is even a tiny thread of "guidance" present and if it is, at how that might happen. Lastly we give indications of what this means for the spiritual context, and show that while the biblical creation metaphor and other stories that describe an external creator-god may be unsustainable, there is a core truth which maintains the rationality of perceiving a creative spirit, and a higher consciousness in the universe with which all life is connected.

Just how special are we?

In a book called "Life's Grandeur" or "Full House", depending where it was published, Stephen Jay Gould dissects our natural tendency to view evolution as naturally leading towards increasing complexity of form, behaviour or larger size. In face of the "obvious" truth that evolution began with bacteria and single-celled organisms and now displays the richness which includes whales, elephants and us – wonderful humanity – he provides analysis, backed up by statistical evidence, that we too are merely an outcome of the mathematics of variation. His contrasting image is that of a drunkard's walk along a street, with a wall one side and a gutter on the other. Random staggering in a space constrained on one side by a limitation (i.e. you can't get smaller than one cell) and open on the other (size and complexity have no simple upper limit) will eventually see the drunkard fall in the gutter. This is an argument for humility. We are not the perfected pinnacle of God's plan. We are just one example of a fallen inebriate – even if we are looking at the stars.

Humility is good for us. It does us no harm to reflect that our time of imagined superiority on the earth is a mere blink in comparison to the 150+ millions of years for which dinosaurs were believed dominant. (Note here that no particular dinosaur is known to have been around for so long. Species came and went, usually in less than 10 million years. For example the records for the most famous of all, T Rex, are based on only 20 finds, with three complete skulls in total, and span just four million years or so.)

Similarly, in face of the apparent success of multi-celled forms, Gould produces evidence that there is a greater biomass of bacteria than there is of surface flora and fauna. Much of this bacterial life lives within the porosity of rocks and in underground water. In addition, bacteria colonise a wide range of environments, including many which would kill animals, such as the deep-ocean fissures in the earth's crust where they live at temperatures above 450°Fahrenheit and pressures 265 times that which we are used to. So who's the big success? Bacteria have been around for over 4 billion years and the more complex single-celled organisms (eukaryotes) had a 2.75 billion year head-start on multi-celled creatures. It is hardly surprising if a great deal was achieved in this vast time-span, especially when bacterial generations succeed each other in hours rather than years. That's a lot of opportunity to try things out.

Although the evidence indicates that humanity has been physically evolved (e.g. upright posture and brain size) for more than a million years, our "more than animal" status is quite hard to quantify or demonstrate. While some evidence of aboriginal cultures may go back as far as 40-50,000 years and be shown for instance in quite remarkable cave paintings, the vast majority of all we are accustomed to think of as human culture and civilisation arises since the end of the last ice-age – about 12,000 years.

Only within this short time-span has mankind made the journey from hunting cave-dweller, or nomadic herd-follower into settled village-dweller with agriculture and animal husbandry. The growth has been rapid and accelerating, from stone tools through pottery to metal-working. Even a technology as fundamental as the wheel (with extensions such as mills and lathes) arose half-way through this settled period. Only recently have we become numerous. At the end of the ice-age there were perhaps a few million of "us".

So where does this leave our theme of spirituality? However hard we might look we will not find fossil evidence for soul or spirit. We might try to assign a spiritual agenda to cave-paintings, but it cannot be more than conjecture. Cultural evidence is limited to the time since settlement and anyway does not constitute scientific proof of anything. Clearly if we are to place spirituality into the realm of genetics and evolution it will not be easy. Nevertheless, we will once again show that there are gaps which undermine the scientific dogma and demand further investigation.

It should not come as a surprise if our answers reflect the recognition contained in our chapters on plant spirits and shamanism that there is a form of consciousness throughout the living world. There is pride and wishful-thinking which leads us into the falsehoods that Gould points out that derive from the human desire to see our species as a peak achievement. However this same pride also manifests as hubris (often masquerading as humility) which elevates the intellect above all other forms of knowing. It causes us to ignore other evidence.

Gould's arguments are so strong, so powerful in their statistics and logical inference as to be totally convincing. Indeed, we have to concede his case that there is no statistical evidence showing any tendency towards complexity of form or function, none for the inbuilt trend towards larger size and none for increased behavioural complexity. We are certain, and will prove from other angles, that evolution does have a "guidance system". So we must and will also show that the guidance system would by its nature have exactly the statistical characteristics that Gould presents. Unfortunately Gould's conclusion is the price we pay for looking assiduously in the wrong place.

Some readers may be hoping that the line we are about to pursue will be supportive of the recently popular "Intelligent Design" approach to evolution. We are reluctant to adopt such a label. For some who use it, ID is simply a more sophisticated version of the biblical creation story. For others ID may not imply a "God" but it carries some other implication that evolution has been guided by an intelligence which sits outside of the living process. We cannot simply align ourselves with either of these since for us nothing is outside. What we see is built in to life, is more subtle and in our eyes more wonderful than either.

It would be helpful to retain the use of the word intelligence, so please understand that for us, intelligence is a quality that is inherent in the living world. This will be one of many areas where we will step outside of a tradition of polarised thinking – science / spirituality, genes / environment, matter / energy, mind / body and in this case, God the external creator as opposed to random chance. As Robert Pirsig argues so powerfully in "Zen and the Art of Motorcycle Maintenance", quality comes first of all, and ahead of the dichotomies of dialectical thought.

Elisabet Sahtouris has pointed toward the simple contra-distinction between science, which starts with matter to generate consciousness, and spirituality, which starts with consciousness to generate matter. The two cannot be separated – at least not in us or the world we live in. Each is inherent in the other. She also points to the parallel distinction between Eastern and Western forms of science. For Western science whatever you can touch is real and for Eastern Science whatever you cannot touch is real (and the touchable is the world of illusion). Here too (using Bede Griffiths' phrase), we see a need for "The Marriage of East and West". We are asking you to see both as equally real and equally unreal. This may require that you step outside your cultural conditioning – not in making that cultural view wrong, but in expanding and adding to it.

We would also like to introduce an idea here which we will explore in greater depth in our remaining chapters. The universe we are presenting is one which is self-creating and self-creative. We would borrow from physics the idea that the universe as we know it started from a "big bang", from a time when nothing existed (in any form which we would recognise). Everything has come about from that starting point and we would wish you to think afresh of the big bang as a creative act, one in which consciousness was present, an act of primal spirit in self-expression, of the first matter expressing its being. We would like you to see every part of creation from then on as an extension of that auto-creative and auto-actualising process in which all that is, experiences itself.

When we come to the living world, and to the development of life and the evolution of planetary ecology inhabited by multiple species, then we are describing what Nobel prize-winning biologist George Wald called the presence of "creative mind throughout biology". It is in this sense that we attribute "intelligence" to the process and only in this sense that we would see a process of "design". However we see this as an increase in the importance and power of consciousness, not a diminution.

The alternative to entropy and competition

A creative view such as this flies in the face of two fundamental principles which have come to us through science and which now inhabit Western culture. The view of Newtonian Physics is that the universe is in a state of gradual run-down. In a process known as "entropy", all the energy from the big bang will go from its extreme of intense compression toward another extreme of dispersion and dissipation. Heat cannot pass from a cooler to a hotter body, so ultimately all matter must eventually end at a uniform temperature. Everything that we experience as life is a merely a blip in this miserable decay.

The biological model is equally grim and gloomy. Alongside the randomness is the over-simplified reproductive "survival of the fittest", which arose in Darwin's mind as an expression of the endless competitive struggle against scarcity which was postulated by Thomas Malthus. Malthus predicted that population growth eventually leads to the point where there are too many people for our resources.

> "The power of population is indefinitely greater than the power in the earth to produce subsistence for man. Population, when unchecked, increases in a geometrical ratio."

This is quite explicit in Darwin's work, as illustrated by the following quotes:-

> "Nothing is easier than to admit the truth of the universal struggle for life, or more difficult than to constantly bear that conclusion in mind. Yet unless it be thoroughly engrained in the mind I am convinced that the whole economy of nature, with every fact on distribution, rarity, abundance, extinction and variation, will be dimly seen or quite misunderstood."

from the introduction to "On the origin of species" – and later

> "It is the doctrine of Malthus applied with manifold force to the whole animal and vegetable kingdoms".

We referred above to Gould's presentation of the success of bacteria. Previously we cited Lynn Margulis' widely-accepted view of the development of eukaryotic cells from prokaryotes and suggested a process in which the eukaryotes became beneficiaries of a co-operation or symbiosis between previously separate micro-organisms. Arguably, the further development of multi-celled creatures extended that process of cellular co-operation to a very advanced level. How does it feel to think of yourself as trillions of bacteria all stacked co-operatively together? We recognise that the notion is slightly whimsical but it is also not without a grain of truth; that we are bacteria's greatest creation. Not only are we single cells in massive co-operation and a long-term host that provides a stable living environment for decades at a time, we have even been perfected to the level where we will purposely manufacture more of their number and sell them by the billion in pots for consumption. Mmm Danone!

It is worth noting in addition, that every bacteria can exchange DNA directly with any other (Margulis again) and that effectively they can be regarded not as species, but as genome-shifting strains. In her more recent work she suggests that evolution includes the trade of entire genomes in more complex organisms, particularly the metamorphosing insects. As mentioned before, the genetic material also includes transposable elements which can move within the genome, and it is also known that the protein sequences can edit and repair themselves. There is no evidence we know of yet that material is exchanged (other than destructively) with bacteria and viruses that inhabit human bodies but it is entirely possible.

Mae-Wan Ho ("Rainbow and the Worm") deals extensively with the physics of an anti-entropic view of life and we have no space for detailed exposition here. Hugely simplified, we will just say that the second law of thermodynamics, from which the idea of run-down derives, deals with isolated or closed systems and deals at the level of heat energy. It does not deal adequately either with systems which store energy or systems which retain information about themselves. Nor does the Law address the question of what life indicates for the boundaries of closed systems or what a conscious universe does to the definition of "isolated". Suffice it to say that we do not accept that the second law provides good guidance for our planet to live by. We would prefer to concentrate on the alternative.

What is more apposite here is the biological view that Dr. Elisabet Sahtouris presents ("Earthdance: Living Systems in Evolution"). She identifies cycles of evolution which can be demonstrated in different types of ecosystems. These have strong implications for our view of a competitive living world and for the notion of limitation and scarcity.

In her view, immature ecosystems (Type I) are characterised by organisms which are themselves not mature and are competing to find space. In more mature ecosystems (Type III) the later descendants of these organisms have evolved in a way which feeds their competitors and which makes them collaborators. The process of life creates a format of built-in negotiation leading to greater stability. Her view transcends the traditional Darwinian view of random mutation and natural selection among individuals. It also takes us beyond the extension of natural selection to the species operating as a whole, as well as the inverse Dawkins view that the competition is between genes, via the species which carry them (as indicated by his book title, "The Selfish Gene").

Sahtouris' view is that the survival of the whole ecosystem depends on the balance of tensions at all these levels. The ecosystem as a whole survives when the balancing process itself works. There is a tension between the impulse for the individual or the species to gain its maximum benefit, and the need for such development not to undermine the success of the whole. The individual or species cannot ultimately be successful at the expense of the whole. For this reason, a plague bacillus which regularly kills its hosts is less well adapted than the bacterium which gives you a sore throat year after year; the probiotic that we sell in pots is arguably the best-adapted of all.

We will revisit this view later, as it is a mirror of other theories which are valuable at the societal level and which describe the evolution of cultures. The diagram here which depicts the cycle Sahtouris describes will be seen as an example of a more generic process. We have added to her labels for some of the stages to widen their context.

Perhaps you can visualise two or three cycles super-imposed and viewed from above, forming a helix (cylindrical spiral) – inhabiting the spiral of development that we are depicting or overlaying the 'target' diagram, propelling its growth from centre to periphery. We have attempted to show this, which you can see as Plate 4 (Page 43c). Perhaps you can also visualise that in the area of individuation and development there might be many ways in which this would happen – the development of new versions of an organism alongside the old, the arrival of an additional organism from elsewhere which adds to the ecosystem complexity, or the development of more advanced characteristics to which other species in the system have to adjust.

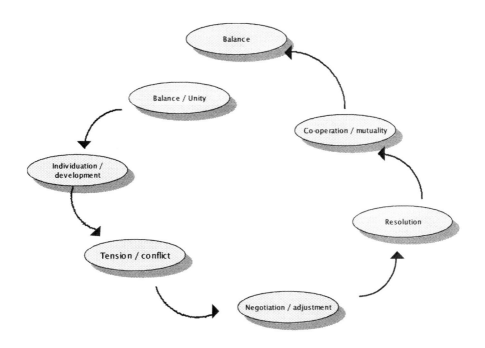

Added to this, there is a need to imagine that the changes in such a cycle may be happening at any of the levels which we encountered when describing the biological complexity. For example an organism might develop a new piece of chemistry that requires adaptation on the part of another species which feeds on it or from it. At another level it might develop a capability such that it is faster, or has better sensing mechanisms. Its rhythms and cycles might change, for instance breeding slower or faster. So change may be generated at any of those levels and may have its impact on other organisms at any of those levels.

Fundamentalist Darwinians might argue that such features are properties which emerge as by-products of a competitive system. This cannot be simply disproved by external observation and this gives their case its appearance of strength. When deeper relationships or the existence of consciousness are not part of the picture, the fundamentalist view can appear sufficient. Our view is that there is abundant cause to see eco-systems as co-creative cycles, not linear phenomena.

Within this co-creation, the system is likely in our view to explore and exploit any direction and colonise any niche available to it. For this reason, it is to be expected that Stephen Jay Gould's statistics would not show a compulsive trend toward complexity. However, this is not the same as saying that the process is purely random – merely that it could not be distinguished statistically from it. It is not the same as saying that complexity is simply a manifestation of "the drunkards walk" – staggering between the minimal wall of single-celled simplicity and the open road of complexity. It is equally the case that an inherently auto-creative and self-exploring consciousness would behave in the way that Gould observes – not staggering, but dancing in free-form both close to and away from the wall.

Readers will make their own judgements whether fundamentalist Darwinism makes a truly convincing case once all the information is included, and when the full picture of the inheritance process is truly observed. For instance, if genomes repair mutations and bring new "genes" (or expressions) into service, what governs the editing process. How do the "editor" genes know which mutations to keep?

Equally, returning to the underlying view of competition for scarce resources, how does Malthus' doctrine stand up when tested against a planet which started from zero in terms of life and food, and which has steadily increased in abundance of forms and complexity of expression? Here too, there is an underlying view which treats Earth as a closed system. As well as not recognising the developmental process of life itself, this apparently ignores the huge input of energy that we receive each day from the Sun. For there to be scarcity in the face of such daily abundance requires either huge failure of vision or massive incompetence. Malthusian thinking gives us a lame excuse that we don't need and we should point out that there has been massive population growth – beyond anything that he imagined – since his time. Nature has shown how it can take such energy and create abundant life from nothing. We need simply and gratefully to join in.

Similarly the doctrine of "survival of the fittest", which is a very crude expression even of Darwin's view, has been responsible for an entire culture of disrespect for nature. We are all familiar with the ecological planetary outcomes of this and it has been used to justify all kinds of abuse from Nazi genocide to corporate greed. It results in a business model which runs counter to the interests of humanity as a whole and leads to a corruption of social values. Malthusian thinking has undermined the core wisdom of Darwin's thesis and left it with a significant weakness; it cannot encompass evolution at the level of entire ecosystems that display intelligent dynamic harmony.

Clearly it is our contention that there is a component within this intelligence that is related to the presence of consciousness. Equally clearly we cannot prove such a thing purely by observation. We need to be participants in the natural world, and it is here that we must remember the views represented in our "talking to trees" chapter – views which were part of wide human understanding in the centuries before science chose to limit what is "knowable". The world has need of a restored balance in this arena and of Goethe's ways of seeing, and pursuing the scientific endeavour.

The bigger picture of coherence

In the previous chapter we detailed the kinds of characteristic that are necessary for coherence to be demonstrated in a large organism such as the human body. But internal coherence also relates to these other questions about development and change at the level of the species. Ultimately it must bring us back to our core theme of the pervading presence of consciousness or information in the universe. We are still pursuing our claim that subtle change can be amplified and reflected in a larger way. The presence of coherent energy-states, and their ability to resonate, radio-like, to the appropriately tuned signal is one of the key elements in this picture.

We referred previously to the difficult task which has faced biologists when they attempt to understand how a single cell differentiates into the many different organs and structures of a complex animal. We indicated earlier how Driesch's experiments on sea-urchins, as well as other's work, showed that an organism can still develop, even after the initial cell is interfered with.

At the start of development, all parts of the embryo have wide-potential to become any structure in the adult organism and there is no indication at that stage as to which part will become what. A piece of embryo removed and transplanted before cell differentiation has occurred will develop in harmony with its new surroundings. However, after differentiation has begun a transplanted cell will continue on its selected course, regardless of where it is grafted. It has also been shown that even if interrupted in its development by freezing or preservation in oxygen-free conditions, an embryo carries some kind of "memory" of which structures its cells are committed to develop into.

Science has searched in vain for chemicals that might be signals for differentiation (morphogens). What seems instead to be the case is that the determined state possesses properties which more greatly resemble a response to the presence of a "field". What seems to be happening, as first suggested by Joseph Needham in 1936, and more recently borne out in experiments by Tatafurno and Trainor, is that there is a vector field present which causes major polarities of electrical activity and major body axes to be oriented according to fields which run first anterior-posterior (that is, mouth to anus along the central tube of ingestion and elimination) and then subsequently dorsal-ventral (that is, between back and front). The third dimension, side-to-side is, as your mirror tells you typically symmetrical in many respects in most multi-celled creatures.

However, such indications leave much detail yet to be found. In addition, none of the above gives a clear indication regarding the development of behaviour. There is room to consider other possible influences. One such has been proposed and is our next topic.

Development of form and behaviour : Morphogenetic fields

A strong challenge to the purity of the view that everything is in the genes, or in the physics and biology, is that which is made by Rupert Sheldrake, firstly in "A New Science of Life", and then in "The Presence of the Past", a hypothesis which he calls "Formative Causation". This theory offers one example of the kind of mechanism that is required for consciousness to direct the process we are discussing. All the detail that we have so far examined still fails to supply us with a real understanding of how an oak-tree is oak-shaped or a liver-cell not a toenail-cell. We have shown that there is no one-for-one correspondence shown between bits of DNA and most observable functions.

There is no correspondence between the physical shape of DNA, or the form of proteins, and the shape of your nose. The genes are carried identically in your liver and your toenail cells. As Sheldrake points out and as we have indicated, the explanation of a purely genetic program for these factors becomes very weak. One formulation of the answer would ask us to be satisfied by such statements as "complex spatio-temporal patterns of physico-chemical activity not yet fully understood", as explanations for quite crucial elements of the process. It would be easier to say "I'm sorry, I haven't a clue."

Biological science developed in opposition to notions such as vitalism, the perception that there was a "current of life", and to un-provable assertions regarding the mind of God. Yet it needed some kind of explanation for the development of form. We have seen that genes may determine many differences in form, but that does not mean for sure that they determine the whole structure, nor that they are the only determinant of the form. We discussed the limitations of purely genetic explanations.

There is some explanation emerging in science that explains increasing size in organisms. There is a particular set of genes known as the Hox cluster that are responsible for staking out the spatial domains of the body plan along the longitudinal axis. This cluster is repeated in increasing numbers in larger animals. (J. Garcia-Fernàndez). No doubt more will be discovered to account for a number of features.

Nevertheless, it is clear that a patterning influence is at work and that DNA is not showing itself adequate to the task. Something makes sure that both your liver and ours are on the right hand side of our bodies. This is generally thought of as some sort of "positional" information which tells cells where they are, and enables them to manufacture the proteins that are correct for different organs and functions. We referred above to the postulation of chemical "morphogens", graded concentrations of chemical guides. None have so far been found, which we believe tells a story in itself but even if they could be found this still leaves the basic question unanswered. What determines the gradient and location of chemical concentration in the first place?

If you have ever seen sped-up video of organism development you might recall that the early cell mass does not stay still and develop in a static, linear way. There are stages where the whole "blob" will rotate and fold in on itself, like turning a split football inside-out. This creates a challenge for all attempts at explanation, such as how do the genes tell a whole mass of cells to fold, but is a particular challenge for gradients.

It is obviously difficult to establishing how such measurements would be made by a developing cell. Where would a chemical gradient start, or end? Relative to what starting point does an abdominal cell detect that it is spleen, liver, lung or rib, when all these are so close. Furthermore there is a duodenum winding past these, and many other organs. There is also some difficulty regarding the number of gradient chemicals required, when there are many different structures involved, and the difficulty of preserving gradients in a way for example, that allows ribs to be separate. Even with electrical fields to support such chemicals, the embryo is not an obviously promising environment for precise positional information and the presence of large amounts of fluid not supportive of positional stability. Again, all of these are good reasons to doubt strongly whether the DNA and cell chemistry alone can explain what is happening here.

An alternative conventional explanation involves the suggestion that there is some form of counting mechanism, by which cells know how many replications they have performed. According to the tally, they select what type of cell they should now form into. We do not know how cells would count. And this theory is hard to reconcile with experimental evidence. It does not fit well with the results of Driesch's egg and larva-tying experiments described earlier, and does not explain at all how undifferentiated tissue moved from one area of the organism to another will develop the characteristics appropriate to its new location, as for example other muscle tissue does when attached to the heart.

As a result of the problems inherent in making the chemical, positional or counting models of development work, and the lack of hard evidence for them, it is appropriate to take a look at the most credible alternative. This is known as the "morphogenetic field", and dates from the 1920's. Physics at that time would have been providing many reasons to think of fields. Electromagnetic fields had been shown in many guises, and are known to be integral to many aspects of physical form. Fields are a helpful means of conceptualising actions which take place at a distance, and with no visible connection.

You cannot see the field which causes a magnet to point north-south It is only the magnet (or other detectors) which are evidence that a magnetic field exists. Science is comfortable with magnetic fields, because it has discovered a wealth of detail regarding the relationship between this field, and electrical activity. It is comfortable because it has generated deep and wide-ranging theories according to which we can successfully predict results.

Morphogenetic fields are no less plausible than magnetic ones, though you would think otherwise if you read the objections of biologists. They are no less visible, and no more so. And if you accept that the detector mechanism could be an in-built intelligence in the developing organism itself, then we have potentially as reliable a detector as the sliver of iron in a compass. This is not by any means enough of a reason to believe that the theory holds true, since the argument is circular. Much more is required. But it is not in itself implausible, any more than magnetic fields are, and does not warrant ridicule. If you had been told that birds can navigate 5000 mile journeys on the basis of invisible lines of force round the globe, prior to the discovery of magnetism, you might have had difficulty with that notion too. We don't yet fully understand how birds detect those fields nor the in-built intelligence that navigates by them, only that they do so. But at this point in time morphogenetic fields have still not received anything like the level of research attention that have been applied to genetic mechanisms, and are hard to provide further evidence for. So what evidence, what indicators can we find?

One indication that there may be such a field comes from Kirlian photography. The Kirlian energy field is not normally visible, but can be made to display on a photographic film, when electromagnetic energy is applied to the subject. When humans are photographed in this way, an energy field is shown to surround the body, in the manner of an aura.

Kirlian photographs of leaves show the "aura" of a complete leaf, and then the similar shape which persists after a part of the leaf has been removed. It has been shown that similar effects occur with other organisms where a part of the body has been removed or damaged. This is not by any means proof of a morphogenetic field, but it is a strong indication that some kind of energy field is present around living systems and that this field persists even (as with these leaves which are detached from their plant) when the organism is not fully alive.

There is a large gap between knowing that there is a field, and showing that this field somehow conditions the development of form. One feature of growth that we are not used to in humans, which occurs in certain animal species as well as in plants, is the ability to regrow limbs, as a starfish or salamander can. A nematode worm will grow a replacement body - almost from any part. It will grow head and tail from a middle-section, and it can grow a right half from a left half (or vice versa), if sliced lengthways. Of course, any gardener knows that plants will grow from cuttings, and one of the common frustrations of British life is that the smallest piece of dandelion root or ground elder that you fail to pull out, will re-grow from deep beneath your lawn. This is not the same as growth from seeds. Whatever "program" is involved, is clearly capable of taking account of what already exists. A true "program", as is attributed to a seed or an egg, starts from a known place. Re-growth starts from anywhere, and yet is responsive to some kind of condition regarding what is, and what is not, already present.

Research shows that such re-growth can occur in humans as when a child's finger-tip was regenerated; it appears that this can take place if the wound is prevented from healing over. One reason why this makes a difference is known to be the presence of an electric current. But this still would not explain how the cells know what forms to take up, which once again cannot be done by counting.

In the absence of research resources being applied to this field of study, there is not much more to say about it. It is as much as we can do, to put it forward as an equally credible alternative to the orthodox assumptions.

Formative Causation

For Dr. Sheldrake though, beneath the old theory of morphogenetic fields lies a deeper explanation which he calls the hypothesis of formative causation. This hypothesis begins from the assumption that morphogenetic fields are as physically real as gravitational or electromagnetic fields. Each kind of cell, tissue or organism has its own kind of field. The field is taken to supply the "memory" of form which would be required to guide the organisation of developing organisms over time.

What Sheldrake sees as being new in his hypothesis, is that the structure of the fields is not taken to be determined by mathematical formulae (which inadequately explain evolution), nor from some simplistic transcending idea in the "Mind of God". The field results from the form of preceding organism, and is akin to a collective memory, one which changes and develops with the contribution of each member of the species. He postulates that the way this would work would depend on a kind of "morphic resonance". Resonance effects occur when the vibrational frequency of one form of energy is picked up by another object, and it too takes on some of the same vibration. When a lorry passes your window, and that window-pane hums the note of the lorry-engine, that is resonance.

Resonance, as a descriptor of action at a distance such as is necessary here has the benefit of supplying a mechanism by which the "sound" of a form might be transmitted. However, there is no obvious equivalent in this context to the air molecules which transmit sound vibrations from one place to another. We would need to find a medium of transmission. Sheldrake states that morphic resonance is different from other resonances, in that it is required to transmit only information, and not energy. This could be true, and it implies that information has no energy value. There is a deeper question regarding the nature of information and organisation and whether ideas have energy, which we will avoid but which you might choose to think about. If information has no energy / is not energy, what is it? For now we will look at the plausibility of morphic resonance while accepting that we do not know what the mechanism might be.

In general, resonance effects occur on the basis of similarity. That is, the size of the window-pane is such that, like a guitar string of the right length, its natural frequency corresponds to one emitted by the lorry-engine. A tuning fork is a piece of metal shaped in such a way as to have a very precise resonant frequency. Resonance occurs on the basis of a rhythmic activity (the movement back and forwards of a piston in an engine, or a pane of glass in the air). All substances are in some form of vibratory movement, from the electrons in an atom to the cycles of cell division, to the motion of planets. So all are in theory susceptible to resonance.

This means of course that the morphic field does not operate on its own. Otherwise a mustard seed in the child's mustard-and-cress tray would just as likely grow up as cress. It is a requirement of this process that the morphogenetic field should act on the ready-made operating structure of the developing system, which is already organised. The image of this is that a cress seed is already "tuned" to receive and respond to "cress vibrations", and mustard correspondingly to its own kind. The postulate of morphic resonance does not deny the chemical activity of genetic material, but works with it, providing an external guide to the development process.

As Sheldrake describes it, all past members of a species influence these fields and do so with a cumulative effect, which increases as the total number of members of the species grows. Under their collective influence, the morphogenetic fields in a new organism are not sharply defined, but consist of a composite of previous similar forms. He describes morphogenetic fields as "probability structures", in which the influences of common past types combine to increase the chances that such types will occur again."

Available space limits the depth to which we can pursue this subject. But to gain a full flavour of the nature of morphic resonance, and to understand a little more of the justification for the theory, we need to step outside of biology.

Rupert Sheldrake asserts that morphic fields operate at all levels of matter. Two areas in which there are reasons to think that they might have application concern the formation of crystals, and the folding of protein molecules. With protein molecules, we are dealing with very long chains of amino-acids. These chains spontaneously fold up into typical three-dimensional structures. Scientists in the laboratory can cause them to unfold, but unless damaged, they will refold into their original conformations.

The surprising thing about this process is that there are a very large number of ways in which molecules of this size might fold. The folding process takes time, and there are so many combinations that to try all of them might take several years - probably large numbers of years. The protein cannot test out which ones require the least energy to maintain the structure in existence and are thus the most energetically stable. The modelling that has been done for this process indicates that there are many different structures that would all fulfill this condition. No theory adequately explains how it is that the protein consistently adopts the correct configuration. It has been suggested that some routes may require less kinetic energy to adopt, but this has not been proven, largely because the calculations required are unbelievably complex. Accordingly, Sheldrake suggests that the hypothesis of formative causation would be appropriate to supply the "memory" which the molecule uses in making its folding "choices".

The other example in chemistry concerns crystallisation. Crystals are regular structures of chemical compounds less complex than proteins. In a similar manner though, it is not possible to predict from first principles what would be the "correct" crystal lattice for a particular molecule to arrange itself into. Nor is there a way of testing whether the selected structure is the most stable. In general, molecules simply will not adopt any other than their normal choice. In that respect crystallisation is a similar phenomenon to protein-folding.

The interesting feature in relation to morphic fields is the creation of new crystal forms, from new substances. Laboratories the world over are engaged in synthesising new kinds of substances, thousands of new molecules each year. So there cannot be any field in prior existence for this newsubstance. It is consistent with the theory then, that the first attempts to cause new substances to crystallise typically take a long time - sometimes weeks or months. It would also be expected that once this has taken place, the existence of a morphic field would cause subsequent attempts at the same process to happen more quickly. This is the case, and it has been observed many times, without any other sensible explanation.

Morphic resonance and behaviour

One other area where there are phenomena that are not mediated purely by genes and therefore hard to explain without some recourse to something like morphic resonance, is that of memory and learned behaviours. Although it is possible that Dr Sheldrake underestimates what the brain is capable of, particularly in the light of recent work on neural networks, he quotes research that is not easy to account for.

How would a behavioural habit be passed on genetically? It is one thing to show that a behaviour could arise over generations by evolution, and be selectively beneficial, and from that to conclude that it is passed on in the genes (even if we do not know how). But what of a habit that was trained in the laboratory, and found in the next generation? The famous Prof. Pavlov, pioneer of the conditioned reflex, trained white mice to run to a feeding place when an electric bell was rung. In his results, the first generation of mice took 300 trials to learn. The second generation took 100, the third 30, and the fourth a mere 10 trials. This experiment was not repeated successfully by him - which could be because the morphic field was already established, and would affect any future group of mice.

Another relevant set of experiments began in Harvard. William McDougall trained white laboratory rats in a water maze where they had to associate the correct choice from two exits with the presence of a light. The first generation of rats learned the maze after 165 errors, on average. Each generation learned more quickly, until after 30 generations only an average of 20 errors occurred. This was shown not to be in any way due to selection for intelligence. Even when McDougall selected the less successful rats to breed from, there was still a progressive improvement from generation to generation.

This experiment was repeated in Edinburgh and Australia. In both cases the rats learned very quickly, and appeared to be starting where McDougall's rats left off. In the Australian tests, they also used rats that were not descendants of previously tested generations, and even then the behaviour was learned faster. This removed any potential, not only for the inheritance through genes (which in the absence of a spontaneous mutation is anyway not compatible with normal scientific descriptions of genetic change) but also for an inheritance of acquired characteristics.

The last example of this that we offer was in the work of R.C. Tryon in California. Tryon was attempting to establish "bright" and "dull" strains of rats, and was selectively breeding to this purpose. He achieved his aims in the sense that he did show that "bright" parents had "bright" children. But he also found that in both strains, the maze-learning results improved from generation to generation.

It is close to impossible to account for results like these without recourse to some form of transmission that is not based in genes and physiology. There are alternatives that would not involve morphic fields - for example that the experimenters were influencing the rats psychically. But it is not clear how this would progress from one laboratory to the next, nor is it apparent why the experimenters (who knew the right answer from the beginning) would increase their influence over time. The only way this would happen, is if the rats were becoming psychically "attuned" to their masters. This is a feasible mechanism, but in terms of normal science equally unacceptable, and desperately weak.

There is a lot more that could be said about morphic resonance and formative causation, and it is worth reading Dr. Sheldrake's full accounts, which go into areas such as language, human learning, and Jung's collective unconscious. He also sees connections with David Bohm's implicate order, which we are not presenting in this book, but recommend as an interesting area for anyone who wants to delve deeper. We are not convinced that the balance between genetics and formative causation lies where Rupert Sheldrake sees it. We think it likely that morphic fields are subtler, and have less effect than he claims, and that more is occurring at the biochemical level as is indicated in Dr Mae-Wan Ho's work. However, for them to exist, and have any effect at all, is a major challenge to scientific orthodoxy. It is probable that something more is involved than is accepted by orthodox science and that "morphic resonance" is somewhere close to the target.

The hypothesis of formative causation is a further example to be added to others in this book, showing that there are forms of energy and connection which need to be taken into account in the proper development of scientific models of the world. These forms of connection share the requirement for "resonance" and for communication processes that are not recognised in scientific orthodoxy. More than that, morphic resonance is entirely consistent with the notion that consciousness is an active guiding force, and it provides precisely the kind of mechanism that would be required in the unseen realms. It fits well with all that we will go on to say about the nature of information in the structure of the physical universe.

The existence of such processes as intuition, resonance, healing triggered by pure energy, not to say those experiences narrated in the context of shamanism, come together with the small-scale biological features which maintain coherence and which are responsive to very small changes of energy. The scientific arguments for genetic determinism and randomness in evolution have been used to reject any possibility of an external creator. We have already hinted that we regard the biblical explanation as a metaphor. It seems unreasonable to us that such beliefs are regarded as primitive or merely irrational. To unsophisticated and pre-scientific cultures they may simply be the best formulations that have been available to encompass relationships that are beyond the intellectual frameworks they are exposed to, as well as being experienced in subtle and internal ways. Bear in mind that the descriptions of many aboriginal cultures and their world-views have been given to us through translations made by Western academics. They are likely to have been filtered through a world-view and language that does not encompass the original expressions. This is one reason we picked Malidoma Somé to speak on behalf of that reality. Such metaphors may deserve review in the light of modern understandings, but those who adhere to them do not deserve to be regarded as moronic.

We listed five "certainties" that we were seeking to challenge. The last of these is that by showing an external creator-god as unnecessary to explain our existence in scientific terms, we can therefore write off all spiritual experience as irrational, or as a side-effect of an incompletely evolved brain. Millions of people have experiences that correspond to our view of a scientific reality. It is very important to recognise that making a creator-god non-essential does not by any means destroy all of the potential for spirit to have meaningful involvement in a scientific reality.

Review

We have reached the close of our section on biology. Having covered a vast and complex area, we would like to attempt a summary of the key elements.

The accepted view in science has become a widespread doctrine which presents Darwin's theory of evolution together with recent theories of genetics, in a narrow and misleading way. We are told, or at least encouraged to believe that:-

Some chemical DNA sequences determine how organisms develop and grow

There is a clear and simple relationship between sections of genetic code and the development of characteristics

The environment in which development occurs is insignificant

Cells are simple blobs of jelly which host the DNA sequences – created by those sequences in order to pass them on

Living systems derive their complex co-ordination through the action of the brain and nervous system

Any appearance of consciousness, intelligence or co-operation is an accidental by-product of random activity in self-replicating chemicals

Changes between successive generations arise from random fluctuations in that process of replication

Any increase in complexity, growth in size or development of capability is a random stagger into a space of available possibilities

This all leads to an accidental evolutionary process in which the forces of competition for scarce resources determine which species will survive.

We have gone to some lengths to summarise the evidence for an alternative view in which:-

Creation can be seen as the out-working of a primary creative consciousness inherent in matter

The choice of which species survive is driven by an exploration by that consciousness of an abundant field of possibility

That exploration is a fundamentally co-operative engagement between the multiple forms of consciousness which inhabit the various species, leading to a spiraling dance into increased complexity and capability

The creative exploration led through self-replicating protoplasm and simple prokaryotic bacteria to more complex co-operative eukaryotes

Single cells are vastly more rich and sophisticated in behaviour and ability than blobs of jelly, are capable of sustaining life without their replicating nucleus and that they are in fact complex living organisms in their own right

When the limits to single-celled capability were reached, nature's exploration continued first with co-operation between cells such as slime moulds and then towards the development of multi-cellular plants and animals of increasing size and complexity

That both the single celled and multi-celled organisms are characterized by processes which drive coherence of function and multiple levels including:-

o vibrational quantum-level coherence and non-local connection

o sensitivity to electromagnetic fields and resonance effects

o photon communication

o bio-computer capability through the liquid crystal nature of cell membranes

       ○environmental influences on protein folding and gene expression

       ○rhythmic cycles of function at every level

       ○chemical messenger systems

       ○electrical nervous systems

Chromosome DNA is not the only part of the cell which affects development

The relationship between any "code" and the characteristics which develop is hard to determine

There are environmental influences on development and "editing" processes which intervene

The mechanics of timing and control are as yet poorly understood

That there are fields of information (parts of the creative consciousness) which maintain information about the forms that may develop – from crystals to organisms

All of this biological richness combines with perspectives from our section on consciousness, intuition and inner knowing. The presence in the world of nature spirits, devas, kontomblés and plant spirits is a demonstration of the ways in which human beings have experienced and continue to experience direct connection with the realm of creative consciousness. The informational connectivity demonstrated by Cleve Backster's plants and bacteria, and the intuitive knowledge of one human being by another are further demonstrations of the universality of this consciousness and of its ability to know itself in all parts from the largest to the smallest.

The cumulative effect of these facts is to show that all levels of living systems are working together in a harmonic and coherent process that consciously created life. This auto-creative or self-creative activity starts from the most simple level of replication. Like a computer in its boot-up process, the first instruction drives the second and third, until millions of instructions are loading and executing in an elaborate operating system. Life-consciousness has developed its own program, exploring and intuiting its way into material existence, developing and embedding its self-knowledge in material form, increasing over time in abundance, complexity and physical capability.

The entire spectrum of this intelligence and creativity is inherent in every one of us. Each of us can connect with the World-Wide-Web of creative consciousness if we choose to do so. Each of us can experience ourselves more and more as a part of that whole. In our next section we will further explore the physics which underlies all of this. We will explore some of the implications for the way we think and for the philosophical views which have embedded themselves in our culture. We will also look at what we understand as "reality". We will see just how science got itself bent out of shape and find some very powerful messages for the ways in which we view ourselves and for what we are as individuals and as collectives in society.

Section 3 : The underlying nature of reality and consciousness

A Moment So Close

funny how it goes with the moment so near
in a little while you can almost feel your fear
even before a time and a moment so close
find another way to open up your heart to me

every now and then there's a moment so close
I can see the future telescope in front of me
isn't it the way for a moment so near
to be further from the past than I would want to be

way up high, the little folks zoomin' by,
ask them why, or if they know the way we'll go?

underneath the skin in a moment so close
little particles a 'runnin' round inside of me
smaller than you go is a moment so near
more than I am comprehending is a part of me

thought it was the light shinin' down from the sun
in a moment it would travel 'cross the universe
couldn't you believe in a moment so real
more than words could say it more than eyes could see you there

Bela Fleck and the Flecktones   *From "Outbound"*

12. Curiouser and Curiouser

"If it was so, it might be; and if it were so, it would be: but as it isn't, it ain't. That's logic."

Lewis Carroll   *Alice in Wonderland*

Absurdity is the only reality

Frank Zappa

Theme

Beneath all that we are accustomed to call "reality" are aspects to the world which are invisible and which are present as forces, particles, waves and information about all of these things. This is the domain of physics. As usual in our text, there is a conventional view of this domain and as previously, it is incomplete either in what it knows or what it customarily presents to us. This section continues our presentation of the added elements which are required in order to give a more complete description of the world.

In this chapter we explore the deep paradoxes which physics encounters when dealing with these matters in order to indicate where the resolution to these paradoxes may be found, and to reveal a further area in which the mechanisms that we describe as "spiritual" are able to operate. Consistent with our approach so far, we once again find that consciousness and information supply the connective threads in this tapestry and in doing so, we lay a foundation for a creatively spiritual human engagement with the world.

Perplexing paradox

It is most important that you do not understand this chapter.

Our goal at this point is to set out with as much clarity as we can manage, just why this is. If it helps at all, we will be in good company. Richard Feynman, who as much as anyone developed the science of quantum physics, said of it

"It is my task to convince you not to turn away because you don't understand it. You see, my physics students don't understand it either. That is because I don't understand it. Nobody does."

Feynman was a nobel prize winner and probably the most capable of all physicists of providing a clear explanation. His book "QED, the strange theory of light and matter" from which the above quote is taken, comes as close to an explanation as any you will read, and manages to be witty and entertaining as well. And yet it is not understandable, because it is fundamentally paradoxical. (If you are so inclined, as a special treat you can experience Feynman's lectures direct on www.vega.org.)

Quantum Electrodynamics (QED) is the most complete explanation to date of how the universe works, how the matter that makes it up is formed, how it behaves. It can explain everything in physics except gravity and it's getting closer to that. Its mathematics are precise in predicting the outcome of experiments on the smallest known elements of matter and the measurements of the universe. It is more precise than Newton or even Einstein's relativity in describing the motion of the planets. To give a feeling of this accuracy, Feynman says

"If you were to measure the distance from Los Angeles to New York to this accuracy, it would be exact to the thickness of a human hair." But he goes on to say "The theory of quantum electrodynamics describes Nature as absurd from the point of view of common sense. So I hope you can accept Nature as She is – absurd."

We are not going to attempt to explain quantum physics in detail. Many of the books referred to do this well and we give a couple of web references to the most up-to-date material. What we need you to grasp is what it tells you about the world, and how distrustful you must be of common sense. Perhaps even more, it tells you where the limits lie to scientific descriptions of the world. This is not just the common sense that told everyone that the earth was flat. Common sense and science both rely on what you can observe and measure. The paradoxes in QED tell you that there are aspects to the world that will never be observable and measurable.

Paradoxes in general also tell you about the limitations of the human mind, of the five senses and of living in a world of time. A reading of the physics literature would also tell you that the cleverest people on the planet (in this arena at least) don't agree about what QED means, or how the gaps can be filled.

They can't resolve the paradoxes either, though we will hear that they are still trying. We will also hear why it may well be impossible.

The Greeks believe that if they could understand the laws of the universe, they would know the mind of God. Einstein used the same metaphor. Physicists are still attempting to find laws which are complete and which remove the uncertainty. Some still believe that the world is ultimately mechanical. Even if it is the biggest and most complicated piece of mechanism you could possibly have, there is a fundamental thought that if you knew all the laws, and could describe completely just where every particle in the universe is, then you could predict just how everything will go from here. It's called determinism. Of course they know now that you could not have that complete description, but they would like to know the laws anyway and some physicists still believe that they can find them. We might not know what the mind of God is thinking, but we would know how it thinks.

The belief within that mechanistic thought process is that there is a plan. If we use the term "Big Bang" for convenience as a term to mean the instant when the Universe appeared from "nowhere", the underlying notion is that the laws would describe precisely how the world reached its current state, how Jon is sitting at a keyboard and you are reading the words he typed. Perhaps it sounds absurd when put like that, but it is an impulse which has possessed mathematicians and physicists for millennia. While the search leads to some amazing knowledge, we need to dissociate ourselves from the belief in determinism. That is a mental trap which has probably delayed our scientific ability to see the real truth. The desire for certainty and predictability runs counter to a more exciting reality which is uncertain and creative. You could even take the view that the psychology of that desire is fearful and disempowering.

The mechanistic view survived intact for a long time after Newton. The cracks began to show as physics discovered that atoms are not like miniature billiard balls, but have smaller components like electrons and that these electrons are little energetic bundles in continuous motion. It broke more completely when Einstein showed that the energy and the matter are interchangeable. This is what it means when you say E (energy) = M(Mass of matter) times C (the velocity of light) squared. It tells you that matter can be converted into energy. We can do this, and doing so makes bombs and nuclear power stations. Energy can also be converted into matter, but that's a bit more difficult because it takes huge

(Hiroshima-sized) amounts of energy to make a smallish ball of Uranium, so we generally leave that job to the cosmos.

This interchange takes us to a core problem. In simplistic terms, when energy is being energy, it moves through the universe as a wave, like light or radio signals. When it becomes matter it can be recognised as particles like photons (particles of light) and protons (parts of the nucleus of atoms). Particles have mass and so one would think that they could be described as having a location at any point in time.

The problem for physics is that while that may be true, you can't measure it. Put simply, the apparatus that you would have to use would affect the particle. (For a graphic illustration of the indeterminacy problem, you can look on "youtube" for Dr Quantum's video of the two-slit experiment) This recognition led to the formulation in 1926 by Werner Heisenberg of his now notorious "uncertainty principle".

This principle says that the more accurately you try to measure the speed of a particle, the less accurately you can measure its position, and vice versa. Heisenberg's formulation showed that the uncertainty in the position of the particle, times the uncertainty in its velocity, times the mass of the particle, has a lower limit, which is known as Planck's constant. This says in mathematical terms that there is no way of measuring that provides certainty, and you can't get closer than a certain point. It does not matter how one tries to measure the position or velocity of the particle, or what type of particle it is. Heisenberg's uncertainty principle is an inescapable, fundamental property of the world".

With this, determinism dies and physics is obliged to work with what's left – our limited capacity to measure the universe. The theory that arises from this, put forward in the 1920's by Heisenberg, together with Erwin Schrödinger and Paul Dirac, is quantum mechanics. Quantum mechanics gets around the inability to provide exact predictions by forecasting a number of possible results for an observation, and saying how probable each outcome is. As a result the universe gains an element of randomness.

It might seem that it is not important to us as individuals if unpredictability is present at the level of particles we cannot see or imagine, but we will suggest it is critical. It will have been clear throughout this book that we are seeking to create spaces and undermine the mechanistic perceptions. In biology we spent a lot of time unravelling the fixed package of genetic predetermination and in providing an alternative to the purely random view of change. What we are doing here is similar. The physical universe is also not determined. And while there is an element of randomness that we have just described, what we will discover is that there is "something besides".

Once again we need to go a little deeper into the detail to understand the flexibility and the space for "something besides". Common sense is confounded by physics because common sense simply doesn't allow for anything to be two different things at the same time. It is more complex than we are capable of imagining. It is similarly difficult to put into everyday language, since our perceptions and language are based in our experience as physical beings. In consequence the means of description ultimately has to be mathematical which is to say, symbolic. In describing quanta as either energy or matter we avoided the truth, which is that they are essentially both at the same time. You could equally well say that they are neither one nor the other. Alongside the uncertainty principle, quantum theory has a "Complementarity Principle" which states that the two ways of describing, as a wave or a particle, complement each other and a whole picture only emerges from the two together.

In quantum terms, subatomic entities are neither fully particles nor fully waves, but rather a confusing mixture known as a "wave packet" in which we can achieve only fuzzy measurements of both. This is why Quantum theory came to find it necessary to predict the probabilities of outcome, depending on the experimental situation. However, the further development of the theory is to treat quanta as vibrating energy filaments known as "strings" and "superstrings". This re-interpretation is the foundation of the current search for a "Theory of Everything" (TOE).

The perceived requirement for a probability-based approach led to an intense debate between two different views of quantum theory. How does anything ever come into being? What stops objects simply fading in and out, or keeps us whole? One view led by Einstein saw this state of affairs as a weakness in quantum theory – that it was only a problem because of our inability to study nature without disturbing her. In his view, the discovery of quantum theory has not made the world suddenly unstable – a view which he famously encapsulated with the statement "God does not play dice with the universe".

Nils Bohr told Einstein that he should "stop telling God what to do", and the camp led by him and Heisenberg took a line more protective of the theory itself. They maintained that the quantum theory was complete and that the instability is fundamental, even at the expense of an adequate understanding of how things become fixed and real. The developmental line followed subsequently by David Bohm argues that some states are more stable than others and that the transition involved

"resembles the idea of evolution in biology, which states that all kinds of species can appear as a result of mutations, but only certain species can survive indefinitely, namely those satisfying certain requirements for survival..."

However it is not clear what those requirements might be.

You may be noticing some parallels between biology and physics in the balance of randomness and stability that are required in order for life as we know it to exist – that is, for there to be something that comes into being and survives, and for that survival not to be fixed for all time but to be capable of further change. Perhaps it is to be expected that these laws of nature would be in some way reflective of each other, but it still leaves a great deal unresolved.

We need to talk some more about the nature of indeterminacy and how it was discovered. In the crucial experiment which was set up to prove whether light was behaving as a wave or a particle (known as the "two-slit experiment") it proved impossible to say either, because the answer you get depends completely on when and where and how it is measured. It is only when it is measured that it becomes describable as one thing or the other (wave or particle). Until then the particle carries, in theory, all possible states in "superposition". It is the act of measurement (or "observation") which "collapses" the probability into a definite state.

Before we can begin to relate any of this to what ordinary folk understand as "reality" we need to take on board two more critical areas of paradox. One is the parable of Schrödinger's imaginary Cat – now as famous as Lewis Carroll's Cheshire cat and whose existence is almost as inconstant. This parable will help us explore the nature of observation and "collapse". The other is the phenomenon known variously as "non-locality" or "quantum entanglement", or the EPR paradox.

EPR represents the initials of three physicists, Einstein, Podolsky and Rosen who were attempting to prove that a definite structure of reality has to exist, in line with Einstein's views given above. They proposed a thought experiment which considered what happens when two particles (for example an electron and a positron) are prepared for the experiment as a pair with complementary properties (e.g. positive or negative "spin"). These properties are not precisely known at the time of preparation, but the fact that they are complementary means that whatever one of them has, the other will be the opposite. You don't need to know what "spin" means for an electron, just that the two particles have to "match".

In the thought experiment, the particles are seen to leave the point of preparation in opposite directions. At some point, when the properties of one are measured, this collapses its probability so that its spin is definite. By implication, the paired particle also becomes instantaneously definite in its properties, no matter how far apart they are.

In relativity theory, nothing can travel faster than light. The information therefore cannot pass from one particle to the other in the instant required. There is no form of preparation which can make the outcome predetermined. As a result, Schrödinger (whose cat we will meet shortly) suggested that the particles need to be regarded as "entangled" – connected in a single coherent state.

This result might seem meaningless, or trivial, or an irrelevant mind-game were it not for two facts. Firstly, David Bohm eventually found a way to turn this thought experiment into a real one and proved that the outcome is as predicted, as we will discuss further in the next chapter. Secondly – while the EPR proposal involves particles that have been artificially prepared together, it has subsequently been shown that any pair of particles, once they have interacted, remain entangled after they have separated. **They become one quantum system, connected even though separated by distance. This is what is meant by non-locality. It means that there are connections at the quantum level which potentially span galaxies and universes, and which we cannot see or detect.** These results show that there is a form of connection in the universe, that potentially covers cosmic distances and that allows information about one element of the universe to be known to another. So conventional physics theory acknowledges mechanisms by which one particle can "know" something about another, irrespective of time and space – the same sort of "impossible" connectedness that our intuitives were experiencing. What physics has not yet said is where and how that information is "held".

That damned cat!

And now for Schrödinger's cat. This is another thought experiment in which an imaginary moggy is shut inside a box. The box is imagined as one we cannot see into, hear from or otherwise detect anything regarding what has happened inside. Inside the box with the cat is a mechanism which, according to the completely random behaviour of a radioactive substance, might trigger the release of a poisonous gas, thus killing the cat. (In another version, there are two triggers such that there is a 50% probability of releasing food or poison.) Thankfully, unlike the EPR experiment, this has remained in the realms of thought only.

The question posed concerns the quantum state of the cat. According to the conventional interpretation, the cat remains in its state of superposition of possibilities for as long as the box is unopened. That is, it is neither dead nor alive, but in the "both / neither" quantum probability state. The probability wave collapses only when we observe the cat. Zen Buddhist readers will notice a certain similarity with the Zen question regarding whether a cat has a "Buddha nature".

There are many interpretations of this conundrum. One is to suggest that since we don't know and can't know, science has nothing to say about it and thus un-asks the question. This would be similar to the master's response to the zen question, which is neither yes nor no but "Mu" – a term which simultaneously translates as "both, neither and not applicable". Another is the core quantum theorist's insistence that the cat's existence is mathematically indeterminate, which offends our common sense since we know (in any normal sense of that word) that its fate was determined before we opened the box, even if we cannot prove it. A third imagines the generation of parallel universes in some of which the cat lives and in others, dies. Under this third theory all of us also branch multiply at every decision point, and so there are billions of Jon and billions of you the reader, in billions of universes. This makes for some good film plots, but has little else to recommend it.

Idealism and the role of consciousness

A more interesting notion is that it is our knowledge, our human idea about the cat, our consciousness that collapses its wave function. This has been resisted by many because it allows consciousness to interfere in the realm of materialist realism, but has achieved acceptance by some, including John Wheeler and Eugene Wigner, who have proposed that human consciousness is the missing link between the quantum particle world and everyday reality. It might initially seem that this is the road we are following, since it ties in quite well with the views we have expressed so far. For us though, it cannot be a satisfactory solution – at least not in the way others are expressing it. Our disagreements would include the following.

1.   Even if you are not taking a purely materialist view, it defies common sense to suggest that if dead, the cat was not determined to be so until the instant we looked. "Reality" knew it was already dead even if we didn't. To suggest that the timing is dependent on us assigns an unwarranted importance to human knowledge and is true only as an artificial mathematical abstraction.

2.   The leap from determining the state of a particle by measurement to determining the state of being for a complex life-form such as a cat that contains trillions of quanta, by distant observation is a misleading over-simplification. The quantum-level event was the either-or of the radioactive particle action. That has been determined and has been "observed" by the poison-release device. Our lack of an external read-out from this device prevents human observers from sharing the experimental observation. The cat's response to poison is something quite different and takes place in a much more complex realm.

3.   The view that it is only human consciousness which can supply the missing link of observation that collapses the probability wave is clearly contrary to the evidence that we give from the plant world, and to state the obvious, it is likely that the cat itself had some feline equivalent of an "Oh bugger" experience before it ceased breathing. No human would have anything to add to that determining observation.

4.   The view we have been constructing is that consciousness is an inherent property of matter – that it has been present from the moment of the big bang and is creatively engaged in self-construction. That being so, even if something else changed the cat's state inside the box – by definition the realm of

consciousness contained the knowledge of what it had done. This is a little like saying that "God knew", but the knowing is "within" rather than somehow held by an external entity. If we ascribe some kind of Divinity to this reality, then that Divinity is inherent in all things.

We believe that our view resolves the disquiet which gripped Einstein and overcomes the difficulty in resolving the questions of how anything initially comes into "being", of how the world acquires the kind of stability which we experience of it and of how we ourselves as experiencers are in a position to do so.

Human consciousness and active potential

Most of our presentation of alternative views up to this point has been in terms of a passive relationship in the spiritual world. Within that realm we observe that humans detect each other, plants detect humans and other plants. We hear that humans detect plant spirits and events in the future. All of that is about knowing and experiencing what is happening or will happen. We are entering new territory here, in which humans may consciously influence outcomes and be part of the creative intention.

 The theory that consciousness influences events at a quantum level, turning possibility into reality by determining quantum behaviour, is known as idealism. It is a powerful notion, and some books which are popular among those who are exploring areas of "new spirituality" have drawn the conclusion that it means each of us individual humans can create all that we want if we think about it hard enough. Films such as "What the Bleep" and "The Secret" have encouraged this mode of thinking and opened up whole areas of aspiration and possibility for their viewers.

While we are not about to say that such views are wrong as such, we do wish to present them in a very different light. You will by now be familiar with our penchant for exploring subtlety and complexity. We are distrustful of the simplicity which masks complexity and denies true perspective. We are seeking simplicity, the simplicity which emerges in the higher ground on the other side of complexity. Nowhere is the need to do so greater than it is here, if we are to avoid misleading people into a false hope and corresponding disappointment. At the same time a true understanding of this creative potential and its relationship with coherence at every level, is the key to huge possibilities for us as individuals and as a planetary collective.

In the more traditional spiritual context, the potential for our thoughts and wishes to influence events takes us into the realm of prayer. If we are to establish a science of the spiritual experience then we would be looking to show that prayer is meaningful and rational. Since huge numbers of people find prayer to be an important part of their lives this is not a trivial issue and deserves to be treated with respect. We will follow this thread further in our next chapter.

Review

Physics tells us that the underlying nature of the universe occupies a state that is describable as both matter and energy and that its state is not completely measurable to be either, resulting in theories that are based on probabilities that events will occur in particular ways. These probabilities do not "collapse" into one outcome or another until "observed".

Within this theory, paradoxes arise. The most important of these paradoxes is that one element of matter can be connected across time and space in an instantaneous way. The universe has already witnessed a relationship (entanglement) and this information is in some way not yet explained, stable and capable of persisting. The connectedness is not dependent on the dimensions that we think of as space and time. Our observations of the intuitive access to information and experimental proof from PEAR of the capability for thoughts to affect the material world show that there is a potential for what is known as "spiritual" experience to take place within the features of this known physical world.

13.From paralysing paradox to creative capability

Deep in the human unconscious is a pervasive need for a logical universe that makes sense. But the real universe is always one step beyond logic.

Frank Herbert

Theme

This chapter brings several strands together. It deals with the advanced physics and mathematics which take us beyond conventional views of reality to reveal the creative flexibility in the universe which is available when we accept its uncertainty and paradox. We find that theoretical physics can support our theme that information and consciousness connect and define the world, and discuss the ways in which this might work. We explore the boundary between physics and biology and examine the processes which facilitate the connections between the information realm and our cognitive experience and which enable small thoughts to have the potential to offer larger consequences.

Scientific limitations

We would hope that it is by now very clear that the view of the world which scientism has been presenting to us is sometimes false and often inadequate. Perhaps it is natural that those who are passionate about their discoveries should over-present them. Most scientists genuinely believe the truth of the world-view they are presenting. Often they are too specialised to see a bigger picture.

It is likewise to be expected in many areas that the both the composition and the presentation of the tune will be influenced by those who pay the piper and we must not forget the huge dependency that science (and therefore scientists) have on the corporate world for their funding. The days of academically pure research are long gone. Where the agenda is not set directly by business it is set by governments with economic agendas. It is what the mass of us have required them to do in the name of our economic welfare. Few of us are pure in this respect, so we need to take our share of responsibility. The least we can do is to recognise that the truth we get from scientism is not unvarnished, so our task of stripping this piece of furniture back to its original wood continues.

In this chapter we will discuss zero-point energy. Much of the investigation of this topic is directed towards the possibility that humans could learn how to release it and that it could become a free source of power. There is little funding to research its relationship with information and consciousness. We will need to do some of this for ourselves.

There is a temptation to present the stories from more mystical sources – the ones which report the abilities of avatars to relocate their bodies at will or to manifest objects from nothing. Machaelle Small Wright, whom we referred to in our chapter on plants tells a powerful personal story in this area. If such things are true, then it suggests that the potential for free energy, anti-gravity devices and warp travel may be found sooner through consciousness research than through technological approaches. However, since our focus is towards the more proven aspects of our topic we leave it to readers to explore this more anecdotal evidence for themselves.

So instead, our journey at this point takes us further into the way that physics understands reality, and how this informs the relationship between our personal consciousness and the world into which we are incarnated. What does all this mean in practice and what are the real limits to our possibilities?

Untangling non-locality and resolving paradoxes

One of the keys to full understanding lies in just how we understand "non-locality". What does this kind of connectedness tell us about our world and what does it mean in practice. When we look more closely at the real EPR experiments, we find that the "faster-than-light" communication between the complementary particles is measurably real. In the version of the experiment conducted in 1997 by Nicolas Gisin, particles ten kilometres apart appeared to be in communication at 20,000 times the speed of light. On a planetary scale, this speed means that communication across the globe takes one-millionth of a second. In effect, this is as near to instantaneous as our accuracy of measurement can determine.

It is a fundamental tenet of relativity theory that nothing can travel faster than light. This fact effectively defines the nature of time within the theory. It was Einstein's leap of imagination, to picture the universe when viewed from the particle travelling at that speed which led him to derive the theory, and with speed of light as the constant, it has to be time (or 4-dimensional space-time as a whole) that bends and becomes relative.

How are these two things, a defined limit and experimental proof that it is being broken, both true at the same time? The first suggestion we would make is the one which typically is required to resolve paradoxes and we will use the famous Zeno's paradox as an example.

This story pits the famously swift Achilles against that poor plodder, the tortoise. The problem is set out like a series of cartoon-frames. In the true and politically correct spirit of positive discrimination, the tortoise is given a start. Now imagine a series of strip cartoon "frames". In the first, the tortoise begins 20 metres in front of Achilles. In the first part of the race, Achilles dashes to the place where the tortoise began. In that time, the tortoise has advanced a little (frame 2). In the next view, Achilles again reaches the tortoise's second mark, only to find that the creature has plodded a little ahead (frame 3). This process is repeated, and Achilles edges closer and closer to the carapace but never, even in an infinite number of such steps, catches up. Each frame would have to be drawn bigger, to allow a scale which even makes visible, the ever-decreasing distance between the contestants, since by the last frame the distance between them is microscopic.

Whether or not you can describe what the precise flaw is in this story, you know that something is wrong with it. It does not match the reality we all live in. You may be mathematically confused, but when a call of nature comes, you will still make it to the bathroom in time, even if required to overtake a tortoise. What Zeno has done, is to take one of the dimensions in the world, and to cause it gradually to vanish. The time dimension in the first frame might occupy several seconds. In the second it would be a fraction of a second, and that fraction would get smaller in each subsequent frame. Not only would you have to draw each frame larger in order to even see the distance between the competitors, but meanwhile the time dimension has become vanishingly small.

The paradox is resolved when we change perspective and re-introduce the dimension of time according to our usual view. If each frame is of the same duration, say one second, and Achilles is travelling at 10 metres per second then Achilles is just behind the tortoise in frame 3 and well past it in the fourth.

Solution 1. An information dimension

So if paradoxes resolve when we change perspective, what would we need to do to resolve the faster-than-light communication that is implied by non-locality? One possibility is that the information which we are detecting in our entangled particles exists in a dimension (or dimensions) of its own. Rauscher and Targ have put forward an extension to relativity theory along these lines. Let's try to explain what that would look like.

If we again use the example of the "spin" property then the two particles are in an indeterminate state prior to measurement as far as the experimenter is concerned. At the point where the measurement is made of one particle, and the experimenter knows the outcome, the other particle is also instantaneously in a determinate state.

This means that the two particles are in a constant state of knowledge about the other. Each possesses the necessary information about their combined / shared state, irrespective of their position in space.

If we were to accept as true the limitation imposed by the speed of light, then we are by definition saying that the information does not actually travel in four-dimensional space-time. It has to be present in a different dimension which contains the others so that there is no distance to travel.

The existence of other dimensions is not unfamiliar to physics. Indeed, when we were discussing J.W. Dunne's experiences with precognitive dreams, we heard that he used relativity theory to explain the events in just such a way. Several physicists have proposed the added dimensions that would be required; Alex Green with a five-dimensional manifold, Elisabeth Rauscher with an eight-dimensional Minkowski space. This has led cosmologist Andre Linde to suggest that consciousness, like space-time, has its own intrinsic degrees of freedom, and that neglecting these will lead to a description of the universe that is fundamentally incomplete. We are not equipped to explain these, still less to judge their respective merits, but it is important that theoretical physics is entirely allowing of the possibility. What is new in this context, is the possibility that the new dimension is the container for consciousness at the quantum level.

We have referred before to the view taken by physics that there are more than four dimensions. Stephen Hawking addresses their existence by asking why we don't notice the extra dimensions, why we can't see beyond three space and one time dimension. He suggests that the others curve up into an unimagineably small space, less than one trillionth of an inch. The value of an additional dimension of this kind is that it takes us outside of the constraints of space or time as we know it and so potentially frees us from the restrictions of relativity theory.

Solution 2. Zero-point energy and the Akashic field

A second and highly popular potential solution to the paradox of faster-than light communication is found in a phenomenon called zero-point energy, and leads to other descriptions involving a "field" of connectedness. Several authors, including Ervin Laszlo, Gregg Braden and Lynne McTaggart have explored this area.

We are approaching the leading edge of physics in this discussion. Although the zero-point energy field has been part of physics for almost a century, it is still far from well-understood. To describe it, we will go back again to the moment of the big bang.

From a physics standpoint the world we observe now has four fundamental forces that hold it together. These are the strong nuclear and weak nuclear forces, both of which operate at the level of the atomic nucleus, plus the electromagnetic force which binds together at the atomic level and the gravitational force which governs planets, stars and galaxies. There is assumed to be a way in which all of these could be combined in a single theory, but none has yet been found.

At the time of the big bang, physicists believe that all these forces were a single "superforce". The physics of this has been demonstrated to be possible in an experiment during the 1980's at the CERN collider. However, the attempt by physicists to find a theory which describes this reality meets a major block because the fundamental particles which supply the force of connection would have to have no mass for the theory to work. (You can think of that as being like something which exists physically but doesn't weigh anything.)

Attempts to unravel this problem are continuing and more details can be found by those with the appetite by reference to the www.calphysics.org website and others. The best information so far from work by Higgs and Haisch, among others, suggests that the properties of some particles, rather than having gravitational or inertial mass as an intrinsic property, only acquire mass as a function of their interaction with their environment. This theory would place the properties of matter and energy outside of the particles themselves and make them, in effect, environmentally determined. This has huge implications. You may recognise the echoes here of the interactions at the cell membrane which lead to Bruce Lipton's pithy comment "It's the environment, stupid!"

What we are seeing here would mean that there is information which has been hitherto regarded as a property of the particle, but which is in fact present in an information field in its environment. Such a field could potentially be the medium of connection between the particles in the EPR experiment.

The existence of zero-point energy had been inferred by Einstein and others before the coming of quantum electrodynamics, but was explored more explicitly by Dirac and others. Quantum physics predicts that in the case where all other energy is removed from a system (that is, when the temperature is reduced to absolute zero because there is no motion any longer in the atoms) there is nevertheless a minimal residual energy at the quantum level because the quanta will continue to vibrate. Because of the number of quanta and the number of modes in which vibration is possible, there is a large quantity of zero-point energy in the universe. Even when all matter is cold, the universe is humming with energy.

The fact that zero-point energy is present throughout the universe and is present at the lowest level of known existence is seen by many to make it a prime candidate for being the underlying mechanism to provide a field that could hold the type of extrinsic information about the universe that Higgs and Haisch are proposing. This has been taken up by non-physicists, and extended to support the belief that zero-point energy is the container for consciousness and has been present since the big bang as an inherent feature of the universe.

The entanglement of quanta within this field – the known connectedness of specific information that exists between one quantum and another after they have interacted - provides the means by which the universe has "evolved" from instability into partially stable physical existence. That is to say, the reason that quantum uncertainty does not cause everything in the world to dissolve, and that there is matter in the universe that we can treat as "real" – ourselves included, is because the zero-point field has increased steadily in the extent of its entanglement. It is as if we were to say that each particle knows more and more about what it is, and retains that relationship with the whole. The energy which allows matter to "become" and then to "be" is held together by quantum entanglement. This provides the stability of what already is, but exists alongside the flexibility of all that is not yet held – the uncertainties which allow something new to be created.

Information about information

All of the above leaves something of a question-mark over the nature of information itself. In a physical sense we don't know what information is. All the signs are that it does not in itself have mass, though there are many unresolved questions about phenomena such as the "dark matter" and "dark energy" which form the bulk of the universe, and which could be involved. It is not at all clear what the relationship is between the energy that is present in the zero-point field and its capability to encode information. It is apparent that physics does not have apparatus to detect that information except where it is a property of a particle, and only to a limited degree even then. As we have just discussed it does not "travel" in any of the senses that other waves or particles are known to.

To be sure, there are other aspects of physics that are hard to describe. Gravity for instance, is a force of attraction between items of matter. It is weak in essence, but strong in effect when large amounts of matter are involved, acting in a fundamentally mysterious manner over large distances. We know of gravity because of what it does. We can describe its action and model the effects that a mass which exerts gravitational force will have on the space-time which surrounds it. We call that a gravitational field, because we know the effects of gravity at different distances from the mass which exerts the force.

Magnetism is similar. If you played with iron filings and magnets at school, you will have seen the effects of a magnetic field made visible. The force exerted by an iron bar, and its shaping of the surrounding space in respect of matter which is affected by it can be seen and measured. Like gravity, we know it by what it does.

In a similar way, we need to understand and know information by what it does. But gravity and magnetism exert a force and that force can be measured. We know what the effects of that force will be on other things. Information does not exert a force. It cannot be measured. When we discussed the quantum cat, we did so in terms of the fact of its life or death. We did not discuss and could not discuss in physical terms, the effect that knowledge of that cat's demise would have upon an adoring owner. It is not measurable. Its force in physical terms is zero, but the effects are no smaller for that.

Nor does information have a field in the sense that gravity or magnetism do. If the cat's owner is on the other side of the world from the cat when he or she learns of its death, the impact is not diminished by the distance. Its impact is detected and has its effect over potentially infinite amounts of space.

Information is not covered by Einstein's universe. We could say that the limits that relativity has defined for speed of travel do not apply to an entity that has no mass. Physics as a whole has nothing to work with if something exerts no force, is not a particle or a wave or even a probability superposition. The information may be real, but doing mathematics with something that you cannot locate, let alone measure, presents a challenge.

Nevertheless, at the quantum level, the mystery of entanglement is an informational event. The two particles are aware, have information about, have knowledge of each other. The information is as real and meaningful as any other part of the world being described. Arguably it is more real, since it is the information about each quantum which tells us what it is.

Even more, if the approaches of Higgs and Haisch are correct, and the inertial or gravitational mass of a fundamental particle are acquired from the zero-point energy environment, then the very formation of matter begins with the information. The implication is that certain fundamentals of the material world are created from that field. It is an echo of the biblical phrase "In the beginning was the Word".

We have been talking consistently about information, but it may be apparent to you that we could as easily have been using the word "consciousness". What we are presenting here is the view that consciousness is the sum total of a body of information. Your personal consciousness is the information that you hold about yourself and your world. The consciousness that we are suggesting was inherent at the time of the big bang, is the sum total of all information about every particle and wave that came into existence. Consciousness has expanded as the universe has expanded and as the quantity of information has grown and developed itself. In our terms, creative consciousness is in a state of continuous self-determination. That auto-creation is as real at the level of particles and waves as we saw it to be in the development of the biological world.

Limits to knowledge

The universe we are depicting is as far from a determinist one as you can get. What we are discovering is that nothing is determined until consciousness creates it. However, that does not mean that everything is totally unpredictable, since everything builds upon what has gone before.

Even without the auto-creative impulse of the universe, it was never truly predictable. We have shown the difficulty determinism has in practice with a paradoxical and quantum-indeterminate world. But people continue to believe that a determinist boat can float, in the expectation that a Theory of Everything will eventually unite all theories underneath the quantum paradoxical world. This belief continues in spite of the work Kurt Gödel published earlier this century, which should have been seen to sink the boat irretrievably.

One of Gödel's specialist areas, was a branch of mathematics called "number theory". This concerns our understanding of the properties that numbers have, and what rules there may be about types of numbers (like prime numbers, even numbers, odd numbers, squares, cubes and so on). The aim, as in the wider scientific areas, was to find and formulate universal laws, ones which would apply in all cases.

In effect, number theory is a specialised language in itself, with symbols that represent numbers. It is a way of saying things in a symbolic way about the properties of numbers. All numbers themselves are symbols. The symbol for 2 of anything can be added to another symbol for 2 of anything, and we know that the answer is 4 of anything, and we are familiar with using number-symbols for that kind of purpose. But you can also have a symbol that represents an even number, and a law presented in terms of those symbols that says, for example "if I add an even number to an even number, I always get an even-number result".

At this point we need to introduce another famous Greek paradox. Epimenides' paradox consisted of the simple statement "All Cretans are liars". There's nothing paradoxical about this unless you know that Epimenides came from Crete. If his statement is true, then he is not a liar. If he is not a liar then his statement is untrue. These conclusions are incompatible, hence the paradox.

The leap that Gödel then made, after recognising that symbols could be used in number theory, was to see whether the symbolic language of number-theory, instead of being used to establish statements about numbers (i.e. rules in number theory), could be used to establish rules about number theory. It turned out that this would be possible if numbers were used to represent statements, and what this meant in a bigger way, was that there is a way in which rules can be established that are about the process of establishing rules.

So far this is not startling. Showing that there can be rules about rules was not a big deal. But Gödel's next question was to ask whether it was possible to prove the statement "This statement of number theory does not have any proof". When he succeeded in proving it he created a paradox similar to Epimenides', because the proof contradicted the content of the statement that it proved. Unlike the Cretan statement it has much wider ramifications. It's a paradox with huge implications for what we are capable of knowing or proving.

The logical process that Gödel used can be extended and generalised so as to show that **all** formal systems would include undecidable propositions. The power of Gödel's theorem is in showing that it will **never** be possible to create a system of rules about the universe without it having the possibility of such internal contradictions and paradoxes. In this one shot, the notion of a determinist universe was blown apart. It makes it plain that the universe is not knowable - not just in the sense that we cannot encompass all knowledge ourselves, nor even in the sense of quantum indeterminacy, but in the sense that **no possibility of total and absolute knowledge exists**. It simply cannot be formulated. Any set of rules would be just like the human world, full of paradox and contradiction, undetermined and undeterminable. Heisenberg showed that we cannot measure everything. Gödel shows us that even if we could, we could not formulate a complete system of rules about it.

Gödel was one of a series of mathematicians who tackled some of the hardest concepts in the field, investigating the nature of infinity, certainty and the limits to human knowledge. Georg Kantor was driven to insanity by his attempt to encapsulate infinity – something which lesser minds might immediately see as a certain route to madness. Ludwig Boltzmann paved the way for the 20th Century investigation into a world of probabilities, proving clearly that there were limits to certainty, but was driven to eventual suicide by the determination of his world and his peers that such an idea must not prevail. Kurt Gödel eventually suffered mental collapse because he sought a way beyond his own theorem. He wished for mankind to transcend the logical limitations that he had proven. Like his friend Einstein, he knew from experience that some breakthroughs in mathematics were reached through intuition and not constrained by the limits of logical reasoning. Unfortunately he tried to prove the existence of this intuitive capability by use of logical reasoning and inevitably failed. The task was impossible, as his own theorem, and possibly a little more common sense, would have indicated. In a deep and desperate irony, he was trapped in his own paradox.

Alan Turing, a fourth in this series of doomed geniuses, took Gödel's theorem further and proved that it had practical consequences in the limitations to what computational machines might be capable of. He showed not only that there were limits to the extent of provability, but that these limits would also make it impossible to know in advance which problems were capable of solution, and which not. So science couldn't even say to itself "we can't know that", and put the problem to one side. Computers faced with such programs would never finish, but we would not know whether it was time to turn them off. Mathematicians might, like Kantor, be stuck forever trying to solve the unsolvable. While Turing's eventual suicide was almost certainly the consequence of appalling treatment by British security services who regarded his homosexuality as a security risk, he too was deeply troubled by questions about the thinking capability of machines, and regarding the true nature of his and other human minds. These deep and unsolvable concerns might well also have been part of his despair.

This strand of intellectual struggle might be just a tragic curiosity, but for the way that it mirrors a wider human struggle to accept that we live in an uncertain world. For a few mathematicians, lovingly obsessed by a world of deep pattern, order and predictability it is perhaps understandable that the failure to create formulae for everything might be unhinging. For the rest of the world the more mundane struggle throughout the last centuries has been to embrace the uncertainty of Gödel's world and to love the creativity that it gives to us. In the place of the order sought by mathematicians, one that is driven by God's word as expressed in numbers and symbols, we find instead a beautiful and harmonious co-creation driven by a Divine spark of infinite possibility. We see this as a more than fair swap. That it also takes place within an intuitive engagement of the kind that Gödel and Einstein experienced, is icing on the cake.

Thus, although it continues to yield useful and practical results, the intention to create a totally objective science, one in which we step outside as observers and encapsulate systems to view and define rules for, is shown by Gödel to be based on a fantasy where absolute knowledge is concerned. Even those systems cannot be guaranteed to be totally consistent. Objective truth is a bar of soap, which will squeeze through our fingers every time. Humans have to learn to love paradox and deep mystery. We find that exciting.

Being and becoming, coherence and freedom

In 1990, a book was published which laid out much of the ground for all that we are discussing here, and which anticipated much that was to be confirmed subsequently. In "The Quantum Self", Danah Zohar began to present the physics which could provide the kind of mechanism which might be the intermediary between the activity of the consciousness and changes which occur in matter.

We have already encountered some of this thinking when we approached the subject from the biological domain, so we are closing a circle from the opposite direction. Danah Zohar discusses consciousness in relation to "condensed phases", which you will recall from our biological presentation as being states that occur in materials in nature and which correspond with the capability of systems to become self-organising

Condensed phases of this kind apply to many systems, and this includes biological ones. Professor Herbert Frohlich of Liverpool University has shown that vibrating, charged molecules in the cell walls of living tissue, which emit electromagnetic vibrations, could be caused to vibrate in unison when energy was introduced to the system. They are so much in unison that they are finally in the most ordered form of condensed phase possible - known as a "Bose-Einstein condensate". The crucial feature of a B-E condensate is that the parts of the system not only behave as a whole, but they become whole; that is, the identities of the component parts merge in such a way as to lose their individual identities entirely.

The purpose of this mechanism is not known, but biological systems have generally evolved to fulfil some survival-enhancing purpose, and it is suggested that the B-E condensate might be a part of the way in which living systems create order. Other scientists have observed such effects, including bio-physicist Fritz Popp, who has discovered that living cells emit a weak "glow" which is evidence of photon radiation. Perhaps auras are not as imaginary as some people would like to have you think!

Other work in recent years undertaken by Dr Stuart Hameroff, and Prof. Roger Penrose has shown evidence that quantum coherence takes place in the tiny microtubule structures which provide a kind of "skeleton" within the brain's neurons. Penrose has advanced quantum theory descriptions of the ways in which this can mediate consciousness. In this, the microtubules are viewed as self-organising (orchestrated) quantum computers, providing "Quantum computation with objective reduction (OR)". The overall theory is often referred to as "Orch-OR". As Hameroff states

"Regardless of whether or not the Orch-OR proposal turns out to be correct (and unlike most theories of consciousness it is testable), it is the type of multi-level, transdisciplinary approach needed to address the problem of consciousness."

It is not important to understand any particular theory at this point – merely to recognise that such possibilities exist scientifically and are worthy of further research. In our biological section we saw that the types of mechanism required for an interface between biology and an external information field do exist. We are now showing the same possibilities emerging from physics.

It is very clear that consciousness - at least for most humans - is a very orderly phenomenon. For example, the very ability to write or read a book of any kind, requires an ability to hold a great deal of information in relationship and context. Particularly with books, which take extended time, maybe weeks to read, you are maintaining a thread which is far removed from quantum "soup". To write a book such as this one required an ordering world overview which has survived two decades in Jon's mind, with four very different drafts and continual deletions, insertions of new information and even modifications of perspective. It is nothing like the same book as at the beginning, but neither is it a different book, even though its style, order and content have changed fundamentally throughout.

This level of organisation demands a great deal of any physical processes that explain it. It is not some trivial accident - rather it is a high-order phenomenon which requires many levels of structure. The Bose-Einstein condensate, and the Orch-OR which has just been described at the cellular level may account for an ability to record states, or to resonate with external energies. (According to Zohar, up to ten million of our ten thousand million neurones may at any one time be in a state capable of responding to quantum-level changes.) But there is a great deal over and above this which governs the recording of information in our nervous systems, from genetic pre-structures through influences of remembered and learned patterns, to momentary modifications of emotional or mental state in response to stimulus.

Heart Coherence

We return briefly to the scientific evidence for intuition and to recent research, particularly that from Rollin McCraty of the HeartMath institute and to the very comprehensive overview by Raymond Trevor Bradley published in the World Futures Journal of General Evolution, which is to be found on the web at http://noosphere.princeton.edu/papers/pdf/bradley.intuition.2007.pdf_.

McCraty not only produces evidence of foreknowledge, but is able to show more of the means by which this is gathered and processed. Along with data showing the intuitive capability, experimenters were able to collect information regarding the electrophysiology of the brain and heart. This experiment shows clearly that it is not only the brain which receives informational input regarding the forthcoming stimulus.

In the tests, subjects were shown randomly selected pictures, some of which were calming or neutral and others known to cause an emotional response. The subject would press a button, and the picture would be timed to display after an interval of six seconds. The results showed consistently that the brain rhythms and heart rhythms would respond to the picture before it appeared on the screen. Perhaps most startling is that typically <u>the heart response occurred a full second before the brain</u>.

In Danah Zohar's model of consciousness, she suggests that the brain has two interacting systems, the coherent Bose-Einstein states that facilitate consciousness, and the computer-like ability of neurones to store and communicate information. One benefit of this view, is that it provides a mechanism by which the "brain-waves" that can be observed on an EEG would be co-ordinated. Many people are familiar with the notion of brain rhythms - the alpha state of calm and meditation, the beta-state of activity and so on. These patterns are quite stable, in spite of the complex moment-by-moment underlying firing patterns of individual nerve-cells. The presence of waves is more easily explained by a quantum "integrating system" - an electrical field that maintains coherence between the brain as a whole, and the low-level activity of neurones.

In a different set of experiments McCraty has shown that there is a direct correlation between the patterns of heart-rate variability rhythms and the brain-wave patterns displayed by an ECG. All these indicators point towards an involvement of both heart and mind in the generation of coherence. He also provides evidence that there is a capability in trained subjects to influence a sample of placental DNA to wind tighter or to unwind in response to focussed coherent thoughts. This has been shown to happen whether the experimenters are near to the DNA or not – effectively opening up a route for both energy healing and healing at a distance.

The Silva trainings which Jon taught began by increasing the levels of student's alpha waves through guided meditation, and initially with assistance from sound patterns to cause brain-wave entrainment. Jose Silva was certain that psychic activity is facilitated by having the brain in an alpha-state, and the success of the technique indicates that this is another route into coherence. We should also remind you of the statements by Howard Martin (Chapter 3) regarding the way in which heart rhythms provide a synchronising pulse throughout the organism, and the correspondence this has with Mae-Wan Ho's view of multiple frequencies of coherent activity.

Holographic models

Raymond Trevor Bradley's paper presents a comprehensive attempt to formulate a theoretical base for intuition. In our view, this is equivalent to providing the mechanisms by which our inner consciousness as a whole interacts with the external world, and therefore for the process of spiritual engagement with it. He draws deeply on the work of others such as Karl Pribram, David Bohm and Edgar Mitchell, which use the understanding of holography to build a model which combines non-local storage of information in such a way as to allow intuitive information to propagate through the world. A full and very readable account of the holographic model can be found in Michael Talbot's "The Holographic Universe". What follows is our highly simplified overview.

Holograms are often misunderstood, and the image that most people have of them is drawn from special visual effects, such as the security foil on the back of a credit card, which displays two images, one of them in 3D. Another well-known simulation is that from the opening of "Star Wars", where a three-dimensional projection of Princess Leia appears in the room saying "Help-me Obi-wan Kenobi". Both of these are applications of holographic techniques, but neither conveys what is of special interest about holography.

To record a holographic image, a laser beam is split in two parts, each put through a lens which diffuses the beam, and one of the beams allowed to reflect from the object to be recorded. The two beams are then allowed to meet, and their waves to interact, on the holographic recording plate. The interaction of the waves resemble the effect that you get with two thin layers of wet silk rubbing together, known as moiré patterns. A set of visual patterns arise which are not the patterns of either set of fabric strands. They are an effect of the interference of those patterns.

The image in a holographic film, in a similar way, stores the information in a manner which is not, to the naked eye, anything like the object being photographed. The image that reveals itself under laser light (or under the bright lights they provide for in-store displays, is three-dimensional, and clearly not located on the surface of the film as a photo would be. When you move, the position of the image relative to the surface of the hologram also moves. This image can also be projected by lasers, as with Princess Leia, in such a way that you could walk around it, viewing it from different angles, even though nothing is actually there but beams of light.

The lack of similarity on the surface of the film to the original object, is important because it does not store information as we traditionally would think to do ourselves. This book contains words in the order we chose to have you read them. It is linear, and provided you know the conventions of Western presentation, it is easy to start at the beginning, go to the end, and then stop. If you tear out a page, then what you have is one piece of the book. This is how we expect reality to be.

What happens in a hologram is different and non-linear. When you cut the film containing a laser holographic image, you can still see the entire image, from either portion. If you cut in half, then quarter, and so on, each piece will provide you with the entire image. You do lose something with each cut, which is the fullness of the information contained. The resolution diminishes as parts are removed, like a cheap digital camera capturing fewer pixels. But the recording is not linear, and shows a way in which information can be recorded, and patterns of energy constructed, that are not in a direct relation to the dimensions from which we view them.

Our linear thinking, as described above, might lead us to expect that our memories would be stored at a specific location in the brain. We might expect that like a computer, the relevant bits of information would be stored next to each other. In 1946 Karl Pribram went to work with one of the great neurophysiologists, Karl Lashley. Lashley had spent three decades researching memory, and in spite of Penfield's evidence, had failed to show any evidence of a linear recording. In fact all that he discovered seemed to contradict this belief.

Some particularly gruesome experiments by biologist Paul Pietsch made a real mess of linearity. Pietsch had discovered that a salamander's brain can be removed in its entirety and experimented first with putting it back the wrong way round, then later with other operations in which he shuffled, sliced and eventually minced the brains. In every case when he replaced the brain, the salamander's functioning went back to normal. Other experimenters have even produced evidence that feeding the minced brains of rats which have learned mazes, enhances the rates at which the receiving rats will themselves learn the behaviour.

Later, Pribram continued to work with the idea that memories are distributed throughout the brain - a belief which seemed to conform to the fact that human patients who had brain surgery, also never showed or reported the loss of specific memories. Similarly, accident victims were not known to forget some people but not others, or half of a novel. Even removal of the temporal lobes, where Wilder Penfield had appeared to find localised memory, did not have any effects of that kind. Pribram's conclusion was that there must be a way in which memories were distributed, but there was no understanding of how this might be accomplished by the brain.

When Pribram became aware of holography, he began to see it as a potential model for the way in which memory could operate, and contain the whole in every part. If the brain could record in a way which was akin to holography, then the results seen by himself and Lashley would be understandable. Seeking to know how the brain would generate the waves necessary to produce an interference pattern, he observed that the electrical communications which take place in the brain do not occur singly. Neurons possess branches like trees, and an electrical message radiates out like the wave ripples in a pond. As Pribram put it "The hologram was there all the time in the wave-front nature of brain-cell connectivity, we simply hadn't the wit to observe it." (Interview, Psychology today, Feb 1979).

Holography also provides a plausible explanation of how the brain stores the enormous amount of information that a human being must acquire over the course of a lifetime. Estimated by eminent mathematician John von Neumann at 280 million million million bits, it would be greater than the number of cells and neurons in the brain, but not, as we saw in chapter 1, greater than the number of potential connections between them. This also indicates that patterns, rather than individual bits of information, would be required for the storage.

It is also worth noting that the Bose-Einstein condensate discussed earlier, in providing a mechanism for coherence of brain-cell activity, would furnish the biological equivalent of coherent laser light that is necessary to generate the interference patterns that such a holographic process would need.

The power of the holographic model increases when we combine the understandings of the brain and memory with what David Bohm took from his standpoint as a quantum physicist. He drew the implication that there is reason to believe that something fundamental is emerging about the nature of the universe, and not just the brain in isolation. Bohm was deeply interested in consciousness and puzzled by the lack of interest displayed towards interconnectedness by Bohr and his followers.

The work of Bohm that achieved his recognition was special study of gases containing high densities of electrons and positive ions, known as plasmas. He found that electrons in a plasma cease to behave as if they are individuals, and start to behave as if they are part of an interconnected whole. (You may recognise the resemblance with self-organising phenomena like the Belousov-Zhabotinsky reaction.) Although their individual movements were apparently random, large numbers of electrons were able to produce effects that were well-organised. The plasma constantly regenerated itself, and would enclose impurities inside a wall, rather as a biological organism encases foreign matter in a cyst. Subsequently, after 1947 when he was made an assistant professor at Princeton, he extended his research to the study of electrons in metals. Here too, he found that the seemingly haphazard movements of individual electrons combined to produce highly organised effects. These were not entangled pairs of particles behaving as if aware of each other, but trillions of particles behaving as if part of some common process.

The classical approach to science leads along a path where the whole of a system is viewed simply as a result of the sum of all the interactions of its parts. The observations Bohm made with plasmons, and the theory of quantum potential indicated that the reverse could well be true - that the whole system organises the behaviour of its parts. He likened the behaviour of electrons in a plasma to a ballet dance, rather than a crowd of unorganised people, thus suggesting that

"such quantum wholeness of activity is closer to the organised unity of functioning of the parts of a living being than it is to the kind of unity that is obtained by putting together the parts of a machine".

As observed earlier, it was Bohm's work which led to the experimental validation of the EPR phenomenon, the paradox of particles "knowing" of each other at faster-than-light speeds, and to the proof of quantum non-locality. He came to the conclusion that the orderliness of the universe was "hidden", just as the laser hologram hides the picture we see. His view was that order is enfolded within the structure of the universe and this became extended as Bohm examined the hologram more deeply, into the perception that the universe itself is a gigantic hologram. This universal whole is viewed as containing / embodying a vast flow of energy and events, in which there is an underlying connectedness and organisation. This view was eventually published in 1980, in the book "Wholeness and the Implicate Order".

There are significant strengths to the holographic model. It provides a notion of an underlying connectedness, even if we cannot actually tell what it is. It provides a framework for aspects of reality that are conflicting and paradoxical, when viewed from the standpoint of other theories. It appeals to the notion many of us have that some sense of a holistic perspective, some alternative to the world-view of determinism and separation is required. It blends with more metaphysical views of the world - with the world of the Buddhist and the meditator.

Chaos and coherence

We have one more element to add to this picture before it is complete. Once again we have a parallel question in physics to that which we asked in biology. What is it that allows subtle and microscopic changes to have consequences which are visible and manifest at a macroscopic scale.

The biological answer was internal to the organism and utilised the capability of a small change to ripple through a field of coherence. Quantum coherence in a zero-point field provides one form of equivalence on a cosmic scale, particularly if the connectivity throughout is non-local and holographic. Anything can affect anything else and the ripples are potentially unending. Nevertheless we would wish to introduce an additional piece of science, which is known by the name "chaos theory".

If you have heard of chaos theory, it is likely to have been presented with an image, a typical example being that the beat of a butterfly's wing in Hawaii could bring about a hurricane in Tokyo. This is rarely explained – partly because it is difficult – and is inclined to seem to most of us both irrelevant and ridiculous. We will try to make some sense of it here, because it could be very relevant indeed.

We have looked a little at the idea of infinite quantum possibility and at the process by which wave-function collapse occurs, and things come to "be". We looked at this alongside the idea of dynamic systems in equilibrium such as the B-Z reaction. Typically though, the world does not behave as a system in equilibrium. It changes.

The attempt to model systems which are not in equilibrium has its own branch of mathematics which, like QED attempts to describe the realm of possibilities, but at the molecular rather than the quantum level. In modelling the real world, there are pressures, forces, dynamics of one kind or another, which interact to make certain outcomes more likely than others. In that description the likely outcomes are ones that possible realities are "attracted" to. For a marble in a bowl, the bottom of the bowl is an attractor. If you spin the bowl enough, the marble may occupy space at the sides, and higher up. But there is a dynamic at play (gravity) which draws the marble back to the floor of the bowl. The use of the word "attractor" should not be taken to imply that there is any will involved. There is no goal. Just as the marble does not care where in the bowl it is, the fact that certain configurations of possibilities are "attractive" only tells us that certain combinations of complex dynamic influences will combine mathematically in particular ways.

Attractors can take many forms - when graphed they can look like loops and whorls and messy spider-shapes. Mathematics does not always look neat or simple. But in the world of the fractal, of complex self-organising systems, we have an extraordinary blend of mind-bending complexity with repeated simple patterns. Like a never-ending series of Russian dolls, we can go from the largest to the smallest scale, and see the same form. But looked at as a whole, the intricacy can be awe-inspiring.

The world of fractal organisation is governed by what have become known as "strange attractors". These are still not well understood, but have one characteristic that is important to us here. The nature of the dynamics is such that although they will move into repetitive, self-replicating patterns, continuing over time to elaborate and extend, the pattern they generate will vary. Snowflakes are known to be never the same twice. The form of a snowflake depends on the initial conditions that form the first crystal. According to the precise shape of the first molecules that crystallise, the detail of the overall pattern will vary such that within the regularity of a hexagonal structure is room for an infinity of variations.

This sensitivity to initial conditions is absolutely crucial to the nature of what is possible in the human world. The butterfly's wings image sounds crazy and unreal, but the nature of dynamic systems that are governed by fractal development and strange attractors, is that a small change at the beginning of a process may magnify through its development such that the end-result is altered dramatically. A more familiar image of such sensitivity might be when listening to a Public Address system, we may experience the point of instability at which a microscopic change to a control, or to the position of a microphone, or in the room acoustics results in an abrupt shift that produces an ear-splitting feedback howl. Just because we cannot see the way in which a butterfly might trigger such a process in the world's weather systems, does not mean it is not real.

Spiritual and practical implications

In the next chapter we will attempt to summarise and present an overview of the entire pattern that is formed by the scientific evidence we have been examining so far.

The implications we would like to draw at this point rest on the recognition that the physics and biology of organic life has many levels of physical structure which together are formed into a whole that is capable of operating coherently. Each whole organism exists in a field of information, or is touched by a dimension that contains the sum total of all knowledge about the state of the universe. Each organism – each of us – is capable of receiving information from that field and has the potential from within its own local consciousness to send out signals that can affect the whole. Our own local process as a self-aware part of that whole is never separate from it. We are a portion of the field.

As a result, each individual has the potential to influence reality. We can create our own "attractors". We can put chosen signals into the quantum coherence of our own forms to influence the way reality behaves. We can put chosen signals into the etheric web of the field and flap the butterfly wings of our own thought.

In such a universe, inhabited by such beings, reality has enormous capability for change. Until we start exercising this capability we will have no idea of the extent of its influence. In this context, the power of prayer, of guided visualisation, of meditative intention and inner communion with "All that is" <u>have</u> to be real.

It is also clear that the extent of our personal inner coherence, and the level of our coherence with the field as a whole, will have a strong influence on the actual impact of any such activity. The timing of the butterfly wing-beat – it's synchronicity with the conditions – may determine whether it causes a hurricane or dissipates in the surrounding turbulence. We will return briefly to this important question in our final chapter.

Through the remainder of this book, we will explore the ways in which this theory affects our individual and social reality, and how it guides our development as cultures and species. We will look at the many elements of human activity and manifestation, and explore our collective potential as a spiritually aware species operating in coherence and creative competence.

Review

In this chapter we have described the mathematical proof with which Kurt Gödel buried the notion of determinism, and shown limits to our understanding that other mathematicians have presented. It is evident that society as a whole has been reluctant to take the implications of these truths on board, but in its place we find that paradox brings with it a world of creative flexibility.

We have discussed the added dimension and the akashic field models that others have presented as possible explanations for faster-than-light communication and as the locations where information about the universe might be stored, separate from the matter and energy.

We have explored the interface between the external realm of coherence and our internal states as the place where small amounts of energy or information might pass between individuals and their external world, as well as seeing the possibility of an entire layer of non-linear connection throughout a holographic universe in which every part holds a portion of the whole. Within this we find the potential for both intuition and prayer, and for a whole layer to contain the non-material or spiritual world of consciousness that we are describing.

14. The Voice in the Silence

In the study of Nature You must always consider

Each single thing as well as the whole

Nothing is inside, nothing is outside;

For what is within is also without.

So hurry onwards and try to grasp

The Universally-open Holy Secret.

Rejoice in this true illusion As well in the serious game;

Nothing alive is ever a one Always it is a many.

J.W. von Goethe   *Epirrhema*

Theme

The theme of this chapter departs from the analytical tone with which we have presented an alternative view of science. Our goal here is to weave our many strands together in order to provide an over-arching story to the unfolding of our spiral of emergence and to give some feeling to our view of life's creative journey.

The story of creation

One of the failures of the education system – at least in our country – has been to make science seem to the majority of pupils both difficult and dull. Despite the huge impact of technology on our everyday lives, and in the face of issues like genetic modification and climate change which raise big questions of public policy on a global level, science does not draw much interest.

For several chapters now we have been looking at some quite complicated ideas. Even though our approach has been mostly to view these ideas as if from 10,000 meters altitude, we are aware that some readers may have found such a journey demanding. We are grateful to every reader who feels this way but has managed to stay with us to this point.

We have tried throughout to sustain a number of threads that loop and interweave and it would be understandable if the overall tapestry is still not totally clear. While weaving those threads we have at every turn needed to justify our thinking with evidence, remove "what ain't so" from the pattern and push back against the forces of scepticism, determinism and flat-earth common sense. We have had to work around the historical separation of biology, chemistry, physics, genetics and evolutionary theory in search of an overarching view of the whole. This coherence is hard-won for writer and reader alike.

We would now like to revisit all those threads without the need at every step to justify our perspective. We want to present a summary of the whole as we see it. We think it's quite a picture. It gives reason to what huge portions of humanity has always known instinctively. It answers the most fundamental questions that we ask about who we are, where we came from and our relationship with the universe. We also think it makes an uncommon sense, a complete sense that satisfies both head and heart.

For the non-scientist reader this chapter will hopefully feel easier as we back away from the scientific detail. For those who have liked a scientific approach please bear in mind as you read this that while this description is intended to reflect the scientific knowledge we have brought together, much of it is not a scientific description. Early parts, if they could be expressed at all, would require purely mathematical formulations. Later parts stretch the boundaries of the language we have evolved well beyond its normal capacities. Please read this description as a mixture of literal and metaphorical expression.

From the All to everything that is

The following description is spoken by a very senior spiritual elder in Lyall Watson's story "Lightning Bird", which tells of a journey into the shamanic world by Adrian Boshier, a young white man in South Africa.

"In the beginning there was bosenaselo, nothingness, a great silence. Then something very strange and difficult took place. There was a voice in the silence. This was the spirit of nothing, a voice that speaks all that we know and see. But of this great spirit we know nothing. It comes from itself, is known by itself and goes out of itself. It is not for us to know."

As a description of the inconceivable, and an encapsulation of our starting point, this is as good as it gets. What existed before the moment of creation we leave to your own intuition and imagination, but our story starts with the Big Bang, when everything that is – an unimagineable force of energy and consciousness – began a process of material existence and self-creation. Starting from no space, no time, no matter, it began to be. You could call it pure consciousness, or essence, or oneness or even quality. For convenience we will call it "The All"; now it was in motion.

About 14 billion years ago as we now measure it, that energy and consciousness formed itself into the smallest of particles and expanded from its point of origin. The field of consciousness expanded, connected in its self-knowing. That self-knowing informed the most fundamental building blocks of materiality. The field allowed that self-knowing to remain intact even as space and time came into being, as the matter-in-creation coalesced, collapsing its wave-function from potentiality into determined form.

In that self-exploration some patterns were stable and some were not. The universe is known to be built on some crucial mathematical relationships, without which we would not be here. When something worked, a ripple was set up in the field of knowing. The All is the ultimate pragmatist. Those ripples, those resonances were known to other parts of the All. Influences spread and propagated. Patterns were established.

Einstein reputedly said that Time exists so that everything should not happen at once. Someone else (we believe) added that Space exists so that everything should not happen to you. Three dimensions of space and one of time seems to have been a stable pattern in which the auto-creative process would continue. Or it may just be the way that we experience it. But three is a more stable number than two. An axis of two is easily broken by a force at right angles. Try sitting on a two-legged stool.

Matter

Over time, that form expanded, changed, differentiated and produced over eons of time, the vast universe containing billions of galaxies. Spirals seem to have worked well and vortex patterns are common at many scales of the universe. The fundamental relationships of the different particles as they formed neutrons, protons, electrons etc., led by mathematical inevitability to the existence of the range of chemical components that we know, ranging from the small gaseous combinations such as Hydrogen and Helium to the heaviest of metals like Uranium and Plutonium which burst from the centres of collapsing stars. Layer built upon layer. Those fundamental relationships, with their configurations of electrons would lead to compound molecules, and stable crystals. Some structures would be stable, some would not. Platonic solids – the five regular convex tetrahedron shapes such as cubes and octahedrons, seemed to work well.

At no time did the All cease to contain the "awareness" of every particle, because the definition and the particle both existed, interlinked, throughout the field. Everything that developed, every gas, liquid and solid was a self-expression of the All, arising from its creative self-exploration. Each part of the quantum entanglement was held in the total awareness and as time went on, more and more of the information became entangled, and more stability ensued.

This exploration was not predetermined, not coming from a plan. The creative process **was** the plan. The exploration was not initially random either, because randomness only exists relative to a predetermined outcome. Randomness and the plan were the same thing – to start with.

Over time – huge amounts of time - more and more patterns became fixed. More material became known to itself and formed into stable relationships which remained intact as yet more of the energy formed itself into matter. Stars and galaxies formed. At the centre of stars lighter elements are fused into heavier ones, a process which still continues in our Sun and produces energy. This energy is available to one particular large lump of molten material that found itself trapped by the Sun's gravitation, circling (or rather ellipsing) 93 million miles from one otherwise insignificant star on the spiral arm of this one galaxy. That lump of material cooled and coalesced and became a planet with an atmosphere. Our story so far has spanned about 9 billion years, two-thirds of the age of the universe, as the oldest rocks are fairly reliably dated at 4.5 billion years old.

Our planet

Over all this time, the balance between what is determined and what is still in creation changes. From nothing at all being fixed, we have reached a point where the material components of the Earth, the atoms, are largely fixed. Randomness is reducing as more and more potentiality collapses into the known, as the universe moves from "becoming" to "being". The creative process now continues at a different level, one which is cooler and subject to the particular local conditions of Earth's gravity, temperature and relationship with its primary energy source. Atoms combine into molecules, which have chemical interactions. A common molecule is water, which covers the surface of the planet.

After a further billion years (give or take a day) the point is reached where the early organic molecules develop the capability to copy themselves. A portion of the All becomes engaged in a local creative process. The field may echo this elsewhere across galaxies, since all remains connected, but the conditions on Earth are particular. This is the only piece we can see physically and in detail. In this piece, the organic molecules eventually form liquid crystal membranes which separate one part of the organic soup from another. Layer builds upon layer. Forms which are successful add to the knowledge of the field.

Organic life

The balance between creative potential and the gradual encoding of stable patterns, which started at cosmic levels of energy and proceeded through inorganic form, is now explored at the level of organic matter. Some of this stability is chemically encoded in genes – chemicals which can perform more complex processes of replication. The All continues to experience itself through the development of organic forms. From atoms and molecules the experience increases in complexity with the construction of membranes into bacteria. Some bacteria subsume others such that the components become organelles within a more complex structure. Some combinations work well and thrive. Eukaryotic cells develop and micro-organisms become common. The earliest photosynthesizers, the blue-green algae, begin the long and gradual process of filling the atmosphere with Oxygen

Everything of this is a vibration in the field of the All, and every part of it is formed from the most fundamental units, from the quanta. Every quantum remains informed by the dimension or field that specified what it is. That knowledge is inherent to the all and all of that quantum information remains interconnected, beyond the three dimensions of space and the fourth of time. Beyond our conception and past our capability to grasp with the mind, the nature of quantum-level coherence is such that vibrations and resonances will propagate through the local field. Resonances became rhythms and cycles. Influenced by the mechanics of gravitational flux and pull and the daily rhythms of light and dark from moon and sun, additional beats are established in the rhythm of life.

Stability continues to be self-defining. That which works makes more of itself and is increasingly capable of managing its environment. Layer builds upon layer. Individual cells also find the stability which comes from co-operative behaviour for mutual gain and bacterial colonies develop into slime-mould collectives operating together, connected by chemical messengers and photon pulses. This principle is built upon as multi-celled creatures come into being.

The strands that are weaving this tapestry of developing life are intertwining at several levels. The Field holds the information that governs the stability of all fundamental particles in their collapsed, determined form as matter (Ch. 12). It also is holding the resonances and patterns of knowing which constitute the morphic field (Ch. 11). Every time that a crystal formed, it created a ripple in this knowing which made it easier for another crystal of the same kind. The same resonances are influencing the development of organic form, and the patterns that organic life will adopt. But now a new level of stability is being developed. The information is not only held stably in the field. It is now being embedded in the "memory" that replicating chemicals have. Those memories are being combined into stable patterns within cells which also have become self-replicating.

There is no real transition process in this story. No single point at which the consciousness of the All "splits" into local consciousness. We are the ones who make such distinctions, it does not. But what is emerging is the capability of the

All to differentiate, to become distinct and to operate at a progressively more local level. In its own way, each rock "knows itself" and holds its form, yet it is not separate from the knowledge of the All. It is a part, but in complete connection with the whole.

Complex organisms

Organic life develops a similar capacity to differentiate at the level of its knowing. As forms develop, the local consciousness becomes identifiable in the ways that people down the ages have described them to be – the nature spirits, the devic kingdoms, the gnomic energies that hold the Field's knowledge of a particular pattern of energy and matter. These resonances, patterns of consciousness, fields of knowing are the local emanations of the All which support the process by which patterns of chemical memory (genes and protein encodings) will form themselves into organic life. The plant spirit for a beech tree and that for an oak will have their own pattern, their own vibration. The All has manifested itself in more complex levels of matter and become visible at the chemical code level, but it also continues at the non-visible level as the Kontomblé, deva and tree-spirit.

All of these processes are also carrying energy relationships that inter-relate through forms of energy such as electromagnetic radiations, electrical potentials and thermal patterns. There are mechanical resonances too, as beats and pulses are established. Fluids ripple with the movement of the life within. Cell membranes continue to function as mediators, detecting messenger chemicals, managing the processes of energy acquisition and waste disposal as well as providing the biological microchip for direct cell-to-cell communication. Synchronisation and coherence are mediated at every level.

In this pattern of growth, the organism develops as a local reflection of the quantum whole. Portions of the information are held in the Field, the Zero-Point fluctuations, the added dimension which touches all others. What the organism "knows" of itself exists both within itself and in the Field. What it knows of the universe it knows both from its own internal information matrix and from its connection to the All.

Increasing complexity in a shared ecology

Organic life develops increasing levels of complexity in form and sophistication in behaviour. The process of self-experimentation and creativity is continuing at the biological level. Layer builds upon layer. Organs become increasingly complex over time in performance of specialised functions. Nerve connections evolve to develop greater centralisation and begin to form brains. The result is larger and larger organisms with greater behavioural range and ever-increasing ranges of environmental niche.

At this point we enter the more familiar territory of evolutionary genetics, but with the recognition that the creative exploration operates within a connected world. The huge flexibility of interaction and responsiveness to change stops short of total randomness. Every organism is aware of every other, but not just as a predator or a food source, or as another sharing its environment. Every organism is influenced by the field as a whole, and similar solutions develop to shared challenges in different areas. Creativity proceeds along lines that are influenced by what has gone before. Within the Field, all organisms are part of the web and carry levels of awareness of the existence of others as also part of the field. Each knows its "kinship with all life".

The song of life

The nature of creation, the continuing impulse for the All to experience itself, is such that each organism is expressing that creativity by surviving and creating replicas of itself. There is an inbuilt thrust to be established, to find stability, to increase the resonance of that particular vibration through the Field and make the harmonics stronger. To an analytical observer that thrust can look like competition or co-operation or like a product of chance as organisms respond to changes in their environment or in each other. In reality it is never disconnected and never truly any of those things which are merely descriptions for facets of a single process which is dynamic and self-correcting.

At the level of biological function, the coherence of all the many dynamics and rhythms, the internal connectivity of cellular structure becomes ever more elaborate. Nervous systems incorporate increasing amounts of information in the form of memory, adding another level of information storage above those held in the Field or stored in chemical codes. The phase coherence of the biological organism reflects that of the universe itself, forming systems which are sensitive to small changes and capable of responding to triggers from multiple environmental sources, including subtle energy stimuli such as that from a homeopathic remedy or spiritual healing. Many of these processes are self-balancing and support internal stability or homeostasis (like temperature regulation or fluid balance). Others are responsive to stress in adaptive ways. Those adaptations can be reflected and recorded in the codes which are passed to a succeeding generation and are capable of having influence on the nature of species change. Such ripples in the internal coherence are also affecting the quantum whole, because the connectivity is never broken. In consequence, the morphic field, the All's memory of how form develops, is influenced, steadily and subtly.

The steady increase in complexity eventually brings the development of intelligence, by which we would mean the ability of an organism to make analytical judgements of the information available to it and to choose behavioural options other than on a purely instinctive basis. The judgement of where programmed instincts stop and internal choices come in is very difficult to pin down, but it is observable that somewhere in the evolution of higher mammals this factor enters in. Only in the human being do we take it for granted that such intelligence exists.

The latest stage in this creative exploration takes place at the level of groups and societies. Our knowledge becomes encoded in culture and again layer builds upon layer as families and groups become clans and settlements, cities and states. The collective consciousness is further externalised in shared behaviours, traditions, mythologies and belief systems. Development occurs through increasingly complex social patterns and via socially adaptive thinking and value systems.

A self-aware species in a self-aware universe

Along with the development of intelligence comes a growth in the ability to be self-aware. Here too, we would not want to argue too deeply about the experience of other species. The crucial point is that humans experience themselves in a way that is conscious of their individuality and aware of their own creativity. Complex language becomes a feature that increases the species adaptability. We also have a unique capability to develop tools which fundamentally transform their environment. The encoding of information also extends its externalised forms in pictograms and written language. Arguably with computers, telecommunications and the web this extends into a substantial system of species-wide connectivity which ultimately makes all information available to all members.

The biblical expression that "God made man in his own image" does not fit this narrative since every part of the process and every level of creation is an expression of the All. However it expresses a degree of truth, in that our awareness of ourselves and our encoding of our own creativity in forms that are available to the whole is a unique reflection of the self-creative and self-actualising nature of the universe as it developed. At this point human creativity begins to reflect the creativity of the All.

Touching the All

We are not presenting human beings as the pinnacle of evolution, but the fact that we are having this communication and the nature of its subject matter are signs of a shift. The carrying of information in the Universe has been developing from the quantum level through the presence of persisting material forms and has become codified in self-replicating chemistry. In complex organisms it has become the ability to carry memory of events and to create new structures by ourselves, over and above those which the All creates "independently" of us. These capabilities, together with the capacity to become a conscious part of the creative impulse and to take a hand in directing our destiny by choice and agreement, almost certainly represent a new level of capability on the planet. The All is operating through us at a level beyond that which is the case for the devic kingdoms firstly as we externalise our creation in social structures and technological creations, but also as people whose "prayers" can also be creative.

Rather than being the pinnacle of anything, we would suggest that this defines us as a species in its infancy. We are at the start of a new phase of development in which the All expresses its creative process through an explicit act where we take on the position of conscious co-creators. We are learning our position in this process, and only just at the dawn of recognition that we even have such a capacity, not even close to knowing how to use it seriously.

In the description we have just given, the word intuition was not used. This is because it was not a development to be included in the story, but a component of creation that was there all along. The intuitive faculty is built in to the nature and the existence of the field of information and only our ability to verbalise and describe it distinguishes us from the rest of creation, which lives there all the time. In this and other aspects of our "mind over matter" capabilities we have also barely begun to crawl.

The view of creation as presented here and the significance of our place in it, involve some significant shifts in thinking from all that has been common until now. We are required to review our thinking about what is "real". There are implications for how we view ourselves individually and how we relate to each other as groups, societies and as a species. There are profound consequences if our view is anywhere near correct for the way in which religion, faith and spiritual experience will evolve in the future. If we truly take on the meaning of our relationship with the All, everything will look different from now on. We will begin to explore that new reality in the next chapter.

Review

This chapter has been the story of auto-poesis, the creative self-expression of a cosmic consciousness from the "big bang" to the development of a self-aware, creative, outwardly intelligent species. It has been the story of the spiral, the progressive layering of increased complexity through physical matter, chemistry, biology and descent with modification, and where that modification exists in both chemical and informational realms. It is a complex story which took the All a very long time to write. Humans are now beginning to be ready to both experience and tell that story as it really is.

Section 4: The Science of Human Experience

I have said that the soul is not more than the body,
And I have said that the body is not more than the soul,
And nothing, not God, is greater to one than one's self is,
And whoever walks a furlong without sympathy walks to his own funeral
drest in his shroud,
And I or you pocketless of a dime may purchase the pick of the earth,
And to glance with an eye or show a bean in its pod confounds the learning of all
times,
And there is no trade or employment but the young man following it may
become a hero,
And there is no object so soft but it makes a hub for the wheel'd universe,
And I say to any man or woman, Let your soul stand cool and composed
before a million universes.

And I say to mankind, Be not curious about God,
For I who am curious about each am not curious about God,
(No array of terms can say how much I am at peace about God and about death.)

I hear and behold God in every object, yet understand God not in the least,
Nor do I understand who there can be more wonderful than myself.
Why should I wish to see God better than this day?
I see something of God each hour of the twenty-four, and each moment then,
In the faces of men and women I see God, and in my own face in the glass,
I find letters from God dropt in the street, and every one is signed by God's name,
And I leave them where they are, for I know that wheresoe'er I go
Others will punctually come for ever and ever.

Walt Whitman   *Song of myself*

15.Reality and the Social Order

"The mental and the material are two sides of one overall process that are (like form and content) separated only in thought and not in actuality. Rather there is one energy that is the basis of all reality ... There is never any real division between mental and material sides at any stage of the overall process."

David Bohm   *Wholeness and the implicate order*

Said Plato:"The things that we feel
Are not ontologically real
But just the excrescence
Of numinous essence
Our senses can never reveal"

Anon

Everything is metamorphosis in life – in plants, animals to man and in him too.

J.W. von Goethe   *Spruche*

Theme

In debating the deep philosophical questions that humans ask about being and becoming we encounter the fundamental question of what the word "real" means and how we know what does, or doesn't meet our chosen definition. We know that the mind is fallible. This chapter explores these questions, and presents the implications of our model of the world for human perceptions of where reality is defined.

We then encounter a stream of development where the emerging complexity in our personal and social responses to life conditions is seen to parallel closely the biological emergence of species and the development of complex ecological balances. We find that the spiral of creation extends further, revealing the dynamic balance between the material, the energetic and the informational aspects of our psycho-social development.

Inner and outer mind

We all experience imagination, dreaming, illusions of the waking senses and errors of perception. Sooner or later, we all notice that other people experience reality differently than we do. Inevitably this leads many of us into fundamental questions of ourselves and the universe. We want to know what is real. We want to know what it is that we truly know.

The view of creation expressed in the last chapter and the presentation throughout this book of multiple levels of awareness and knowing have profound implications for our understanding of reality. In the universe we are presenting it is hard to distinguish Descartes' "I think therefore I am" from its reverse "I am, therefore I think", from Popeye's "I am what I am". Or is that Buddha?

All definitions are up for grabs. Some of the most fundamental particles – the very fabric of the universe - have their definition held in the zero-point field, the information dimension. Our biological being is the outcome of a number of vibrations in the quantum soup, responding and interacting to multiple stimuli beyond our conscious awareness. Our consciousness is everywhere, and nowhere. Information about ourselves that we think of as personal, is held somewhere beyond what we think of as our physical body.

Beyond this, the information that is available in this external field or dimension is also beyond present time. Both the past and the future also seem to be available judging both by common personal accounts and by J.W. Dunne's documentation of his own and other's experiences.

The fact that everything "known" is somehow co-ordinated by a field of information puts a very odd slant on what we have considered to be "real". The Oxford Dictionary has its first definition of the word as "Actually existing as a thing or occurring in fact, objective, genuine". Most people are more comfortable with "real" having something of solid substance behind it, but the blackbird song outside our window is also regarded as real. The description of the universe presented here greatly blurs the boundary between subjective and objective and places the determining features of the material world at least partly in a non-material realm. Arguably this has been true ever since wave-particle duality, but we suggest that it is now somehow more personal. It doesn't just affect what you and I know of the world around us; it goes to the very root of who we think we are.

The end to realism and idealism

This book is not intended as a history of philosophy. But there are some core strands of thinking which need finally to resolve and find a new place in human consciousness. Most of philosophy, most of science and most of human thought has operated for millennia on the basis of dualities; the either / or of subject-object, mind-matter, good-true, reason-emotion, body-spirit distinctions. None of these work effectively in a consciousness-driven universe, except when we apply them within quite specific boundaries. They are useful distinctions which make conversation easier and support an analytical process. But they are not reality itself. As Robert Pirsig puts it, in "Zen and the Art of Motorcycle Maintenance"

> "This eternally dualistic subject-object way of describing the motorcycle sounds right to us because we're used to it. But it's not right. It's always been an artificial interpretation imposed on reality. It's never been reality itself."

It is for this reason that we have emphasized throughout, the requirement for a third dimension beyond these dualities as depicted in our 'target' image and as represented in the spiral vortex picture.

The philosophical investigation into what can and cannot be known and into what is real is ancient and deep. The idea that things can be real only when they are observed was most famously epitomized in Bishop Berkeley's view that the tree in the quadrangle ceased to exist when no-one was there to observe it. Ronald Knox satirized this view:-

> There was once a man who said `God
> Must think it exceedingly odd
> If he finds that this tree
> Continues to be
> When there's no one about in the Quad.'

But was answered by an anonymous respondent

> Dear Sir, Your astonishment's odd:
> I am always about in the Quad.

> And that's why the tree
> Will continue to be,
> Since observed by Yours faithfully, God.

The central notion of idealism can be summarised as saying that all things are an expression of mind, or dependent in some way upon mind. You might see a reflection of Berkeley's view in the notion that only humans can collapse the wave-function that determines the fate of Schrödinger's cat. There are many subtle variations on the theme of idealism, but they tend to have a central agreement that some kind of observer is required (one mind, many minds, the mind of God etc..)

Plato is seen as the architect of the "realist" view, in which the existence of objects has nothing to do with humans or observers of any kind. The objects are deemed to have a reality of their own, in which forms are related to particulars – the actual instances of objects and properties. A particular is regarded as a copy of its form as in the example that a particular apple is said to be a copy of the form of Applehood and the apple's redness is a copy of the form of Redness.

There is a certain resonance here to the idea of a morphic field. The realist view has things existing independent of any sense of an observer. Even a reference to "the mind of God" would be in the sense that particulars could be held there, but actual forms are not dependent for their existence on God as a perceiver.

Humberto Maturana and Francisco Varela have taken a different angle of approach to this question. Their theory of what can be known is developed from the roots of biology. Where philosophy has argued its various points of view based largely on pure reasoning and analysis, these authors have examined the development of cognition and behaviour from the most primitive organisms to humankind.

In their beautifully argued book – far too detailed and subtle to summarise – they reach the conclusion that cognition is a "bringing forth of the world through the process of living itself". Their view, like ours is of a world which is self-creative; in common with Elisabet Sahtouris they use the term "autopoietic"). They provide thorough evidence and analysis that our reality is not "out there", and neither is it simply an internal construct that we develop as individuals. Rather it is a world in which they suggest that any individual who understands what they have said "will be impelled to look at everything he does – smelling, seeing, building, preferring, rejecting, conversing – as a world brought forth in co-existence with other people."

In consequence, reality has no independent point of reference. There is no external certainty available to validate our descriptions and assertions. The reality that humans live in is something we have constructed together and there is no absolute Truth. In their presentation, our neighbour's certainty is as legitimate and valid as our own; the act of recognition that accepts this fact is the act of love. It is the biological basis of social life, a biological dynamic with deep roots leading to operational coherence in the social realm.

Reality is socially constructed

The recognition that we do not simply construct our knowledge of reality inside us, and that reality does not consist either of the "things" of the world, is an echo at the social level of the underlying fabric of the universe. In the zero-point field, information is held outside of the things or the beings who experience them, as we saw when discussing quantum entanglement and in the work of Higgs and Haisch (P. 229). In this social realm there is a similar sense of the information existing in a realm of its own, independent of us. Even science is a social construct and not an absolute truth. Scientific objectivity also relies on consensus between its practitioners. In its absence there is no agreement about facts and no scientific "truth".

This thinking is to some degree present in older work by Berger and Luckmann. The title of their book "The Social Construction of Reality" sums up their viewpoint concisely. They present the way in which knowledge is held socially. Not only is society itself constructed by a process of social legitimization, but the individual's view of personal identity is framed within society's terms and his / her view of the world is framed by concepts which society itself provides.

You can see this for yourself in your view of identity. Please answer the following question. Who are you?

Now please answer it at least twice more, with different answers. You can play this game for as long as you keep coming up with new responses, or until you realize that none of the answers truly define who you are.

It is almost certain that your responses will include items such as your name, your gender, your job, your family status, your age and your relationships to others. You may possibly have reached the point where personal preferences or inner qualities began to be listed. Apart from a few of the more objective statements such as gender and age, the typical responses one gives this question have a social context and are, in effect, given to us by the way in which society views us. And even when it comes to inner qualities, these are not free from social construction.

Another theorist, George Kelly, working in the arena of personality came to the view that our individuality is formed according to the constructs we find to be significant, and where we measure ourselves and others to be on those constructs. Greatly simplified, George Kelly regarded each human being as a scientist attempting to predict the behaviour of the world around them. In his words "A person anticipates events by construing their replications". These predictions would take place on the basis of a repertory of measures that are personal to the individual. That is "A person's construction system is composed of a finite number of dichotomous constructs." For one person, an important measure applied to other people might be based on the construct "for me / against me". To another person that measure might be irrelevant, whereas the construct "communicates / does not communicate" might be very important.

Kelly predicted and showed that the level of empathy between one person and another would be based on the similarity in constructs that they use to predict or evaluate the world. It is clear that constructs might arise both as a result of personal experience and choice and by virtue of being provided by a shared culture. For example, to a person brought up among the Amish, the constructs of "Behaves like Amish / Not like Amish" might be important in their attitude to people. Their attitude to things might be similarly culture-related as "Referred to in the Bible / not….". A Tibetan Buddhist would not share these constructs. Nor would he/she start from the same concept of what is "real".

Eastern religions have traditionally taken a different approach to reality. As Bede Griffiths describes it

> "There is no objective reality outside us as opposed to a subjective world within. There is one reality, which manifests itself objectively outside us and subjectively within, but which itself is beyond the distinction of subject and

object, and is known when the human mind transcends both sense (by which we perceive the "outside" world) and reason (by which we conceive the mental world of science and philosophy) and discovers the Reality itself, which is both being and consciousness in an indivisible unity."

No doubt Griffiths, from his background as a Catholic Priest, also saw this as a parallel to the notion of restoration to oneness through Christ. But the Eastern formulation of this also comes closer to that of Pirsig. Our divided view and our experience are seen to derive from ignorance and illusion; that division exists only in us, not in Reality. Restoration to oneness with God is the underlying solution expressed as Buddhist "Nirvana" and Hinduist "Moksha".

From the above brief examples it is evident that the approaches we are taking have been pre-figured by thinkers and present in some religious perspectives on the spiritual world down the ages. The scientific evidence may only be coming together now, but there are thinkers who had the analytical understanding to see it coming and / or the spiritual experience to feel it and there are other cultures in the world whose approach starts from a much more helpful standpoint than the now-embedded Western scientific paradigm. The views being presented in this book pull these strands together and provide additional cohesion. We do not claim to have invented them. What interests us now, and in the remainder of this book, is what do we now do with the knowledge?

A new way to frame reality

The historical emphasis from science on a particular form of observation has made any kind of unified view quite impossible. As said here before and often complained of elsewhere, the dualistic view is self-justifying. It makes a (quite spurious) claim to "objectivity" in such a way as to exclude human experience and knowing from any possibility of delivering "truth". The objectivity is spurious because that choice of perspective is a subjective one. Perhaps more importantly, it is quite simply out of touch with the scientific nature of reality. Remember, we have used science itself, both in our method and in our reasoning, to establish that the "mind" and the "matter" are not in any way separable. Put another way, we have provided scientific evidence for the existence of those things which people describe as "spirit", "essence" and "soul".

Throughout our text we have documented the scientific evidence that supports the view which is also expressed by many others that consciousness is an inherent part of material reality, totally inseparable from it. As we have shown, there is a significant level of understanding of the foundations for this relationship. While it may lack much fascinating detail it is sufficiently advanced for us to work with in practice. With this established, it is time for the western world and the scientific fraternity to embrace the new reality and to let go of the old one. It is no longer fruitful for there to be philosophical debates about realism and idealism, when both are equally true (or untrue). It is no longer of any value to maintain the pretence of a meaningless objectivity in science beyond the boundaries where it has justification. As Bede Griffiths argues (echoed by many others through titles such as "The Tao of Physics" and "Dancing Wu-li Masters) there is a need for a Marriage of East and West.

We took this apparent diversion into the territory of knowledge construction and value systems (constructs could also be described as values) for two big reasons. The first, which we will examine in a moment, concerns the way in which the spiral of development continues beyond the biological realm. Since our proposal is that material existence is a process by which the "All" experiences itself, the existence of culture and large-scale society is a significant part of its development. This is taking place in a small blue-green planet at the outer edge of just one among billions of galaxies, but that fact does not reduce its significance, even if we are the first to do so. If that is the case we are still potentially an influence in the establishment of a morphic field for the rest of creation. More crucially it is also of considerable interest to human beings. A large part of human evolution is now taking place, not through changes in our biology, but by means of the cultures that we create. As we are all too aware, that human social and intellectual emergence has a huge impact on the whole of planetary life. A scientific understanding of who we are requires a model for this cultural development and the growth of our own knowledge. As we are about to see, the human aspect of spirituality and belief has its own evolutionary path.

Our knowledge, our values and the perceptions we carry of what is "real" are secondly of major significance when it comes to our individual and collective choices around religion, or around non-religious spiritual orientations. We will deal with this in the next chapter. The choices available to us are the very stuff of our lives and the way in which we may now see our own potential are exciting both personally and collectively. This will be the climax of our story.

Cultural evolution : Memes, vMEMEs and social dynamics

Having challenged Richard Dawkins at various points in this book, it is a pleasure to be able to acknowledge a major contribution that he has made. Recognising that he is unable to provide any genetic explanation for human culture, he has introduced into our language a fresh and potent concept, the "meme". The meme is a unit of cultural information that propagates itself across the ecologies of mind and produces the content of belief systems. The memes that we are particularly interested in are those that drive the values governing how people think, which we will call vMEMES. You may detect some resonance here to Construct Theory. Why do people value what they do?

The theoretical structure that we are about to introduce has the name Spiral Dynamics Integral (SDi). It is based on theories developed by Prof. Clare W. Graves and articulated in this form by Prof. Don Beck, by Christopher Cowan and in the Integral perspective of Ken Wilber. SDi is a wonderful example of simplexity; a theory in which simplicity emerges elegantly on the far side of complexity.

Many scientists have difficulty in accepting as a science any discipline that has to do with society as a whole or with the psychology of its members. But while it is clearly not an arena for the kind of experimentation that a chemist might perform, it has many of the elements that govern other accepted sciences – study of form, breakdown to components, collection of data, statistical analysis, verification against real-life examples. We will draw out some parallels between the way that genetics and evolutionary theory reveal dynamics in biological development, and the features of cultural development as it affects individuals and all sizes of social group. The mechanisms which balance the forces governing individual vs group and competition vs co-operation dynamics occur again here. So too does the progressive development of life through dynamic co-operation and increasing levels of behavioural sophistication that we saw in the Sahtouris loop. All of these are in play.

SDi is also one of the most scientific of approaches to society because of the way in which Clare W. Graves developed it. Where many theories emerge from people thinking about society, Clare Graves started from the collection of data. Based on questioning huge numbers of people about the values they hold and the conditions governing their lives, his theory emerged from the data itself. It is in the finest traditions of first observing, then measuring, then analyzing the results. At the same time it satisfies all the demands we can make for explanation of high-level patterns and of an intuitive feeling of rightness to a living process, with high predictive success and many effective toolkits for supporting change.

A theory which does all of these things will inevitably have much complexity within it. Those who seek full technical understanding are encouraged towards Beck and Cowan's authoritative exposition. For a narrative overview, Don Beck's CD set (www.soundstrue.com) offers a more accessible approach. Our presentation inevitably must be high-level and simplified. No change there, then.

The codes and principles that underlie spiral social evolution can be viewed as a form of psychosocial genetic material. Just as a biological being is required to respond to its context and its surrounding ecology in order to thrive, so too are individuals and social organisms. Just as changes occur in biological organisms over generations as adaptations are incorporated into the form and repertoire of the species, human thought systems also change and elaborate over time. Where a biological life-form deals with variability in climate, habitat or food source, the human individual too, responds to life conditions. Those life conditions are partly grounded in physical survival - the difference between tundra and rain-forest - but increasingly relate to survival in the social context itself as societies grow in size and complexity from village to megalopolis. The social genetic material is in the value codes, the vMEMEs which live within individuals and which govern their individual and collective management of change. We are not dealing with different types of people, but with thinking systems in people that express their way of coping with varying life conditions.

The codes and principles also have to deal with the in-built tension that exists between social cohesion forces and individualization forces. (Anthroposophical readers might recognize here Rudolf Steiner's Social and Antisocial forces in the human being.) Both are necessary and healthy. On one side are the gains that accrue from stable social structures with the associated tendency that society has to require conformity to shared values. On the other is the need for individual creativity and adaptation, the need that society itself has for those who can lead or pioneer responses to conditions of change and the natural impulse in human individuals for self-expression and self-actualisation. As Steiner would say, the healthiest societies exist when the community is reflected in the individual and when the creative strength of each individual manifests within the society.

The balance between these pressures is not static though. It varies with the external life conditions. It also creates its own push-pull. Each stage of development reaches a threshold at which the internal social conditions themselves demand a fresh response. As a result, it does not swing like a pendulum between the two, but expands and grows, shifting to a new level as it does so.

We can make this more intelligible by describing the levels of the spiral. The developmental process we are charting reflects the evolution of human society over time. It also reflects developmental changes in the human psyche from the simplest and most infant-like, towards the most fully developed levels of human capability. However, please be vigilant as you read these descriptions, for the reasons we are about to give.

What Spiral Dynamics isn't

Many psychological systems seek to establish typologies – different classifications of humans. These are the introvert / extrovert types of model in which people are unchangeably one or the other. The SDi layers are not types of people. They are thinking systems, coping mechanisms and value-sets that people may adopt and relinquish in relation to their life conditions.

The view of evolution in which humans are seen as the pinnacle of creation could also be mirrored in the perception that the different layers or stages of the spiral represent a hierarchy, and a ladder which humans should aspire to climb. Where the movement through the spiral might be seen as representing progress, this is only the case where the life conditions themselves are developing that way. Where they are not, it is entirely right for individuals and societies to remain in layers that are adapted to those conditions, or even to revert to earlier stages when conditions deteriorate. Each coping system and behavioural repertoire remains in the population and has value in supporting the layers beyond.

Similarly, since each of us is reading the description to follow from our own perspective, there is a tendency to filter. We might unconsciously assess each layer according to our own value set. Layer 3 may view layer 6 as unfit to survive. Layer 6 may view layer 3 as primitive and selfish. Layer 5 may see no value at all in the thinking systems at layer 2. But each is important and fulfils a necessary function. While each of us may have our centre of gravity in one layer, we retain those before and are most likely growing towards those to come, and may need any of them if we are to adapt to change. You are encouraged to read the description from a "value-neutral" perspective if you can. Try to appreciate the positive qualities of them all.

The last warning is that you should not confuse any of these descriptions with anything that might relate to a particular race, colour, creed, gender or political orientation. Human beings in any of these classifications can and do operate in any of the vMEME systems that we will describe. Indeed, the original motivation for introducing the use of colours to describe the various value systems was in order to provide a more meaningful way to understand the complexities of the South African transition than that which was offered by skin-colour and racial designations, which actually obscured the real issues and inhibited creative solutions. So having established that this is not a typology, not a hierarchy, not a ladder, and does not intend judgements about certain categories of human, let's look at what Graves' theory actually says about human emergence. You may find it helpful to look at the colour diagram facing Page 43 as we do so, as well as referring to the table that follows.

Colour	Life Conditions	Adaptive Capacities	Core values	Pinch points
Beige	A. Survival bands	N. Instinctive hunter-gatherer	Keeping Alive	Conflict and insecurity
Purple	B. Safety in numbers and collective wisdoms	O. Interpreting nature's ways. Kinship and elder wisdoms	Bonding, making sense of the world and safety	Lack of freedom for self-expression
Red	C. Self-expression and strength	P. Taking power over the world, Heroism	Impulsive, pleasing self, attention and respect	Bullying, exploitation and slave-empires
Blue	D. Seeking purpose and order	Q. Legal and governance systems	Finding a right way to live. Order and purpose	Constricts innovation. Control through guilt
Orange	E. Strategies to prosper by	R. Striving, analytical, technological, scientific	Success, status, capability, autonomy	Manipulation, greed, inequality, lack of care
Green	F. Seeking equality and fairness	S. Sensitivity, sharing and caring, community	Inner peace, equality, consensus	Over-conformity, limits to development
Second Tier Systems				
Yellow	G. Integrating and aligning systems in flexible ways	T. Knowledge, overview & integration	Competence, Functional flexibility, Natural flow	Material focus, lack of collective feel
Turquoise	H. Seeking synergies and holistic viewpoints	U. Intuitive and spiritual awareness, seeing self and whole together	Supporting the whole Making spiritual sense	? Individual mastery ? ? One size fits all ?

What Spiral Dynamics is

The full perspective of Spiral Dynamics reveals a complete model of human psychological and social development. It is underpinned by a recognition that there are also biological mechanisms, rooted in brain and neuro-endocrine chemistry. These affect the way in which value systems emerge and are expressed and the choices that people make within them. This model explains our changes in terms not of WHAT we think but of HOW we think. The content which Richard Dawkins describes as a meme arises from value systems or vMEMEs. Content as different as core Christianity, Moslem fundamentalism and strong Marxism may all be expressions of the same layer of values, the one which we will describe below as seeking order and overarching rules to live by. This distinction of content from value systems brings a fundamental re-orientation in our understanding of how communication should take place, and how conflict might need to be managed.

The oldest, simplest and most primitive of human adaptive levels is that which existed when the earliest hunter-gatherers were foraging the earth, dealing with day-to-day survival challenges. The social form is of a band or family, responding in a largely instinctual way to the demands of existence. Clare W. Graves codified the conditions as life conditions "A" and social form (or capacities) "N". The level A-N has been arbitrarily assigned the colour beige for ease of reference. Beige is close to an animalistic level of existence and is now rarely seen in the original sense described above. However it continues to exist as a code within people. If conditions arise through external emergency and social breakdown, or when people within a larger society are living at the margins of survival, beige survival codes can become predominant for the affected individuals, living in cardboard shanties and out of plastic bags.

Human beings aspire to predict and manage their lives and to increase their security in the environment. Throughout history populations have become more dense bringing a need to manage the potential conflicts between bands or families. Security increased through safety in numbers. Nomadic tribes adapted to work with migrating herds. Settled living brought the possibility of more sustained husbandry. In this way, the conditions of the beige layer give rise to the pressures which encourage people to co-operate and band together. In banding together, shared views are established and group processes and structures evolve. Society evolves cultures of elder tradition and codified responses to seasonal changes through ritual and rhythm.

The intuitive understandings of the world's mysteries are embedded in culture and shared belief and managed through mythical and symbolic relationships with ancestors, nature spirits and cosmic forces. This level is codified with conditions B, social form O and has the SDi colour purple. The colours, while otherwise arbitrary, do oscillate between warm shades for the more individualistic levels and cooler, bluer ones for the more socially cohesive and unifying layers.

Human beings also aspire to express their individuality, their sense of self. The ritual and conformity may come to be, or to feel excessively constraining. Individuals may perceive new responses to life's demands which stretch the shared boundaries of the tribe. Conditions may demand change which requires strong leadership or the tribe may feel the need to expand its sphere of influence. The need for safety and security take a back seat to the impulse towards power, strength, heroic expression and creation of new forms; the life conditions codified C come into existence. The response to these conditions is a power-driven and hierarchical social coping strategy P. The settled tribe is replaced by a feudal or warlord structure, a level codified as red. At its larger manifestation this leads to the type of empire that occurred under Genghis Khan. In human development this happens in infants when two-year-olds start to discover their own identity. For both individual and society the expression of these impulses is healthy, and needed for full engagement with life's adventures and risks.

Ultimately, the expression of self and power is not fully satisfying to the individual, who with age is likely to also seek meaning and stability, and the desire for a more permanent sense of purpose and belonging. For the society excessive red can become unhealthy. Power corrupts. Within society red bands become mafia-like. When a whole society is feudal, people will eventually come to think about fairness and balance and about life's higher cause.

The counterbalance to self-expression is self-sacrifice for such a higher cause. The counterweight to abuse of power is legal constraint and accountability to higher values, and higher powers ("God's laws"). Typically the most common expressions of this level with its requirement for order (conditions D) and structured response (Form Q) are strong religious hierarchies such as those seen in Catholicism and Islam, and / or strong legal structures with police forces and judiciaries (e.g. mid-20th-century Communist bloc Europe) . This cool blue level thus contains hot red impulsivity and channels it within the higher good. It is the (ideally) benign authority which supports children to come through their "terrible two's" and to integrate constructively with their fellows, accepting deferred gratification, fair sharing and caring and the authority of rules, parents and teachers.

By now you may be getting a sense of the pattern. Can you see what tensions will arise within a cool, order-driven structure? Perhaps it is apparent to you that once again the individual forces will need to assert themselves. The rules can become stultifying and create similar feelings of entrapment to those which came from the rules at the purple B-O level. Excessive Blue can become a police state or a theocracy. In Blue, society may have succeeded in making progress as a whole but "what about me?"

Potentially excessive blue structure can lead to fear of innovation. The emergence of new ideas and technologies may be experienced as a threat. Extremes of this type of constraint would be the Amish and Mennonite communities, but perhaps more visibly to readers from Anglophone cultures would be seen in the English novels of the nineteenth century as the new technologies of the industrial revolution took people out of traditional work roles, undermined the social economic structures and created opportunity for entrepreneurs. This was not a simple or quick transition, and the elements of red such as the British Empire and the explorers opening up new territories were working in the UK within a context of blue "God Queen and Country" for a long time. But eventually the new order which has emerged contains those forms within something different, a success-driven culture of entrepreneurs. Science and technology are crucial to this layer, the life conditions designated "E", the coping systems "R" and the warm colour of Orange. America has epitomized this development. Its "anyone can become president" ethos and its business culture are quite plainly visible. The legal structures have not gone. Orange cultures are heavily dependent on the underpinning of blue structures. When those break down you get Mafia Dons, corrupt police and ghetto gangs. Equally, like other layers, Orange can over-express and become unhealthily dominant.

At every level, the previous codes and values do not disappear. They remain present in the culture and they remain alive in individuals. They are the base on which newer levels build, they are transcended and included, and we are all blends of every level. Anyone who has watched a British state occasion such as the opening of parliament will observe strong elements of purple ritual underneath the blue formalities, and the remnants of red feudalism alive in the Lords and the monarchy. The history of the relationships between these forces is encoded in the forms of the ritual, and the way in which the monarch is allowed entry to "her parliament". While it is independent, it operates in her name and she speaks even today of it as "my government".

In the sixth layer we first encounter the F-S mix of the emerging of people-driven egalitarianism to counteract excesses of entrepreneurial greed or technological alienation arising in Orange. This layer is codified with the cool colour green, which happens to match with some other implications of the green agenda, but these should not be seen as the same. The best means to address ecological "green" issues may not necessarily be those formulated from the SDi green layer. One danger of the way in which vMEME green reacts to orange can be the perception that it is not just extreme orange which is damaging, but all orange. Since the economic surpluses which support green caring social agendas are highly dependent on technology, this can be counter-productive. As said, we need to be aware of both positive and potential negative consequences of any unbalance expression.

A momentous leap

In 1974, during early days of introducing his findings to the world, Prof. Graves wrote an article in which he described humankind as "preparing for a momentous leap". To some degree, the emergence of the seventh layer reflects the same dynamic tensions and impulses as others. At the same time, Graves' description reveals an additional feature which he found in his data. His view was that the first six layers should be grouped together as a single tier and that a new tier was showing up. The first two layers of this second tier are designated yellow and turquoise.

The transition to second tier could be described as bringing an added dimension. The first-tier layers are not aware of the complexity of human social emergence. For a long time societies were quite unaware of the existence of those significantly unlike them. Rome began as a red empire, dominating the many more purple tribal societies across Europe. It attempted and failed an internal transition to a blue republic for its own citizens, but its principal perception of those it conquered was that they were potential slaves in one form or another. Rome's prosperity was built on red and it reverted to being an empire. Our blue missionaries sought to bring our values and our God to a world they simply regarded as ignorant and deprived. Even now, the Earth shows clear evidence of the way that our orange technocracy regards pre-technological societies as primitive, dispensable. They and their habitats are ripe for exploitation in the belief that this will be good not only for us, but for them. First tier layers do not value one another.

In the second tier a fuller perspective is emerging. The transition from green to yellow rebalances the collective egalitarianism of the former, and recognizes the need for flexibility, freedom and flow throughout multiple thinking styles. Yellow is the first memetic layer at which value systems are sufficiently aware of the whole. The development of Graves theory is itself a signal of the emerging Yellow vMEME collective. It is a second-tier perspective. Thus the Yellow view begins to recognize the interdependence of humanity and the planet. It is a new level of survival, where what is at stake is not the individual human, but the collective humanity. Yellow is still new even at the time of writing. It has been estimated that in 1996 perhaps 2% of the human population show significant signs of yellow values and that at the time of writing (2008) this may have risen to around 5-7%.

Thus the last layer that we will describe is even more a dawning light on the horizon, and not a huge feature of our planetary mix. The vast majority of humans are still living in red and blue life conditions and through those value systems. Many readers of this text are likely to live in the worlds where Orange technology features strongly and it is easy to overlook the fact that the Western countries where Orange is strong are still numerically a minority of humans.

Turquoise, as the second layer of second-tier in some degree revisits the first tier second layer of purple. It re-integrates human awareness that there are levels of existence which are not visible at the material level. It is more capable of seeing the intuitive strand of human intelligence that was previously present in shamanism. It revisits the understanding that arises when we know where we have come from, and what our ancestry is. It recognizes the holistic nature of the world, the interdependence not just of all humans, but of all life on the planet. We need to share our world not only with each other, but in a balanced ecological relationship. In seeking to integrate the material and the non-material worlds, it has a transcendent view. It is hopefully apparent that this book views the world through a lens which is reflective of the emergence of Turquoise values. Like Graves theory in its time, our perspective arises now as one of many emerging signs of a new vMEME horizon.

This presentation simplifies SDi greatly. Describing seven bands can obscure the fact that each one has stages within, which are the transitional times as cultures enter the new band, as they become centred in it, and as they reach the exit conditions of moving to the next phase. Understanding the difference between underlying values and the content with which they may be expressed can sometimes be difficult. And in truth, this is a science still in its early stages, with a great deal more of the subtlety to learn. The technology of application of this theory to individuals, organizations and cultures, while already powerful, is nonetheless in its infancy.

For those who are curious to explore this rich territory we recommend the publications referred to earlier, and the website www.spiraldynamics.net . There are many powerful practical applications of the theory that assist individuals, groups, companies and societies to manage the complex transitions that they face. Regrettably these are also beyond our scope here. We should make it clear that the description we have given addresses perhaps 20% of the explanatory depth that SDi offers and which is probably only apparent in the full Beck and Cowan text. The full power of Graves theory is still waiting to emerge. Our view is that when it does, it will eventually be seen as a paradigm that is as important to our understanding of humans and society as Darwinism has been for biology. One illustration of its power is to be found in the book "The Crucible" by Don Beck and Graham Linscott which describes the application to South Africa's transition from Apartheid. Copies are hard to find but we are hopeful that a new printing will be available in the near future.

One purpose in describing SDi was to show how the principles that we saw in biological development are repeated at the level of maturing individual psychology and in the development of social organisms. Although we have given space to describing the layers, the underlying dynamics are of greater significance. But we hope to have done enough to indicate the way in which the balance of individual and collective success is held within the dynamics of changing societal life. We also hope that it is highly visible that the repeating cycles of co-operation and increased complexity that Elisabet Sahtouris describes are operating again here.

The other feature which some readers may by now have anticipated, is to recognise that we again reflect the particle level and the biological levels in the way that information is held both within and independently of the human individuals. This chapter is about the way that we construct "reality". The values at each level of SDi are held by people, but also become encoded in rituals and forms, in doctrines and accepted wisdoms and in shared views. Some are encoded in the language like the red "it's a dog eat dog world". The reality is socially constructed and the value memes become a part of a collective consciousness.

Whether held in language, habit, shared experience or collective folk wisdom these parts of consciousness are all in the realm of information rather than material things. We would also suggest that it is consistent with every other level to expect that the codification is also "in the ether", and would reflect both Jung's phrase "the collective unconscious" and our presentation that we are embedded in the field of the All. As we have reached the most recent levels of the spiral, the emergence of a global information network technology is facilitating increasingly rapid transition through the levels and adding a conscious, externally embedded level to the collective unconscious. The other feature that web-like technology increasingly shares with the "All" is that the flow is in both directions. Just as we influence the "All" through our own existence as part of it and through choices such as prayer, the technological information field has also democratised our ability to influence and share with one another. The planet's driving stories are now on Television and in Facebook and YouTube.

Spirals: past into future

There is a reason why the image of spiral form occurs regularly in nature and is appropriate also to a dynamic of social development. There is extensive literature on the significance of the Fibonacci series and the golden mean as providing a mathematical reason why spirals are a recurrent natural form. The concept boils down to the fact that as a spiral develops, it retains its shape as it is added to at its open end. Nature builds on itself and layer builds upon layer. Nothing is discarded. That which is already there becomes fixed and embedded, held within the development of the whole; it carries the record of its own past. What is newly added is influenced by the shape of what exists. The space for its growth is partly preconditioned and partly open.

The opening part of this chapter examined the history of attempts to understand what "reality" is, and to discover boundaries to what can be regarded as Truth. Throughout this book we have repeatedly encountered the brick walls that science has constructed around the search for Truth. We have seen that arbitrary choices have brought a focus on components at the expense of wholes, and on the aspects of life which can only be seen when the organism is dead. The frequent question that people ask about the existence of a soul, is whether it has material reality? Does it have mass, and where does it exist? One suspects that the question is much more often asked by those who believe there is no such thing, in order to present challenges to those who know there is.

An alternative approach to science (and reality) has been in existence all along. Wolfgang von Goethe is remembered as a poet and playwright, but only because his scientific work, which he regarded as his major achievement, has been treated as an irrelevance rather than accorded the respect it deserves. Goethe was concerned to observe the nature of things, but then to find the true essence of natural phenomena which is not given in immediate sensory observation, but appears after painstaking research within the observables as a "higher nature within nature" It is the "ideal in the real...the idea in the phenomenon," which, according to Goethe, it is the researcher's task "to seek out".

Goethe was responsible for introducing the term "morphology" into biology and developed theories of colour (his understanding of wave theory was unfairly ignored as particle physics developed) and of plant and animal form. These theories are concerned with the whole rather than the part, and so approach knowledge from the opposite direction to conventional science.

The Goethian approach to form has been continued by such notables as Rudolf Steiner (Harmony of the Creative Word) and Wolfgang Schad (Man and Mammals). These viewpoints restore the perspective that science requires an understanding not just of mechanisms, but of the patterns and energy relationships that determine the forms that life takes. Mechanisms are not explanations and the story that they tell is incomplete.

Gregory Bateson, in his book "Mind and Nature" makes a very persuasive case for the need to understand "the patterns that connect". Where much of science looks at things and processes, and expects that the patterns will emerge from them, Bateson like Goethe recognizes that there is an underlying unity which is not revealed by comparative anatomy or description of form. It requires an understanding of relationship. By definition relationships can never be encoded as properties of things. They have to be external and exist between things. The intuitive understanding of such connectivity is just as important to our true knowledge of the world. Einstein, Gödel and Feynman all recognized the part intuition played in their ability to develop theory from observation and the scientific literature abounds with stories of intuition and dreaming as a source of breakthrough. Alfred Russell Wallace and Charles Darwin were first and foremost naturalists who <u>observed</u>.

Bateson tells a story of a very powerful computer, to which a man asks a question about its mind – "Do you compute that you will ever think like a human being?" After a period of self-analysis, the machine produces its answer. "THAT REMINDS ME OF A STORY". As Bateson points out, stories are a way in which humans encapsulate knowledge of relevance. The connecting strands between events and phenomena are in multiple realms of connectedness. As he puts it "If I am at all fundamentally right in what I am saying, then thinking in terms of stories must be shared by all mind or minds, whether ours or those of redwood forests or sea anemones."

The world of science needs to understand not just the events that happen, but the story that links those events. In Steiner's "Harmony of the Creative Word" he too quotes Max Planck's statement "Anything that can be measured is real; anything that cannot be measured is not real." It should by now be abundantly plain that there is much that is real in any normal understanding of that word, and yet not measurable. Steiner's presentation of the world of form is startling in its contrast with modern science. His language seems flowery and ill-defined. A scientific skeptic will tear its subjectivity apart in seconds. (Reminder : Skepticism is another subjective choice.) And yet the overall picture of life which emerges from his methodology and likewise from Wolfgang Schad has an elegance and consistency which adds considerable meaning to the "patterns that connect". We suspect that there is a further spiral that reflects development of form as seen through the three dynamics that they identify of Metabolism / digestion, Circulation / Rhythm and Nervous system / Brain. This is a realm for other experts, but is an indication of the "story" to be told, the story science does not yet tell.

Much of our text has examined the complexity of living systems. The current scientific view seeks to understand complexity by finding simple components. Biologist and mathematician Brian Goodwin, author of "How the Leopard changed its spots" argues the need for a science which can encompass complexity and echoes the views of Ian Stewart and Jack Cohen in "The collapse of chaos", an excellent and insightful book which guided some of our descriptions of genetics. Goodwin's view is that a new scientific methodology is required which can incorporate the intuitive and holistic in its way of knowing. His term for this is a "Science of Qualities".

There are so many levels in the mechanisms we have examined. The spiral of life from fundamental particles through chemical elements, cells and organisms to societies and cultures has to be understood in its entirety, and this is not an easy task. But we hope that what has emerged provides some of the fundamental relationships that become visible when the whole is viewed together, and that some simplicity and tentative sense of "qualities" is visible in the recurring patterns.

Qualities, in our view, would include the recurring balance between stability and creative flexibility, the interplay between chaos and order, and the interaction of the material world and the world of information. They would include the balance and tension between the forces that support individuality and uniqueness, and those which encourage consistency and stability across groups. They would include the existence of an energy connection that mediates the interaction between material and information realms, recognizes that these are completely embedded in each other and thus embeds each organism interactively within the field of creation. In the image of the spiral, the place at which creation and stability interact is at the open, emerging end of the spiral form. It is the place where new elements are added to the building blocks of the old.

In early sections of this book we presented the evidence for intuitive capability. We showed the consistency of world-view through the cultures which have maintained an intuitive relationship with the world, and among those from our culture who have entered into that realm. It should be obvious that a view of the world in pieces has led directly to our inability to understand the consequences that will follow from our many technological actions. It is not science itself which brings this about, but an attitude that underpins science and narrows its viewpoint. That attitude is a choice to define reality in ways which deny the intuitive and reduce our capability as a culture to understand ourselves and our relationships with the world. The results in ecological damage are self-evident.

There is a corresponding impact to our understanding of who we are and of our place in creation. If human beings were less robust (and less inclined to trust their own experience above science) the sense of alienation would be much worse than it is. But we would hope it is as clear to others as it is to us that both science and society would benefit greatly from a more accurate framing of reality. If there were full recognition of the extent to which our understandings exists beyond the things we look at, and often independent of the material of our own bodies, we could begin a fresh and more rich engagement with every aspect of life.

In our closing chapter we will return to the central theme of spirituality and the ways we have available to restore meaning and empowerment to our relationship with the world. Religion may seem like a victim to the growth of science, but it too has been complicit in putting power outside of human beings and human realms. Science created disconnection with its mechanistic views. Some religious forms have discouraged connection and personal authority by placing rules, historical texts and hierarchies of priesthoods between people and their spiritual experience. Our last chapter will seek to re-establish the values which are present at the centre of all the great faiths and to find a unifying sense of empowerment for all in the ways that they choose to interact with the realm of consciousness.

Review

In this chapter we have presented the basis on which we understand reality. At both a personal and social level, human beings construct their reality in terms of the things that they value, the thinking structures which they see as enabling their psychological and social survival and well as their physical well-being. Kelly's constructs and the Gravesian value systems are both elements in the way that we work together to co-create what is regarded as "real". In either case, the information exists between people, in a personal and cultural field.

The outcome is that just as the entanglement of particles places information beyond the physical boundaries of the particles themselves, just as morphic fields affect the development of biological form, our perceptual systems have an external existence that exists in the information realm. The spiral continues at this level as all others to be an interaction between the physical, the energetic and the informational. Some information is cultural and explicit. Some is intuitive and held in the space of photon coherence and subtle effects. All of these work together to create the "mind" of the all and our experience of it.

16.Holistic Spirituality

One of the things that today's science lacks is an effective theory of complexity.

Jack Cohen and Ian Stewart   *The Collapse of Chaos*

We have lost the core of Christianity. We have lost Shiva, the dancer of Hinduism whose dance at the trivial level is both creation and destruction but in whole is beauty. We have lost Abraxas, the terrible and beautiful god of both day and night in Gnosticism. We have lost Totemism, the sense of parallelism between man's organisation and that of the animals and plants. We have even lost the Dying God.

Gregory Bateson   *Mind and Nature*

Joy, beauteous spark of godhead,

Daughter from the heavenly fields!

Drunk with fire, our footsteps tread

Your holy sanctuary that heals.

With your magic fresh cohering

All that our ways would split and shred

Human brotherhood appearing

Where your gentle wings are spread

Friedrich Schiller   *To Joy*

Theme

We hope that this book will be read by scientists and that it may expand the thinking of those who, while open-minded by nature and intention, have been conditioned to a conventional view largely because the alternatives have been under-communicated. But our primary desire is to reach those who have an inner knowing that there is "something there" and who are sharing this with others through religions that even they know to have been shown as out of touch with scientific knowledge or who are attempting to find their own path outside them. One of less acceptable facets of "The God Delusion", of Carl-Sagan's "Demon-haunted universe" and of other attacks on spiritual beliefs is that they tend to suggest, with varying degrees of vehemence, that masses of human beings are stupid. We find it deeply distasteful to confuse lack of knowledge, poor education and culture-led lack of choice with stupidity. When we started this journey, we indicated the direction we would take in addressing this information deficit, and described the strands that would weave into our tapestry. It is time for one final re-cap to draw together all that we have done.

The holistic manifesto

This book has been full of our heroes. They are heroes because they have sought the Truth. They have been willing to endure the hostility and criticism that comes when you follow an unconventional path.

When reality is socially defined, so too is sanity. Promoting an alternative view of reality in some cultures is risky. For every one of these heroes there are others who didn't make it and thousands more who are encouraged to doubt their sanity and the validity of their experience. This book is for those who might also not make it unless our definitions change and for those who feel obliged to keep their spirituality in the closet.

One hero not previously mentioned is Dr. William Bloom, among the most lucid, compassionate and authentic of the pioneering voices. William has been championing the holistic agenda for decades now. In his recent book "Soulution: The holistic manifesto" he argues the case for a coming-of-age in the trend towards alternative views of religion, spirituality and health. He draws out the many strands of commonality and coherence in what sometimes appears from the outside to be a mixed bag of practices and belief systems and shows the maturity of the world-view that emerges.

We hope that a more balanced understanding of scientific reality will make a significant contribution to this shift. Over time, perhaps it will reduce the confidence of those who have scorned and dismissed holistic health and non-orthodox paths to the world of the divine. With luck it will increase the confidence of those who in their hearts know what they know, but have been embarrassed by their difficulty in proving it and have not trusted themselves as they deserve to.

William Bloom quotes a British survey in 2000 which indicated that 70% of people believe that there is "something there" – personal God, life force or whatever. Only 9% of people believe that their own path to God is the only way. 33% believe that there is a way to God outside organised religion and a similar number believe that all religions offer a path to God. A 2007 US survey indicates that even in a country often seen as strongly fundamentalist, 70 percent of Americans affiliated with a religion or denomination said they agreed that "many religions can lead to eternal life," including majorities among Protestants and Catholics. Among evangelical Christians, 57 percent agreed with the statement, and among Catholics, 79 percent did. Among minority faiths, more than 80 percent of Jews, Hindus and Buddhists agreed with the statement, and more than half of Muslims did.

Evidence exists to suggest that other parts of Europe are similar to Britain and if this finding is anywhere near representative of humanity as a whole, it suggests established religions are suffering more than the sense of spiritual belief in general. It also indicates that there are many people who are in some sense unfulfilled, undirected or "closet" believers.

The non-material world of connection and information

At the core of our challenge lies two thousand years of flawed philosophy, which chooses to view the world as if we are separate from it, and as if it consists solely of things. The world also contains qualities, information and values. All of these are real and all have an effect on the real world but are excluded from scientific discourse.

From that philosophy, further viewpoints developed which are designed to exclude humans and their experience from any evaluation of what may be regarded as "true" or "proven". This is claimed to increase objectivity when it is in fact a subjective choice. It excludes any possibility of there being unseen connections between humans and other aspects of the world. In this and other ways science forces itself to deny what turns out to be real.

In contrast, the reality which we have shown is that humans are connected to the natural world. We can know things intuitively that are not possible through our standard senses.

Within that connected reality we have shown that our view of present and future is misleading and that information is available from the future. We have shown that minds can access information over considerable distances of space, without apparent limit. We have shown that they can direct enquiries with apparent precision towards other individuals, even when they do not know their location. We can know beyond the accepted boundaries of time and space

Plants also have the capability to sense their environment and so do bacteria. The evidence indicates that all living things possess this capability. Humans are not the only "minds" inhabiting the Earth.

All of this evidence indicates the presence of an information network or field of consciousness that is available to all living things and through which we can both receive information and send influence.

Within the realm of information that we cannot see using normal senses, there are beings in existence which are part of the natural world and which influence it. There are also fields of consciousness within plants and animals that govern the growth of organisms and that can be communicated with individually and can mediate in healing.

Within that realm of information lies the capability to influence those organisms by means of energy "vibrations" and resonance effects. One means of doing so is homeopathy, which was developed using entirely scientific methods. As well as bringing about healing through controlled and targeted application of specific remedies, homeopathy has demonstrated links between generations other than those mediated by genetic DNA. There is evidence to support all of the major approaches to spiritual and energy-based medicine.

The biological realm and the human organism

Genes do not have a one-to-one correspondence to characteristics.

There aren't enough genes to explain by themselves the way that an organism develops.

The conventional presentation of what "genes" are is misleading.

Influences are passed from generation to generation by other means besides chromosomal DNA.

The determination of development is not only controlled by genes, but by other elements of genetic material.

The determination of development is subject to environmental influences and is flexible rather than fixed.

The conventional presentation of the role that genes perform is also misleading.

Layers and complexity

There are many levels of function and complexity in a typical higher mammal such as a human being.

Complex functionality is present at the level of individual cells – cells are not blobs.

Cells contain organelles performing parts of the cellular function. These have probably developed via the accumulation of simpler functions in component bacteria.

Many aspects of cell functionality are mediated through the cell membrane, which is a liquid crystal.

The development of life progressed from simple (prokaryote) bacteria through complex (eukaryote) bacteria towards bacterial colonies functioning in a co-ordinated way. Co-ordination was mediated by photon communication and chemical messengers and was responsive to environmental triggers.

Further development came via the development of multi-cellular organisms of increasing complexity, with increasing differentiation of cellular function, and with formation of organs and structures. Co-ordination built on the earlier layers with the addition of synchronising rhythms, nervous system pathways, electrochemical connection and connective tissue with jump-conduction of protons through the liquid-crystal continuum. Organisms maintain a degree of quantum-level coherence that makes them rapidly responsive to small-scale triggers.

The small-scale triggers may include the detection of subtle energies including ZPF / thought-field influences and vibrational energies such as those provided by homeopathy and other forms of "energy medicine".

The heart is a driver for rhythmic co-ordination and is in large degree a "controller" to the brain rather than controlled by it

Some of the interaction between mind and body is mediated by neuro-chemical messengers which distribute control and emotional experience throughout the body. The heart and emotions influence the organism and are not simply side-effects of brain activity.

Multiple levels of synchronisation and control are interleaved in the organism, creating a holistic and indivisible totality which cannot be understood merely as a combination of its parts.

Subtle energies influence the body throughout, supported by such self-organising phenomena as pumped phase coherence and Bose-Einstein condensates which mediate the relationship between the physical body, internal consciousness and the inherent fields / dimension of information.

There is external evidence of long-range order, efficient and symmetrical energy transduction and high sensitivity to external cues combined with "noiseless" communication.

Every cell in the body, and the organism as a whole are embedded together in the field of consciousness, influenced by it and influencing it.

Evolution

The evolutionary process has been a self-actualising (autopoietic) creative process in which all species of organisms have balanced their individual creativity with the creative growth of the totality, the primary creative consciousness, in a blend of competition and co-operation.

The Darwinian model for evolution is not wrong, but its origin in Malthusian thinking has over-emphasised the element of scarcity and competition and has not allowed for a sufficient degree of environmental influence on the creative dynamic.

The autopoietic nature of the universe provides an inherent drift towards increasing levels of complexity as all possibilities are explored.

Developing complexity is supported by a cycle of individuation and mutuality which spirals through successive levels of biology and speciation

Morphogenetic fields, or other such qualities in the "information field" bring repetitive use of elements and patterns, and variations in the blend of informational (sensory), rhythmic (breath / heartbeat) and action metabolism elements among differentiated species.

There is no evidence that humans are the peak of the evolutionary process, nor that it is complete. There is equally no evidence that we are not. It would be entirely consistent with this evidence for human beings to be the source of the entire field of creation and to have created everything we experience as a collective dreaming. How would we know? While not our view, this possibility should not be dismissed.

Physics and philosophy of science

The underlying mathematics of Kantor, Boltzmann, Gödel and Turing show a flexible and paradoxical universe with no bounds to creative possibility.

The subject-object dichotomy that we inherited from Greek thinking is false and leads to spurious choices of what is regarded as "knowledge" or "proof".

A scientific method which views the world excessively through its components and by taking life apart, leads to inadequate perceptions of the whole. It is incapable by itself of delivering a complete understanding of life, and to be complete needs to be complemented by the "Goethian" approach.

As it becomes clear that the information which connects all of creation is held somewhere in the "spaces between" material particles or living entities, our science must find ways to observe these spaces.

Quantum physics shows that our natural view of reality is inadequate. There is much taking place that we cannot detect with our senses.

There are in-built limits to all rules and predictive models as shown by Gödel's theorem and Heisenberg's Uncertainty principle.

At the lowest level of matter, everything is a form of energy which started in an indeterminate state and might have been particles or waves.

All that we see is the result of a process by which some energy has been "determined" as taking a stable form. We, and the matter that we interact with, are parts of what has already been determined.

The "determining" process is inherent in creation. From the outset (e.g. "big bang") consciousness was present as the prime cause.

The relationship between matter and consciousness (and between organisms and the whole of creation) takes place outside of the four dimensions of space and time that we normally work in.

One popular possibility for the way this works is through the "zero-point" energy-field (ZPF). Information is thus held in the "environment" and is instantaneously available to everything, everywhere. The alternative possibility, that there are additional dimensions, is also capable of explaining a world of consciousness. Either model will support our case for connected consciousness.

The relationship between human consciousness and the information realm may well be mediated through the presence of pumped systems or B-E condensates in the brain or body-mind.

There is evidence that coherence is supported by alpha brain-rhythms and heart-rate patterns, that our detection systems are at least partly mediated by the heart, and that this detection can take place pre-cognitively.

Information storage, both within the brain and in the field of consciousness has properties which are holographic and holistic.

Human ability to use thought to significantly affect physical reality uses these mechanisms to provide a small trigger which creates an "attractor" within a system of unfolding chaos. Morphic field resonances may also operate at global or universal levels as attractors within such systems and could be intensified by larger numbers of people.

The psycho-social realm

Human beings build their view of reality based on external information, most of which is socially defined.

Human beings construct predictive and adaptive models for their choices and behaviour which are in the form of constructs (polarities) and values (vMEMEs).

In a parallel to biological evolution, similar patterns are present in social evolution that balance individual and collective interests.

In a parallel to the world of physics, our social reality arises and his held outside of individual organisms. It too inhabits the "spaces between".

As with biological development, social forms are adaptive responses which reflect the life conditions around them. These coping strategies are based on identifiable values systems.

The development of social systems reflects the spiral patterns of individuation and co-operation observed to arise when Satouris cycles are repeated at higher levels

Just as complex biological organisms contain the earliest biological forms (bacterial components and single cells) within them, and are built in a way that transcends and includes previous developmental levels, so too is the psychosocial realm. Earlier vmemetic systems remain available and can re-emerge if required.

Where do we go from here?

Having drawn together the scientific themes it is now time for a similar exercise in respect of what it means for humans and for humanity. It would be entirely consistent with the presentation of our memetic evolution that we would at this point in time require humanity to explore more deeply and to cohere around a holistic view of society with a strong spiritual component.

The characteristic beliefs and actions of the emerging H-U Turquoise 'Holistic' value MEME, as listed in Beck and Cowan's "Spiral Dynamics" are:-

- The world is a single, dynamic organism with its own collective mind

- Self is both distinct and a blended part of a larger, compassionate whole

- Everything connects to everything else in ecological alignments

- Energy and information permeate the Earth's total environment

- Holistic, intuitive thinking and co-operative actions are to be expected.

From the outset we have indicated that our intention here is to pull a big story together – a story in which the narrative is largely provided by the work of others. We have our own perspective and have selected from among our particular heroes and influences. Others have trodden similar paths, creating their parts of this story, contributing to the whole and we wouldn't be here without them.

At the same time, we started with the intention to provide a sense of cohesive scientific underpinning that would respond to a specific challenge. We wanted to provide a rational basis for spiritual belief and give meaning to fundamental human activities of relationship to the living world and faith in the creative power of intention and prayer.

All the elements for this are present in Beck and Cowan's list. Except one. There is nothing in their list which indicates that human beings have the power to influence the energy and information that permeates the Earth's environment and that the connectivity of it all includes a spiritual (consciousness) component. That part is perhaps the oldest of all in our tale, having been founded in aboriginal thinking and in the oldest of religions. It has lived through the centuries and survived even in Western thinkers who took the "mystical" path – other heroes like Teilhard de Chardin and Bede Griffiths. It has been true forever and everything has built upon its Truth.

Caroline Myss, another hero and spiritual leader quoted early in our story describes the new generation who are carving out the territory described by William Bloom as "mystics without monasteries". Dr. Jean Houston – a great dramatist of the mythological and author of some of the best books and workshops on expanding our capability to fulfil ourselves in this multi-layered reality – described us as "modern shamans". Andrew Harvey has called for the holistic community to become "spiritual activists". We would add to this the call from Goethe and Steiner for spiritual scientists. The world needs scientists who are informed by a complete view of reality. It urgently needs a spiritual science, not just a material one. We live in a single world, not in two separate spiritual and material worlds. There are no winners in a battle for supremacy between science and spirit. This book is about integration, about making whole in ourselves and our social constructs what was always whole in reality.

The future of Religion

In the face of this emerging consciousness, what is the position of what used to be known as "religion"? Richard Dawkins's "God Delusion" is very scathing in expressing his hostile attitude to religion. It is easy to be intolerant of intolerance. We would prefer to take a more allowing and constructive line, one which is reflective of the spiral development.

We won't pretend that we can make a good fit between our views and the fundamentalist approaches to any creed. It is obvious that our view of creation implies great flexibility; the voice of the Divine is not fixed and could not possibly be contained in any text as a literal truth for all time. In a world where the voice of the Divine is the continuing sound of creation, The Koran, the Bible and the Torah have to be viewed as something other than "God's rule-book". This does not make them, in our view, less valuable as sources for humanity's collective wisdom.

At the same time, in a multi-faceted creation all are equally the "word of God" as written down by humans using available language – in many cases highly spiritual humans with close connection to the Divine. All have the right to be regarded as authentic efforts to encode the spiritual needs of the time, in the context of the life-conditions and using constructs that were meaningful and relevant to the people who would hear those words. They are expressions of the cultural memetics that expressed the value systems of their time. For example, in the context of scientific evolution the Bible's version of creation makes little sense as a literal description, but as a metaphor for the creation story as we narrated it in chapter 15 it works quite well. The fall from grace and "expulsion" from the garden also makes some sense if viewed as a metaphor for the development of thinking systems that separated us from direct intuitive knowing. We expelled ourselves from Malidoma's world.

As Clare W. Graves, the developer of Spiral Dynamics said, "Damn it all, a person has the right to be who he / she is." It is arrogant for us to tell others what to believe and it only invites hostility. They have based their lives in the constructs which are necessary responses to their life conditions. These will change of their own accord when the life conditions make it safe for people to do so. The current political approach of the West towards Islam has done very little to create such conditions of safety and Global capitalism's economic dominance continues in many places to delay the emergence of better conditions. American advice to Russia after the fall of communism completely destroyed its blue structures because of their communist content. Instead of propelling the desired emergence of orange entrepreneurial freedom, it removed healthy controls and threw the country back into criminal red. The interventions in Iraq and Afghanistan are equally ill-thought-out and arguably equally contaminated by greed. We suggest that it is not helpful to tell people what they should believe.

We also believe that the alternative to religious power-structures and hierarchies will evolve in time. As more people discover a direct experience of the spiritual world and establish their own intuitive relationship with the All there will be a shift of churches and faith groups towards being communities of spiritual equals with less need for intermediaries in their conversations with Creation, but increased value for those who can facilitate the personal journey involved as people wrestle with what will remain a challenging developmental process. The definition of priesthood will therefore change and many priests are already making this transition.

Every day more and more people are exploring the spiritual alternatives, prompted by curiosity, good experiences with holistic therapies, star autobiographies and TV shows. There is generally no road-map to follow and myriad possible directions to go. In our resources list we give a few thoughts on people, books and magazines we consider worth attention, but our experience, wide as it is, is far from exhaustive.

We also recognise that each individual will have their own path – often quite different from ours. Advice is extremely difficult to offer and potentially unhelpful, so we will restrain ourselves to a few fairly generic comments. While this is not a self-help book and some may feel that we are straying from the real agenda, we hope that we are introducing some readers to a new world, and feel an obligation to offer a few compass-points in the hope that it will aid navigation.

Choosing therapies

When choosing therapies, there are clear advantages in choosing the well-established ones where the methodologies have long track-records. At the same time, Juliana practices a range of quite new approaches and we know of many others which have developed recently such as Tapas Acupressure Technique and EFT which are even candidates for learning aspects of self-healing. Many of the newer forms, including Plant Spirit Medicine, TAT and EFT have roots anyway in older traditions such as acupuncture.

We would suggest that the person is more important than the technique. It is also inevitable that many problems may have multiple levels involved. Long-term issues may benefit from a series of approaches at different levels (energetic, physical tissue, spiritual, emotional, mental etc.) in order to heal completely. Many therapists have developed their own unique combinations of approach to cover a wide range. This is sometimes presented by critics of the complementary approach as a sign of wooliness and confusion when in fact it is a recognition by those with experience that the holistic approach works best because it recognizes the complexity of our bodymind and works better when all layers can be addressed appropriately. It is no more confused than the conventional view that surgery, physiotherapy and pharmacology all have a part to play. Personal recommendation is usually worth more than qualifications. In all cases our advice would always be to talk to any practitioner you think might be right for you. A practitioner who is impatient with your questions or fails to relate to them cannot be right for you, and few will begrudge the time to explain what they do. Trust your instincts and go with the one who most leaves you with a feeling of "rightness" in your body.

Exploring alternative paths

We would give similar advice regarding workshops, books, tapes and internet "stuff". It is not a question of who is right or wrong but of who is right for you. There are few intentional charlatans in our experience. There are many honourable and capable people. But there are also people who are "half-way up the mountain" and who lack the humility that comes with knowing how much they still don't know. There are people who think their way is the only way or that what was right for them must be right for you. There are those who enthusiastically overstate what they are capable of delivering. There are those who are caught up in glamour and excitement and some who have had amazing experiences and have been blown off-balance. Some are excessively caught up in their own culture of sales techniques and spiritual economics.

In our version of reality we have removed many of the measures by which people have previously distinguished what is "real" from what is not. Measuring things against objective science used to seem helpful and we are undermining that. This is not the place to give our views on astrology for instance, or on psychic channels, angelic messengers, avatars, gurus or teachers. In the new conscious-connected reality so much becomes possible that was previously ludicrous. How do you know where the boundaries are? It is not our place to tell you; our views may only be correct for us.

So who do you trust?

One of the most lucid writers in this area is Sandy Stevenson and we would echo her advice (Paradigm Shift Dec. 2007) that before connecting yourself with any belief system or energy, and before changing anything about yourself there is a need to apply discernment and examine your inner truth. This starts with the common sense instruction that if you are not sure, don't do it. You can ask (pray) for pointers to come to your attention. Learn to be in touch with your gut-feel. Most of us have known a time in our lives when we over-rode our instincts and said "yes" when we felt "no".

William Bloom has similar cautions about distinguishing between spirituality and psychic powers. There are people who have special abilities but they are not necessarily wise about how to use them. He quotes one oriental healer he encountered who showed remarkable abilities, but who later showed himself to be an addicted gambler who could not keep his hands off women. We ourselves have experienced remarkable psychic channels who lost the discipline of knowing when they were bringing information "from the All" and when they were in their own thoughts and emotions. They held the discipline when giving sessions. Someone like that can give amazing, accurate and insightful readings, but getting any closer to their lives can reveal their own struggles and can even be a nightmare. By all means consult one, but don't take them home.

The bottom line of this strand of thought is to never surrender your power or authority – no matter how amazing the person seems to be. No-one who is in integrity will ever ask you to do so. They may give you strong advice but will never manipulate or threaten you with negative outcomes. We also recommend the work of David Hawkins, and the use of kinesiology as a means to determine what is true from what is false. His book "Power vs Force" is full of insights, his CD sets are excellent and kinesiology is one way of finding out what your "inner knowing" rather than your mind is telling you. Developing intuitive skills is valuable in this and many other ways.

One disadvantage of scientific logic is that it provides no tools for working with the things that you are unaware that you don't know. Many people have had the experience of agreeing with decisions that they knew in their bones were not right, but had no logical arguments against. They have held back from expressing their inner knowing or argued themselves out of what they felt to be truly right for them, Businesses have failed from what they didn't know about the competition's plans. That's one of the things intuition is for – the decision that looks right today, but will be proved totally wrong in hindsight when the unanticipated change in conditions became visible. There are technologies that support us to factor in what we don't know we don't know and benefits in perception that goes beyond linear time. We believe that our personal decision-making has improved hugely since we started using our intuition properly.

Any warnings here are given as a backdrop to our encouraging you to explore. There is a rich world waiting in which you have potentials that you may have never imagined. Among those potentials are those which are promised by "The Secret", by "What the Bleep" and by countless books, CD sets and workshops. We want to talk about the many approaches on offer to "creating your dreams" and "finding abundance", as well as talking about why prayer does not necessarily work as people expect it to. We are not criticising the films mentioned. Their core message is aligned with ours and "bleep" echoes some of the science. It is unavoidable that they make some aspects sound over-simple, and we wish to address that gap here. But consistent with all that we are saying, the more people adopt the approaches offered the easier it becomes for everyone as the resonances increase and the "field" grows.

The power of manifestation

Both religion and science have conspired to put power outside of us. In religion the prayer is to an external deity, sometimes through an intermediary or with preconditions that we are told must be fulfilled. We ask in the name of the prophet or the Son; we may have to make a sacrifice or other action in order to be in the necessary state to receive.

Science puts all power entirely beyond the human individual, apart from that which can be exercised in physical terms. Our only way to make a difference is then through direct action on our fellows, or by technological dominance over the natural world. To use Dr. David Hawkins' distinction, this is about force rather than power. The balance needs to be redressed in favour of true personal empowerment.

You might ask whether we are qualified to write on this subject. Have we manifested everything we have ever wanted? Are we multi-millionaires? The answer to both questions is "no" but we feel we are learning and the second is not our focus. Beyond that we would encourage you to put aside such judgements until after reading what we have to say below. There are others who do cite having achieved one or both of these things as justification for charging large sums to teach you how to do the same. Some may have made their money that way in the first place. Others may have achieved all they have anyway, or only because their visualisations gave them the confidence they needed.

We would like to delve a little deeper and would suggest that your personal relationship with the forces of creation is – dare we say it again – complex. It is not so complex as to prevent success, but it does require a high degree of consciousness, understanding and discrimination. It may also take some time.

Our thesis has been that small triggers - as small as thoughts – can create a resonance that in a context of coherent systems and "butterfly wing" chaos may have big outcomes. We believe that they can, but there are many factors standing in the way of a simple cause-and-effect relationship. We will list many and analyse a few.

All we see of the evidence suggests that "thoughts" are held and stored throughout the body. The whole psycho-endocrine story supports this. The coherence of the body is maintained at multiple levels. Your thoughts transmit into the universe on a continuous basis – intentional, conscious or not. Prayer, or creative visualisation, or any of the techniques in this arena only form one portion of your "output" to the universe. If your whole body is out of alignment with your chosen prayer (we will use the word prayer to cover all techniques from now on) then instant success is unlikely. Coherence matters.

Indeed, one of the things that you might need to pray for and work on is the creation of internal coherence. Simply praying for abundance may not work if your whole life is based in a belief, experience and practice of struggle and low self-worth. Your body-mind is sending conflicting messages. If you are in continual self-talk about hopelessness, if your daily conversation with others states that you are expecting the worst and if you always plan on that basis then your message is incoherent. It may take some work to create an increased level of personal coherence. Our experience is that in the meantime it is good to work with what seems within our grasp, and what we feel ready for. If you currently believe that you don't deserve millions, then don't pray to win the lottery. There are abundant examples of people whose lives were destroyed by winning.

Dr Miceal Ledwith presents a further perspective on prayerful coherence, maintaining that the creative force within our thoughts is not made effective through our conscious mind. In his view the scale of our conscious thoughts are as a gnat to an elephant in their capability to impact the field. Dr Ledwith speaks as a former leading Catholic academic, with both priestly and intellectual perspective on prayer. In his particularly delightful way he draws attention to the difference between Jesus' perspective on prayer "Believe it and it is already yours" and the common act of a grovelling plea for something to be given to us. Describing oneself to the Divine as unworthy and then begging for scraps is not an act of true belief. It represents a failure to position ourselves within the field of the Divine and be in accordance with the Old Testament teaching (Psalm 82) that "Ye are Gods", which Jesus cited as his defence when accused of blasphemy. For prayer to be fully effective and coherent, we have to BE different, not simply to change a conscious thought or two. This is the reason why true spiritual masters have had to do a great deal of work on themselves.

Another aspect to our thinking, echoed by many other spiritual teachers and contexts, is the nature of personal incarnation. We subscribe to the view that each person makes a choice of when, how, where and why to incarnate. This is the personal part of the creative All. (Caroline Myss' "Sacred Contracts" articulates this whole area very well). If this is right, you came with a purpose and an intention. The more you are in touch with that intention, or the more closely you are "on plan" the greater the likelihood that you will a) pray for something consistent with that plan and b) that the conditions in the universe are right to support it. Your plan might not have involved financial wealth; focussing on that might cause you to miss the riches you really had set out to discover.

Within all of this is a process where each of us harmonises with our own "destiny" and the destiny of others who are in the midst of their own creation and who are co-creating with you. Your little drop in the ocean is just one little ripple among many. The right drop at the right time will be powerful. To the importance of internal coherence you can add the need to develop coherence with the wider world. Our ripples need to add to one another until they become a tidal wave. We have indicated that the world is co-creative and auto-creative. We see human future as conscious co-creation.

There are aspects of this which are present in the traditions of sacrifice and preconditions. The expression often suggested to balance any personal prayer is "Thy Will not mine, oh Lord, be done". This expresses the understanding that our prayers need to be for the good of all. If we are all interconnected, that which is bad for "you" cannot ultimately be good for "me". In the formulation we have given there might be an alternative "Our Will, not Mine" flavour to this, since we each need to own our portion of the Divine within us. Ultimately though, we all have to recognise we are just a portion of a whole. In accepting that "We are Gods", the WE aspect is important

The idea of sacrifice also expresses a relationship of supplication. This does not mean that it is performed from fear, and probably was never intended as a form of barter even if it appears that way. For some cultures it may have been a means of creating and channelling collective will. It is also important to have within us an attitude of being grateful for what we already have as this sets up an appropriate resonance for the act of receiving. It is part of how we recognize that "It is already ours". Our context would be that supplication and sacrifice can be a part of the balance in our empowerment – that we intentionally make our individual will smaller, that we give back in order to harmonise with what we seek and that we strengthen our desire by affirming that it is important to us, so we will give something up in order to make it happen.

Our last statement in this context concerns the importance of action. You may know the joke about the man who prays continually for a lottery win and complains loudly to God about not having won despite years of prayer, only to hear the voice of thunder saying "Meet me half way – buy a bloody ticket!"

There is another joke which looks at prayer from the opposite side. In the midst of horrendous floods, a devout man sits on his roof, praying to God to save him. A boat comes past and offers him passage, but he says "No thank you, God will save me." Two days later he is getting anxious, but when the helicopter comes, he shouts up "No thank, you, God will save me." Finally after nearly a week, when he is dying of hunger, he shouts at God "Why have you not saved me?" only to receive the response "I sent a boat, I sent a helicopter, what more do you want?"

The messages here should be obvious. If you are praying that someone will give you a piano, then clear the space for it in your room. If you pray for something and it comes in a slightly different form, but achieves the ends you need – have the common sense to say thank you, and acknowledge the success of your creation. If you want a successful business, by all means pray, but do the work on the ground. The game here is incarnation and we do not achieve everything in the spiritual realms alone. Giving form to the spirit is the human task and we are fond of the statement from Mohammed "Trust in Allah, but first tether thy camel."

The Will of God

It is tempting to avoid this territory, but since the question is almost inevitably in people's minds we have to deal with disasters and suffering. The question asked of God is "why?" and it does not vanish when we are dealing with this great co-creation that we are participating in. We are no better placed to give an authoritative answer than anyone else. All we can do is indicate how the question relates to the universe we are describing.

We do not know if the All could have done things differently than it has, but we know for sure that it didn't. The creative process that we are in the midst of contains a balance of creation and destruction when viewed from the human perspective. From the point of view of the All, nothing is destroyed, things merely change form.

Disasters and suffering are a human perspective. That statement is not intended to trivialise – it hurts us as much as other people and we are just as inclined to be fearful for or protective of ourselves and our loved ones. Even so, we live in a world where consciousness incarnates and as we have said, we go back to consciousness when that is over, so nothing can truly be lost. Perhaps that is some consolation.

Nor does that view suggest that we should not do anything about suffering. Maybe it is part of our collective plan that we need to learn how to work with the forces which are destructive. The Earth was created as a ball of molten rock and humans don't yet know how to cool volcanoes or prevent the collision of tectonic plates. Even those things we might be expected to do better with, such as food distribution, seem to present a big challenge.

Most of us do what we can, and the world does seem to be getting better from a human point of view. There are more of us than ever living today, and many are managing a degree of peace, prosperity and happiness. We are collectively beginning to work with the imbalances where these achievements have been in some way at the expense of our planet. Creation is a "work in progress". Human beings are a potent force in that creative work and there are great opportunities for us to do better still. Accepting our personal empowerment when we work in alignment with spiritual purpose will make an enormous contribution towards an outcome that meets human goals (and that includes our goals for a healthy planet).

We heard a story today which reflects our view of possibility, connection and creative attitude. A friend of ours who makes jewellery has been ill for some time. It has been a painful business, but she carries on making very nice jewellery. Another friend recently went with Juliana to an exhibition of this work and bought a necklace for £55 from the person helping run the stall.

When the maker returned to the stall she was pleased to see that the piece had sold. She had only included it at the last minute, but knew the price and realised that £55 was precisely the amount needed for a really nice belt that she had seen while away from the stall. However, when she looked later for the £55 she could not find it anywhere, so she gave up on the belt, concluding that it apparently "wasn't for her" after all.

Later on that day, someone told her about a healer in another town two hours away and she had a strong feeling (intuition) that this person could help her. She decided she wanted to go and was told that this healer charged £55. So she began again to search for the missing money, eventually finding the notes crumpled in the rubbish and packing from the stall. Soon afterwards she went to the healer concerned who had a big impact on her health. She is feeling better today than she has for a year.

This is just today's example of the many stories we encounter which reflect the reality that we feel we share with those who are open to the flow of the universe and trusting its promptings and their intuition. If our friend had overridden the failure to find the £55 and bought the belt anyway, she probably would have hesitated to afford the healer, but she didn't. She might also have not taken the slightly unexpected sale as a "gift" that she was entitled to use for something special for herself. But she did.

It is also precisely true that Juliana came and relayed this story to Jon at exactly the moment that it appears in drafting this narrative. It was a perfect example, at the perfect time, of how we see the "Will of God", or the "mind of the creative" working into the Universe. We have no idea what becomes possible when much larger numbers of the human race find their empowerment to work with this reality, but we cannot see any limits. The future is up to all of us.

A springboard for the future

The implications of the picture we have painted in this book are many and huge. We would like to close with just a few of them

There is a big change required in science, which has to revisit its assumptions and find a way to work constructively with the third realm beyond subject-object or mind-matter dichotomies. It will need to incorporate the study of qualities and consciousness, to incorporate Goethe's approach to knowledge. There needs to be a rebalancing of the "take it to bits" model of enquiry with the "look at what it is and understand it as a whole" method. There are far-reaching consequences for funding and for our decision-making about how to use the results. There is a great deal that society is accepting from scientists today that it will need to question more deeply. The very definition of "science" and "scientist" will need to expand to meet our context.

The model that we have for education is strongly geared to the same philosophical underpinnings. Children are trained to accept so-called "facts" and to distrust their personal knowing. Intuition and creativity are being educated out in all but a few places. The recent recognition from British government research that the Steiner-Waldorf system is delivering better outcomes is a pointer to the way we need to go. We have close experience in this world and if anything the research underplays the achievements. Plutarch made the statement "The mind is not a vessel to be filled but a fire to be kindled" (later rephrased by and attributed to Yeats). This truth has been badly neglected. Nor is it just children's education. Adults could be usefully trained in many skills – intuition, cognitive expansion, conflict resolution, relationship building and parenting being a few among them. All are areas that the global collective is less capable of than it could be and all are trainable. We have the power of major communications media to assist in this.

The educational process serves an economic model that is equally flawed. Most values that can be assigned in our accounting systems are assigned to things and the non-material exceptions (such as good-will and brand value) are not balanced by down-sides. The consequences of corporate or government decisions for the environment, for ecological balance and for climate impact cannot be factored in (though small attempts to quantify carbon footprint are being attempted). There is little capability for assessing social consequences – even the more obvious ones like crime and health costs. Still further away from the balance sheet are valuations of Spiritual Capital – a theme developed by Danah Zohar and Ian Marshall in their book of the same name. It is becoming obvious that we literally cannot afford to continue in this way and we have less time for the change than anyone would wish. This will require vast mobilisation of resources.

These resources would be much more available if they were not being used for ineffective, inappropriate and ultimately destructive modes of conflict resolution – otherwise euphemised as "defence expenditure" and often looking like conflict creation. This is not to discount the value of many peace-keeping and policing operations, but there is an inevitability that if you keep giving people guns, they'll want to shoot them. The gun lobby argument is "Guns don't kill, people do." The reality is that people with guns kill. The choice is therefore between removing the people and removing the guns. It's not difficult to see which of these is preferable. A huge global arms industry is a debit in the balance of our spiritual capital. How else can you look at it? But this is a vast economic power-base. It will not surrender its position – we have to starve it of energy and allow it to find new ways to use its technical muscle. The biblical image of "swords into plough-shares" is as good as ever.

Beneath these attitudes is a way of thinking about the natural world, the planet itself. Whatever phrase, in whichever language might have been used by the Creator to Adam and Eve, we do not accept that the Divine order is represented by the current exercise of "dominion" and the roots it verbally shares with "dominate". We need to adopt an attitude of stewardship and partnership. Even the concept that we can "own" land needs to change. Anything that we take hold of, we must also take responsibility for. This is something more than mere ownership.

Our political choices in the West towards other world-views, based on arrogance, dominance, economic exploitation, and rooted in religious and cultural imperialism are costing us everything. We will need a big shift. It is not beyond us. If South Africa can back away from its dreadful history in not much over a decade then anything is possible. The part played in that change by Spiral Dynamics and by Don Beck personally is a significant background element, documented in Don's book "The Crucible". This is because the shift we need to make is fundamentally values-based and brings a change in global life-conditions. Values, like qualities and consciousness need to be re-integrated into our political expectations, our institutions and those we appoint to them. Don's work to change life-conditions continues through partnerships in the

Middle-East. We hope he will be supported, and pray for a similar success.

Health management concepts have to change. Another huge economic power-base is in pharmaceuticals. We would not want to be without antibiotics or analgesics. There are phenomenal capabilities in surgery and diagnostic technology that add greatly to human health. There is no immediate threat to the pharmaceutical industry as the world of health will not change overnight. But our state medical systems are based on fixing people who are ill and not on finding out how to keep us healthy. Unfortunately the pharmaceutical industry is a stakeholder in your sickness. This cannot be a sound or sustainable model. If the shareholders in that industry value their investments, they will want to begin broadening their base into wellness, and into the integration of alternative approaches. They will need to become stewards of the collective immune system.

Thank you and Farewell.

It is no light task to write a book based in science, and however much we would have liked to make it light and easy, much of it inevitably is not. We have emphasised our liking for the simplicity which emerges on the far side of complexity and we had to take you through the complexity to get there. Even skimming as we did, we again acknowledge the patience and tenacity of all who made it through to here.

We have fulfilled the task that we set ourselves and believe that we have delivered on our promise to put a sound scientific base underneath human spirituality in its many and diverse forms. We have countered the negative aspects of "The God Delusion" and met the challenge that Richard Dawkins' and others of scientism's advocates have issued. We have summarised an emerging world-view that is becoming irresistible. It is on its way from ridicule through opposition and will one day be seen as self-evident. In doing so we have opened up a fresh world of human potential.

The science of the past was based on a human philosophical choice to step outside of creation. We bit on the fruit of the tree of knowledge and cast ourselves out of the garden because we disconnected ourselves from the remainder of the world. It couldn't work and it hasn't worked.

In the closing paragraphs of "A Brief History of Time", Prof. Stephen Hawking makes observations regarding the possible discovery by physics of a complete and unified theory of how the world works. He suggests that scientists have, until now, been too occupied with the development of new theories that describe what the universe is to ask the question why? At the same time, he is concerned that the people whose business it is to ask why, the philosophers, have not been able to keep up with the advance of scientific theories. His hope is that if a complete theory is discovered, it should in time be understandable, at least in principle, by everyone and not just scientists and that we will all be able to take part in the question of why the universe exists. If we found that answer, he says ".. it would be the ultimate triumph of human reason - for then we would know the mind of God."

This notion is the most fundamental of all flaws in science and the others all stem from it. We don't believe that such a theory will ever be found until it acknowledges consciousness as a physical reality. But even if there is such a theory, it will not tell us why we are here or what we need to do. Knowing the origins of the universe may be really fascinating, but our place in it as human beings has everything to do with consciousness, with creativity and with empowered choice. If we are to know the "mind of God", then that knowledge will be complete only when it includes our inner journey, and our ability to connect our own consciousness with the cosmic flow.

In this, religion and mysticism have always been right - it is through meditation, contemplation, intuition and receptivity that we harmonise with the greater will. But even the religions and the mystics have often been short of the mark. The breakthrough, the triumph, is that we first hear the harmonies and then add our voice to the chorus. The answer to the questions "Who are we", and "Why are we here?" is that we are individualised parts of the collective consciousness, learning to experience our ability to create together. Our task is to recognise our purpose and decide to participate consciously.

We are all in a position to become mystics without monasteries, to view ourselves as modern shamans. Holistic spirituality has arrived and is here to stay. It is inclusive of all religions and faiths, all ways to the Divine. This is our exciting challenge for the future and the ultimate triumph of human reason and non-reason. Our task is not to know the mind of God. It is collectively to include ourselves in and empower ourselves as what we already are. It is for each of us and all of us together to become the mind of God.

Jon and Juliana Freeman
Dorset, England
July 2008.

Index, Glossary , bibliography etc.

<u>Acknowledgements</u>

Written at Oscar time, with some sympathy for those who are recognising that it is impossible to acknowledge the hundreds of people who touch our lives and without whom things would be different, but whose gratitude impels them to try, to the embarrassment of all.

Jon would wish to acknowledge his father for always asking questions and for his dedication to making life better, together with his mother for the love of music and for showing that the world is full of feeling. Acknowledgements to those who have lived around me and had to bear with unpredictable life paths, obsession, brain-on-a-stalk behaviour and other handicaps. Jack, Yannis, Joby – this is my excuse and my apology.

To Charles Paul Brown – the first to say "Write your book". Sorry it took so long, Chuck. To the creators of the Oxford University Human Sciences degree, to Vernon Reynolds, Bryan Little, Godfrey Lienhardt and other tutors way back when who won't even recognise my name – thank you anyway for intellectual inspiration. Along the way, in addition to those whose work is mentioned elsewhere, Leonard Orr, Jacob Bronowski, Jose Silva, Ram Dass, Marshall Rosenberg, and Rudolf Steiner. Among those mentioned elsewhere, particular personal acknowledgement to Jean Houston, Don Beck and William Bloom. Thanks also to the Prophets Conference – Robin and Cody – for bringing great people within my reach. Very special thanks are owed to Marcos Frangos whose close attention has improved the text and reduced typographical errors, but most of all whose dear friendship, and Joanne's too, nurture and encourage our work. Thanks to other readers whose constructive comments were very helpful, Dr. Howard Smith, Michiel ("Jan") Doorn, Dr Vinicio Sergo, Dr. Christopher Cooke. Thank you to guiding spirits, guardian angels and nature beings. It is awesome how many different forms consciousness may take. For musical inspiration while writing, special thanks to Bela and the Flecktones, Gary Burton and John McLaughlin – all exemplars of the creative coherence and dynamic equilibrium that Mae-Wan Ho calls quantum jazz - plus gratitude also to Johann Sebastian and Ludwig v B. for order and impulse.

Finally and most obviously to Juliana – co-creator, supporter, healer, partner, friend, lover and beloved. More than words can say.

Juliana would like to acknowledge all the beings that have supported her growth and unfolding – her mother for the family sensitivities to the world of spirit and her father for his enthusiasm and love. To my early teachers – Raymond Armin, Peter and Simon who opened me to the unseen worlds; Betty Balcome for her training of my psychic abilities; To Eliot Cowan, whose presence, as well as his profound teaching, changed my life. There have been many other people who have influenced and assisted me and I thank you all. My most profound thanks and appreciation to all the wondrous beings that have graced my life up to this point and who I deeply desire will continue to walk beside me: the angelic beings, the nature spirits, plants and crystal beings, my spiritual teachers and mentors and all those whose presence is felt even when not seen. This world would be far less sweet without you all.

To Jon – for the courage and integrity to always speak your truth even in the most difficult circumstances and for daring to write this book. For your constant loving support and your willingness to give your time and energies for the benefit of others. For all that you are. With my love and devotion.

Bibliography, references and resources.

All quotations used are copyright of the authors and publishers listed. We are most grateful for the permission to include their material, where used. In other cases, works are listed because they were inspirational or influential. Further suggestions appear below.

Robert Hunter "Attics of my Life". Ice Nine Publishing. From Grateful Dead "American Beauty".

Norman Shealey and Caroline Myss from "Anatomy of the Spirit", Bantam Books 0553-50527-0.

MonaLisa Shulz from "Awakening Intuition", Bantam Books 0-553-81212-2

Candace Pert from "Molecules of Emotion", Simon and Schuster UK Pocket Books 0671-03397-2

J.W. Dunne from "An experiment with Time". Recently re-published by Russell Targ with Hampton Roads Publishing Company. 1-57174-234-4

Peter Tompkins and Christopher Bird from "The Secret Life of Plants", Penguin 01400-3930-9

Bob Jahn and Brenda Dunne from the Princeton Engineering Anomalies Research www.princeton.edu/~pear   More up-to-date work and DVD's available from www.icrl.org

Malidoma Somé from "Of Water and the Spirit". Penguin Arkana 0-14-019496-7. Copyright ©1994 by Malidoma Patrice Somé. Used by permission of Jeremy P. Tarcher, an imprint of Penguin Group (USA) Inc.

Machaelle Small Wright from "Behaving as if the God in All Life Mattered", Perelandra books 0-9617713-0-5

Peter Caddy and Dorothy McLean from the Findhorn website, www.findhorn.org

Eliot Cowan from "Plant Spirit Medicine", Swan Raven & Co. 1-893183-11-4

Alberto Villoldo reference to "Dance of the Four Winds". Destiny Books 0-89281-514-0

Stephen Harrod Buhner from "The Secret Teachings of Plants", Bear & Co. 1-591-43035-6 . Special thanks for a particularly extended quote.

Deepak Chopra "Quantum Healing". Bantam New Age 0-553-17332-4

Bruce Lipton from "The Biology of Belief", Mountain of Love Productions 0-9759914-7-7

Jack Cohen and Ian Stewart "The collapse of Chaos" Penguin 0-14-017874-0, while not quoted directly was very influential on our approach to genetics. Funny too.

Douglas Hofstaedter "Godel, Escher Bach". Deep intellectual entertainment. Penguin 0-14-005579-7

Mae-Wan Ho is quoted from her website www.i-sis.org.uk Her book "The Rainbow and the Worm" is published by World Scientific 981-02-3427-9

Richard Dawkins is quoted from "The Blind Watchmaker" Penguin Books 0-14-008056-2

Stephen Jay Gould's "Life's Grandeur" is referred to. Even if we disagree, a great and interesting science writer. Jonathan Cape 0-224-04312-0

Robert M Pirsig "Zen and the Art of Motorcycle Maintenance" is one of the best, most profound books of the last 100 years. Vintage 0-099-32261-7

Elisabet Sahtouris from "EarthDance", iuniverse.com 0-595-13067-4

Rupert Sheldrake "A New Science of Life" Grafton Books Paladin 0-586-08583-1

Richard P. Feynmann "QED" Penguin 0-14-1-2505-1

Raymond Trevor Bradley. Overview of Heart Coherence material in World Futures of General Evolution 63:61-97, 2007 and on http://noosphere.princeton.edu/papers/pdf/bradley.intuition.2007.pdf

Danah Zohar. "The Quantum Self". Bloomsbury 0-7475-0271. See also "Spiritual Intelligence" and "Spiritual Capital".

David Bohm "Wholeness and the Implicate Order" Ark 0-7448-0000-5

Michael Talbot "The Holographic Universe" Harper Collins 0-586-09171-8 Not quoted, but a full – even holographic - account of that theory.

Lyall Watson "Lightning Bird" Hodder & Stoughton 0-340-27999-0 Out of print

Don Beck and Christopher Cowan. "Spiral Dynamics". Blackwell 1-55786-940-5

George A. Kelly "A Theory of Personality". The Norton Library 0-393-00152-0

Humberto Maturana and Francisco Varela "The Tree of Knowledge" Shambala 0-87773-642-1

Gregory Bateson. "Mind and Nature" Flamingo 0-00-654119-4 "Steps to an Ecology of Mind" University of Chicago 0-226-03905-6

Bede Griffiths reference to "The Marriage of East and West" Mediomedia 0-972-56271-0

William Bloom reference to "SOULution: The Holistic Manifesto" Hay House 1-4-19-0342-8.

Stephen W. Hawking reference to "A Brief History of Time" Bantam Press 0-593-01518-5

Recommended sources of further information

Further information about Eliot Cowan and Plant Spirit Medicine in the US at www.plantspiritmedicine.org and PSM in the UK www.plantspiritmedicine.org.uk

Don Beck's CD's (www.soundstrue.com) are probably the most accessible introduction to the detail of Spiral Dynamics integral. Other overview material is available via www.spiraldynamics.net and www.wie.org/spiral . The Beck and Cowan text listed above is full and authoritative. The work in the Middle-East can be found on www.humanemergencemiddleeast.org

All of Caroline Myss' work has exceptional depth and authenticity. We would particularly recommend "Sacred Contracts". Much of her work is also available through audio on Soundstrue. www.myss.com

Jean Houston's work is expansive. Her psychological understanding and her ability to interweave the mythological and archetypal layer of human consciousness bring special richness to this picture, as does her interweaving of artistic perception. Her work on expansion of human capability is dynamic. Try "Jump Time" and "The Possible Human". Seeing her live is an entertainment as well as an inspiration. Her websites are www.jeanhouston.org and www.socialartistry.com .

Brenda Dunne's work continues at the laboratory for International Consciousness Research. www.icrl.org .

Sandy Stevenson's website www.lightascension.com is a place to encounter some of the new-age spiritual approaches and to see what some of the beliefs around non-incarnated spiritual support for humanity have to offer. This is probably the most esoteric of our suggestions and the most likely of them to challenge the more scientifically-minded, but we include it because we see Sandy as probably the most grounded and authentic "channel" that we have encountered. Her book "The Awakener" is an excellent introduction to this area.

Mae-Wan Ho's Institute for Science in Society website www.i-sis.org.uk is a huge source of understanding for those who want to keep track of scientific abuses in areas such as genetic engineering as well as giving access to her

DVD's and other work.

William Bloom. Authentic, open-hearted and thoroughly grounded spirituality. To be found at www.williambloom.com . His regular thoughts are to be found in the Cygnus books newsletter. Cygnus are a great source of well-priced alternative books www.cygnus-boooks.co.uk . Check out "The Endorphin Effect".

Howard Martin and Rollin McCraty can be found through www.heartmath.com

Alberto Villoldo can be found on www.thefourwinds.com Lots of excellent material.

Machaelle Small Wright is at www.perelandra.com. First-class plant-derived energy-based health products. Inspirational manuals on gardening with the plant spirits.

David Hawkins. Deep understanding about the nature of Truth and our ability to discern what it is and live by it. "Power vs Force" Hay House 1-56170-933-6. Exceptional CD set "The Discovery" for those who want a coherent view of a path to enlightenment. A man who giggles and chuckles at life. Greatly misunderstood and misrepresented. Read him or listen to him but don't read about him. www.veritaspub.com

Miceal Ledwith – humour and wisdom, plus much interesting information on the recent "orbs" phenomena. www.hamburderuniverse.com

Daily thought, entertainment and inspiration for being in touch with the personal aspect of individual creativity. Check out Mike Dooley's daily thoughts on behalf of The Universe www.tut.com .

Juliana has also written a series of lovely little illustrated books which introduce children and adults to the world of the plant spirits. See them on Amazon or on her website.

Juliana's website is www.julianafreeman.com

Jon's website is www.jonfreeman.org

INDEX